NUTRITION AND MEDICINES IN NATURE

ENV BOOKS SERIES

NUTRITION AND MEDICINES IN NATURE

Editors

Dr. Jairam Singh
Physician and Surgeon
Bharti Clinic
Jamaalpur Maan, Raja Ka Tajpur, Bijnore - 246735
(UP) (India)

&

Dr. Pawan Kumar 'Bharti'
Society for Environment, Health Awareness of Nutrition & Toxicology (SEHAT)
B-225/5D, Top Floor, Subhash Gali, Road No. 7, Block B
Ashok Nagar, Shahdara, Delhi - 110 093
(India)

DPH

DISCOVERY PUBLISHING HOUSE PVT. LTD.
INDIA

Published by:
Namit Wasan

DISCOVERY PUBLISHING HOUSE PVT. LTD.
4383/4B, Ansari Road, Darya Ganj
New Delhi-110 002 (India)
Phone : +91-11-23279245; 23253475; 43596065
E-mail : discoverybooksindia@gmail.com
discoverypublishinghouse@gmail.com
namitwasan9@gmail.com
web : www.discoverypublishinggroup.com

First Edition: **2020**

ISBN: 978-93-88854-39-9

Nutrition and Medicines in Nature

Printed at:
Infinity Imaging Systems
Delhi

Preface

In humans, an unhealthy diet can cause deficiency-related diseases such as blindness, anemia, scurvy, preterm birth, stillbirth and cretinism, or nutrient excess health-threatening conditions such as obesity and metabolic syndrome; and such common chronic systemic diseases as cardiovascular disease, diabetes, and osteoporosis. Undernutrition can lead to wasting in acute cases, and the stunting of marasmus in chronic cases of malnutrition.

Human beings have long depended on medicines from Nature to prevent and treat illnesses, and today the World Health Organization (WHO) estimates that up to 80% of the global population still relies on plants for primary health care.

For many of the 150 million tribal peoples, Nature provides a potent pharmacy that they can rely on, thanks to their detailed botanical knowledge; the upshot of a profound attunement to their ecosystems for thousands of years.

Medicinal plants, also called medicinal herbs, have been discovered and used in traditional medicine practices since prehistoric times. Plants synthesise hundreds of chemical compounds for functions including defence against insects, fungi, diseases, and herbivorous mammals. Numerous phytochemicals with potential or established biological activity have been identified. However, since a single plant contains widely diverse phytochemicals, the effects of using a whole plant as medicine are uncertain. Further, the phytochemical content and pharmacological actions, if any, of many plants having medicinal potential remain unassessed by rigorous scientific research to define efficacy and safety.

The present book updates the subject content of Nutrition sources, Nutrient Deficiency, Nutritive importance of Probiotics, foliar nutrition in green gram, Nutrition value of tropical Apple, Pharmacological aspects of Rheum emodi; treatment of diabetes by medicinal plants; Antimicrobial Therapy by Plant Molecular Medicine.

Thanks are due to publisher and contributors from various institutions and universities.

The book will be helpful for the researchers, academia working in the field of Nutrition sources of the future, Nutrient Deficiency, Nutritive value and importance of Probiotics, foliar nutrition in green gram, Nutrition value of tropical Apple, Pharmacological aspects of Rheum emodi; Scenario of diabetes and treatment by medicinal plants; Antimicrobial Therapy for Multi-Drug Resistance by Plant Molecular Medicine.

–Editors

(envbooks@gmail.com)

Contents

Preface

Introduction

Section-I: **Nutrition**

1. **Spirulina - Nutrition of the Future** 3-22
M.R.A. Manimala

2. **Nutrient Deficiency in Plants** 23-32
Prasann Kumar, Shipa Rani Dey

3. **Nutritive Value and Importance of Probiotics** 33-53
M.R.A. Manimala

4. **Foliar Nutrition in Green Gram (*Vigna radiata* L.)** 54-81
V. Aravinth

5. **Apple of Tropics:** ***Its Production and Quality Assurance with Special Reference to Nutrition*** 82-96
Prasann Kumar, Shipa Rani Dey

Section-II: **Medicines in Nature**

6. **Rheum Emodi as Valuable Medicinal Plant and its Pharmacological Aspects** 99-111
Showkat Ahmad Bhat, Gurjinder Singh, Sabhiya Majid Tehseen Hassan, Tariq Parvez Azad

7. **Scenario of Diabetes and Medicinal Plants as a Source of its Treatment** 112-144
Showkat Ahmad Bhat, Gurjinder Singh, Sabhiya Majid Tehseen Hassan, Tariq Parvez Azad

8. **Recent Advances in Antimicrobial Therapy for Combating Multi-Drug Resistance by Plant Molecular Medicine - A Review** 145-160
Dhananjay Pandey and A.K. Gupta

Index 161-166

Contents

Introduction

Nutrition is the organic process of nourishing or being nourished, including the processes by which an organism assimilates food and uses it for growth and maintenance.

Nutrition is the science that interprets the interaction of nutrients and other substances in food in relation to maintenance, growth, reproduction, health and disease of an organism. It includes food intake, absorption, assimilation, biosynthesis, catabolism and excretion.

The diet of an organism is what it eats, which is largely determined by the availability and palatability of foods. For humans, a healthy diet includes preparation of food and storage methods that preserve nutrients from oxidation, heat or leaching, and that reduces risk of foodborne illnesses.

In humans, an unhealthy diet can cause deficiency-related diseases such as blindness, anemia, scurvy, preterm birth, stillbirth and cretinism, or nutrient excess health-threatening conditions such as obesity and metabolic syndrome; and such common chronic systemic diseases as cardiovascular disease, diabetes, and osteoporosis. Undernutrition can lead to wasting in acute cases, and the stunting of marasmus in chronic cases of malnutrition.

Animal Nutrition

Carnivore and herbivore diets are contrasting, with basic nitrogen and carbon proportions vary for their particular foods. Many herbivores rely on bacterial fermentation to create digestible nutrients from indigestible plant cellulose, while obligate carnivores must eat animal meats to obtain certain vitamins or nutrients their bodies cannot otherwise synthesize.

Plant Nutrition

Plant nutrition is the study of the chemical elements that are necessary for plant growth. There are several principles that apply to plant nutrition. Some elements are directly involved in plant metabolism. However, this principle does not account for the so-called beneficial elements, whose presence, while not required, has clear positive effects on plant growth.

A nutrient that is able to limit plant growth according to Liebig's law of the minimum is considered an essential plant nutrient if the plant cannot complete its full life cycle without it. There are 16 essential plant soil nutrients, besides the three major elemental nutrients carbon and oxygen that are obtained by photosynthetic plants from carbon dioxide in air, and hydrogen, which is obtained from water.

Plants uptake essential elements from the soil through their roots and from the air (consisting of mainly nitrogen and oxygen) through their leaves. Green plants obtain their carbohydrate supply from the carbon dioxide in the air by the process of photosynthesis. Carbon and oxygen are absorbed from the air, while other nutrients are absorbed from the soil. Nutrient uptake in the soil is achieved by cation exchange, wherein root hairs pump hydrogen ions (H^+) into the soil through proton pumps. These hydrogen ions displace cations attached to negatively charged soil particles so that the cations are available for uptake by the root. In the leaves, stomata open to take in carbon dioxide and expel oxygen. The carbon dioxide molecules are used as the carbon source in photosynthesis.

Although nitrogen is plentiful in the Earth's atmosphere, very few plants can use this directly. Most plants, therefore, require nitrogen compounds to be present in the soil in which they grow. This is made possible by the fact that largely inert atmospheric nitrogen is changed in a nitrogen fixation process to biologically usable forms in the soil by bacteria.

Plant nutrition is a difficult subject to understand completely, partially because of the variation between different plants and even between different species or individuals of a given clone. Elements present at low levels may cause deficiency symptoms, and toxicity is possible at levels that are too high. Furthermore, deficiency of one element may present as symptoms of toxicity from another element, and vice versa.

Nutrients

The list of nutrients that people are known to require is, in the words of Marion Nestle, "almost certainly incomplete". As of 2014, nutrients are thought to be of two types: macronutrients which are needed in relatively large amounts, and micronutrients which are needed in smaller quantities. A type of carbohydrate, dietary fiber, i.e. non-digestible material such as cellulose, is required, for both mechanical and biochemical reasons, although the exact reasons remain unclear. Some nutrients can be stored - the fat-soluble vitamins - while others are required more or less continuously. Poor health can be caused by a lack of required nutrients, or for some vitamins and minerals, too much of a required nutrient.

Macronutrients

The macronutrients are carbohydrates, fiber, fats, protein, and water. The macronutrients (excluding fiber and water) provide structural material (amino acids from which proteins are built, and lipids from which cell membranes and some signaling molecules are built) and energy. Some of the structural material can be used to generate energy internally, and in either case it is measured in Joules or kilocalories (often called "Calories" and written with a capital C to distinguish them from little 'c' calories). Carbohydrates and proteins provide 17 kJ approximately (4 kcal) of energy per gram, while fats provide 37 kJ (9 kcal) per gram, though the net energy from either depends on such factors as absorption and digestive effort, which vary substantially from instance to instance. Vitamins, minerals, fiber, and water do not provide energy, but are required for other reasons.

Molecules of carbohydrates and fats consist of carbon, hydrogen, and oxygen atoms. Carbohydrates range from simple monosaccharides (glucose, fructose and galactose) to complex polysaccharides (starch). Fats are triglycerides, made of assorted fatty acid monomers bound to a glycerol backbone. Some fatty acids, but not all, are essential in the diet: they cannot be synthesized in the body. Protein molecules contain nitrogen atoms in addition to carbon, oxygen, and hydrogen. The fundamental components of protein are nitrogen-containing amino acids, some of which are essential in the sense that humans cannot make them internally. Some of the amino acids are convertible (with the expenditure of energy) to glucose and can be used for energy production, just as ordinary glucose, in a process known as gluconeogenesis. By breaking down existing protein, the carbon skeleton of the various amino acids can be metabolized to intermediates in cellular respiration; the remaining ammonia is discarded primarily as urea in urine.

Carbohydrates

Carbohydrates may be classified as monosaccharides, disaccharides, or polysaccharides depending on the number of monomer (sugar) units they contain. They constitute a large part of foods such as rice, noodles, bread, and other grain-based products, also potatoes, yams, beans, fruits, fruit juices and vegetables. Monosaccharides, disaccharides, and polysaccharides contain one, two, and three or more sugar units, respectively. Polysaccharides are often referred to as complex carbohydrates because they are typically long, multiple branched chains of sugar units.

Traditionally, simple carbohydrates are believed to be absorbed quickly, and therefore to raise blood-glucose levels more rapidly than complex carbohydrates. This, however, is not accurate. Some simple carbohydrates (e.g., fructose) follow different metabolic pathways (e.g., fructolysis) that result in only a partial catabolism to glucose, while, in essence, many complex carbohydrates may be digested at the same rate as simple carbohydrates. The World Health Organization (WHO) recommends that added sugars should represent no more than 10% of total energy intake.

Fiber

Dietary fiber is a carbohydrate that is incompletely absorbed in humans and in some animals. Like all carbohydrates, when it is metabolized it can produce four Calories (kilocalories) of energy per gram. However, in most circumstances it accounts for less than that because of its limited absorption and digestibility. Dietary fiber consists mainly of cellulose, a large carbohydrate polymer which is indigestible as humans do not have the required enzymes to disassemble it. There are two subcategories: soluble and insoluble fiber. Whole grains, fruits (especially plums, prunes, and figs), and vegetables are good sources of dietary fiber. There are many health benefits of a high-fiber diet. Dietary fiber helps reduce the chance of gastrointestinal problems such as constipation and diarrhea by increasing the weight and size of stool and softening it. Insoluble fiber, found in whole wheat flour, nuts and vegetables, especially stimulates peristalsis – the rhythmic muscular contractions of the intestines, which move digest along the digestive tract. Soluble fiber, found in oats, peas, beans, and many fruits, dissolves in water in the intestinal tract to produce a gel that slows the movement of food through the intestines. This may help lower blood glucose levels because it can slow the absorption of sugar. Additionally, fiber, perhaps especially that from whole grains, is thought to possibly help lessen insulin spikes, and therefore reduce the risk of type 2 diabetes. The link between increased fiber consumption and a decreased risk of colorectal cancer is still uncertain.

Fat

A molecule of dietary fat typically consists of several fatty acids (containing long chains of carbon and hydrogen atoms), bonded to a glycerol. They are typically found as triglycerides (three fatty acids attached to one glycerol backbone). Fats may be classified as saturated or unsaturated depending on the detailed structure of the fatty acids involved. Saturated fats have all of the carbon atoms in their fatty acid chains bonded to hydrogen atoms, whereas unsaturated fats have some of these carbon atoms double-bonded, so their molecules have relatively fewer hydrogen atoms than a saturated fatty acid of the same length. Unsaturated fats may be further classified as monounsaturated (one double-bond) or polyunsaturated (many double-bonds). Furthermore, depending on the location of the double-bond in the fatty acid chain, unsaturated fatty acids are classified as omega-3 or omega-6 fatty acids. Trans fats are a type of unsaturated fat with trans-isomer bonds; these are rare in nature and in foods from natural sources;

they are typically created in an industrial process called (partial) hydrogenation. There are nine kilocalories in each gram of fat. Fatty acids such as conjugated linoleic acid, catalpic acid, eleostearic acid and punicic acid, in addition to providing energy, represent potent immune modulatory molecules.

Saturated fats (typically from animal sources) have been a staple in many world cultures for millennia. Unsaturated fats (e. g., vegetable oil) are considered healthier, while trans fats are to be avoided. Saturated and some trans fats are typically solid at room temperature (such as butter or lard), while unsaturated fats are typically liquids (such as olive oil or flaxseed oil). Trans fats are very rare in nature, and have been shown to be highly detrimental to human health, but have properties useful in the food processing industry, such as rancidity resistance.

Essential Fatty Acids

Most fatty acids are non-essential, meaning the body can produce them as needed, generally from other fatty acids and always by expending energy to do so. However, in humans, at least two fatty acids are essential and must be included in the diet. An appropriate balance of essential fatty acids—omega-3 and omega-6 fatty acids—seems also important for health, although definitive experimental demonstration has been elusive. Both of these "omega" long-chain polyunsaturated fatty acids are substrates for a class of eicosanoids known as prostaglandins, which have roles throughout the human body. They are hormones, in some respects. The omega-3 eicosapentaenoic acid (EPA), which can be made in the human body from the omega-3 essential fatty acid alpha-linolenic acid (ALA), or taken in through marine food sources, serves as a building block for series 3 prostaglandins (e.g., weakly inflammatory PGE3). The omega-6 dihomo-gamma-linolenic acid (DGLA) serves as a building block for series 1 prostaglandins (e.g. anti-inflammatory PGE1), whereas arachidonic acid (AA) serves as a building block for series 2 prostaglandins (e.g. pro-inflammatory PGE 2). Both DGLA and AA can be made from the omega-6 linoleic acid (LA) in the human body, or can be taken in directly through food. An appropriately balanced intake of omega-3 and omega-6 partly determines the relative production of different prostaglandins, which is one reason why a balance between omega-3 and omega-6 is believed important for cardiovascular health. In industrialized societies, people typically consume large amounts of processed vegetable oils, which have reduced amounts of the essential fatty acids along with too much of omega-6 fatty acids relative to omega-3 fatty acids.

The conversion rate of omega-6 DGLA to AA largely determines the production of the prostaglandins PGE1 and PGE2. Omega-3 EPA prevents AA from being released from membranes, thereby skewing prostaglandin balance away from pro-inflammatory PGE2 (made from AA) toward anti-inflammatory PGE1 (made from DGLA). Moreover, the conversion (desaturation) of DGLA to AA is controlled by the enzyme delta-5-desaturase, which in turn is controlled by hormones such as insulin (up-regulation) and glucagon (down-regulation). The amount and type of carbohydrates consumed, along with some types of amino acid, can influence processes involving insulin, glucagon, and other hormones; therefore, the ratio of omega-3 versus omega-6 has wide effects on general health, and specific effects on immune function and inflammation, and mitosis (i.e., cell division).

Protein

Proteins are structural materials in much of the animal body (e.g. muscles, skin, and hair). They also form the enzymes that control chemical reactions throughout the body. Each protein molecule is composed of amino acids, which are characterized by inclusion of nitrogen and sometimes sulphur (these components are responsible for the distinctive smell of burning protein, such as the keratin in hair). The body requires amino acids to produce new proteins (protein retention) and to replace damaged proteins (maintenance). As there is no protein or amino acid storage provision, amino acids must be present in the diet. Excess amino acids are discarded, typically in the urine. For all animals, some amino acids are essential (an animal cannot produce them internally) and some are non-essential (the animal can produce them from other nitrogen-containing compounds). About twenty amino acids are found in the human body, and about ten of these are essential and, therefore, must be included in the diet. A diet that contains adequate amounts of amino acids (especially those that are essential) is particularly important in some situations: during early development and maturation, pregnancy, lactation, or injury (a burn, for instance). A complete protein source contains all the essential amino acids; an incomplete protein source lacks one or more of the essential amino acids.

It is possible with protein combinations of two incomplete protein sources (e.g., rice and beans) to make a complete protein source, and characteristic combinations are the basis of distinct cultural cooking traditions. However, complementary sources of protein do not need to be eaten at the same meal to be used together by the body. Excess amino acids from protein can be converted into glucose and used for fuel through a process called gluconeogenesis.

Water

Water is excreted from the body in multiple forms; including urine and feces, sweating, and by water vapour in the exhaled breath. Therefore, it is necessary to adequately rehydrate to replace lost fluids.

Early recommendations for the quantity of water required for maintenance of good health suggested that 6-8 glasses of water daily is the minimum to maintain proper hydration. However the notion that a person should consume eight glasses of water per day cannot be traced to a credible scientific source. The original water intake recommendation in 1945 by the Food and Nutrition Board of the National Research Council read: "An ordinary standard for diverse persons is 1 milliliter for each calorie of food. Most of this quantity is contained in prepared foods." More recent comparisons of well-known recommendations on fluid intake have revealed large discrepancies in the volumes of water we need to consume for good health. Therefore, to help standardize guidelines, recommendations for water consumption are included in two recent European Food Safety Authority (EFSA) documents (2010): (i) Food-based dietary guidelines and (ii) Dietary reference values for water or adequate daily intakes (ADI). These specifications were provided by calculating adequate intakes from measured intakes in populations of individuals with "desirable osmolarity values of urine and desirable water volumes per energy unit consumed."

For healthful hydration, the current EFSA guidelines recommend total water intakes of 2.0 L/day for adult females and 2.5 L/day for adult males. These reference values include water from drinking water, other beverages, and from food. About 80% of our daily water requirement comes from the beverages we drink, with the remaining 20% coming from food. Water content varies depending on the type of food consumed, with fruit and vegetables containing more than cereals, for example. These values are estimated using country-specific food balance sheets published by the Food and Agriculture Organisation of the United Nations.

The EFSA panel also determined intakes for different populations. Recommended intake volumes in the elderly are the same as for adults as despite lower energy consumption, the water requirement of this group is increased due to a reduction in renal concentrating capacity. Pregnant and breastfeeding women require additional fluids to stay hydrated. The EFSA panel proposes that pregnant women should consume the same volume of water as non-pregnant women, plus an increase in proportion to the higher energy requirement, equal to 300 mL/day. To compensate for additional fluid output, breastfeeding women require an additional 700 mL/day above the recommended intake values for non-lactating women. Dehydration and over-hydration - too little and too much water, respectively - can have harmful consequences. Drinking too much water is one of the possible causes of hyponatremia, i.e., low serum sodium.

Alcohol (Ethanol)

Pure ethanol provides 7 calories per gram. For distilled spirits, a standard serving in the United States is 1.5 fluid ounces, which at 40% ethanol

(80 proof), would be 14 grams and 98 calories. Wine and beer contain a similar range of ethanol for servings of 5 ounces and 12 ounces, respectively, but these beverages also contain non-ethanol calories. A 5 ounce serving of wine contains 100 to 130 calories. A 12 ounce serving of beer contains 95 to 200 calories. According to the U.S. Department of Agriculture, based on NHANES 2013-2014 surveys, women ages 20 and up consume on average 6.8 grams/day and men consume on average 15.5 grams/day. Ignoring the non-alcohol contribution of those beverages, the average ethanol calorie contributions are 48 and 108 cal/day. Alcoholic beverages are considered empty calorie foods because other than calories, these contribute no essential nutrients.

Micronutrients

Minerals

Dietary minerals are inorganic chemical elements required by living organisms, other than the four elements carbon, hydrogen, nitrogen, and oxygen that are present in nearly all organic molecules. The term "mineral" is archaic, since the intent is to describe simply the less common elements in the diet. Some are heavier than the four just mentioned, including several metals, which often occur as ions in the body. Some dietitians recommend that these be supplied from foods in which they occur naturally, or at least as complex compounds, or sometimes even from natural inorganic sources (such as calcium carbonate from ground oyster shells). Some minerals are absorbed much more readily in the ionic forms found in such sources. On the other hand, minerals are often artificially added to the diet as supplements; the most famous is likely iodine in iodized salt which prevents goiter.

Macrominerals

Many elements are essential nutrients called dietary minerals. Some have roles as cofactors, while others are electrolytes. Elements with recommended dietary allowance (RDA) greater than 150 mg/day are, in alphabetical order:

- Calcium, a common electrolyte, but also needed structurally (for muscle and digestive system health, bone strength, some forms neutralize acidity, provides signaling ions for nerve and membrane functions)
- Chloride; electrolyte; see sodium, below.
- Magnesium, required for processing ATP and related reactions (builds bone, facilitates peristalsis)
- Phosphorus, required component of bones; essential for energy processing
- Potassium, an electrolyte (heart and nerve functions)

- Sodium, an electrolyte; common in food and manufactured beverages, typically as sodium chloride. Excessive sodium consumption can deplete calcium and magnesium, leading to high blood pressure.

Trace Minerals

Many elements are required in trace amounts, usually because they play a catalytic role in enzymes. Some trace mineral elements (RDA < 200 mg/day) are, in alphabetical order:

- Cobalt required for biosynthesis of vitamin B12 family of coenzymes. Animals cannot biosynthesize B12, and must obtain this cobalt-containing vitamin in their diet.
- Copper required component of many redox enzymes, including cytochrome c oxidase
- Chromium required for sugar metabolism
- Iodine required not only for the biosynthesis of thyroxine but also — it is presumed — for other important organs as breast, stomach, salivary glands, thymus, etc. (see Extrathyroidal iodine); for this reason iodine is needed in larger quantities than others in this list, and sometimes classified with the macrominerals
- Iron required for many enzymes, and for hemoglobin and some other proteins
- Manganese (processing of oxygen)
- Molybdenum required for xanthine oxidase and related oxidases
- Selenium required for peroxidase (antioxidant proteins)
- Zinc required for several enzymes such as carboxypeptidase, liver alcohol dehydrogenase, and carbonic anhydrase

Vitamins

Vitamins are essential nutrients, necessary in the diet for good health. (Vitamin D is an exception, as it can be synthesized in the skin in the presence of UVB radiation, and many animal species can synthesize vitamin C.) Vitamin deficiencies may result in disease conditions, including goitre, scurvy, osteoporosis, impaired immune system, disorders of cell metabolism, certain forms of cancer, symptoms of premature aging, and poor psychological health, among many others. Excess levels of some vitamins are also dangerous to health. The Food and Nutrition Board of the Institute of Medicine has established Tolerable Upper Intake Levels (ULs) for seven vitamins.

Medicine in Nature

Human beings have long depended on medicines from Nature to prevent and treat illnesses, and today the World Health Organization (WHO) estimates that up to 80% of the global population still relies on plants for primary health care.

For many of the 150 million tribal peoples, Nature provides a potent pharmacy that they can rely on, thanks to their detailed botanical knowledge; the upshot of a profound attunement to their ecosystems for thousands of years.

Thousands of years of patient observation and experimentation are evident too in the Innu people's awareness that earache can be successfully treated with the inner scrapings of beavers' scrota. "There are medicines out there that I know about," said an Innu man. "In the country I am an environmentalist and a biologist."

In tribal communities the role of 'biologist' is often performed by shamans: highly revered mediators between the living and the supernatural worlds, they combine the diagnostic and curative power of plants with spiritual healing. They use the psychoactive properties of plants to induce altered states of consciousness which allow them to commune with the spirits of natural phenomena in order to determine the cause of their patients' illnesses and ask advice on the appropriate treatment. "When for the first time you sniff the powder from the yãkõanahi tree, the xapiripë spirits begin to gather around you. Gradually, they reveal themselves," says DaviKopenawa, a Yanomami shaman from Brazil.

It is the oral traditions of tribal societies that have trained generations of shamans. Tribal languages are those of the land, suffused with vocabularies that contain complex geographical, geological, medicinal and climatic information. The Kallawaya, highland farmers and travelling healers in Bolivia who have a vast knowledge of wild plants and their therapeutic uses, have their own 'secret' language, called MachajJuyai, believed by some to be the language of the Inca kings. Encoded within this tongue is medical knowledge that has been handed down from father to son. Of the 7,000 languages in the world, however, around 4,000 are now endangered. "Every language and culture shows us something about the way a people has evolved to deal with the world," says linguist Daniel Everett. "So when a language dies, we lose ways of life, solutions to problems and classifications of plants and animals."

Were it not for the plant knowledge of tribal peoples, many vital medicinal compounds might still be unknown. Certain plant products, used initially as poisons by South American Indians, have become important in Western medicine. One example is the poison curare. Used on the tips of blowgun darts to render prey immobile, it has been appropriated as a muscle relaxant for humans and has made possible techniques such as open-heart surgery. As it is widely believed that the medicinal value of many plant species is as yet unknown to Western scientists, it makes sense to place greater value on the knowledge and experience of peoples who have been studying their flora and fauna for millennia.

Valuable as the botanical knowledge of tribal peoples is, perhaps even more so is their holistic approach to health. Wellbeing is seen not just as the absence of illness, but as a state of emotional, physical and spiritual harmony. Man is not an island: humans are dependent for their health on harmonious connections to each other and to the Earth.

This is a philosophy that takes into account the whole person, as opposed to the more reductive approach of allopathic medicine, which tends to consider an individual as composed of separate parts. As the industrialised world becomes increasingly aware of the adverse physical and mental effects of separation from Nature – one study has shown that gall-bladder surgery patients who had views of Nature from their hospital beds took less pain medication than those who had views of a concrete wall – the need to integrate the genius of Western medicine with the holistic understanding of tribal peoples becomes ever more urgent. And with new pathogens threatening to cross the species divide, the hope is that new medicinal plant compounds will be found.

Historically, most drugs have been derived from natural products, but there has been a shift away from their use with the increasing predominance of molecular approaches to drug discovery. Nevertheless, their structural diversity makes them a valuable source of novel lead compounds against newly discovered therapeutic targets. Technical advances in analytical techniques mean that the use of natural products is easier than before. However, there is a widening gap between natural-product researchers in countries rich in biodiversity and drug discovery scientists immersed in proteomics and high-throughput screening.

Medicinal Plants

Medicinal plants, also called medicinal herbs, have been discovered and used in traditional medicine practices since prehistoric times. Plants synthesise hundreds of chemical compounds for functions including defence against insects, fungi, diseases, and herbivorous mammals. Numerous phytochemicals with potential or established biological activity have been identified. However, since a single plant contains widely diverse phytochemicals, the effects of using a whole plant as medicine are uncertain. Further, the phytochemical content and pharmacological actions, if any, of many plants having medicinal potential remain unassessed by rigorous scientific research to define efficacy and safety.

The earliest historical records of herbs are found from the Sumerian civilisation, where hundreds of medicinal plants including opium are listed on clay tablets. The Ebers Papyrus from ancient Egypt, c. 1550 BC, describes over 850 plant medicines. The Greek physician Dioscorides, who worked in the Roman army, documented over 1000 recipes for medicines using over

600 medicinal plants in De materiamedica, c. 60 AD; this formed the basis of pharmacopoeias for some 1500 years. Drug research makes use of ethnobotany to search for pharmacologically active substances in nature, and has in this way discovered hundreds of useful compounds. These include the common drugs aspirin, digoxin, quinine, and opium. The compounds found in plants are of many kinds, but most are in four major biochemical classes: alkaloids, glycosides, polyphenols, and terpenes.

Medicinal plants are widely used in non-industrialized societies, mainly because they are readily available and cheaper than modern medicines. The annual global export value of the thousands of types of plants with suspected medicinal properties was estimated to be US$2.2 billion in 2012. In 2017, the potential global market for botanical extracts and medicines was estimated at several hundred billion dollars. In many countries, there is little regulation of traditional medicine, but the World Health Organization coordinates a network to encourage safe and rational usage. Medicinal plants face both general threats, such as climate change and habitat destruction, and the specific threat of over-collection to meet market demand.

All plants produce chemical compounds which give them an evolutionary advantage, such as defending against herbivores or, in the example of salicylic acid, as a hormone in plant defenses. These phytochemicals have potential for use as drugs, and the content and known pharmacological activity of these substances in medicinal plants is the scientific basis for their use in modern medicine, if scientifically confirmed. For instance, daffodils (Narcissus) contain nine groups of alkaloids including galantamine, licensed for use against Alzheimer's disease. The alkaloids are bitter-tasting and toxic, and concentrated in the parts of the plant such as the stem most likely to be eaten by herbivores; they may also protect against parasites.

Modern knowledge of medicinal plants is being systematised in the Medicinal Plant Transcriptomics Database, which by 2011 provided a sequence reference for the transcriptome of some thirty species. The major classes of pharmacologically active phytochemicals are described below, with examples of medicinal plants that contain them.

Cultivation

Medicinal plants demand intensive management. Different species each require their own distinct conditions of cultivation. The World Health Organization recommends the use of rotation to minimise problems with pests and plant diseases. Cultivation may be traditional or may make use of conservation agriculture practices to maintain organic matter in the soil and to conserve water, for example with no-till farming systems. In many medicinal and aromatic plants, plant characteristics vary widely with soil type and cropping strategy, so care is required to obtain satisfactory yields.

Preparation

Medicinal plants are often tough and fibrous, requiring some form of preparation to make them convenient to administer. According to the Institute for Traditional Medicine, common methods for the preparation of herbal medicines include decoction, powdering, and extraction with alcohol, in each case yielding a mixture of substances. Decoction involves crushing and then boiling the plant material in water to produce a liquid extract. Powdering involves drying the plant material and then crushing it to yield a powder that can be compressed into tablets. Alcohol extraction involves soaking the plant material in cold wine or distilled spirit to form a tincture.

Traditional poultices were made by boiling medicinal plants, wrapping them in a cloth, and applying the resulting parcel externally to the affected part of the body.

When modern medicine has identified a drug in a medicinal plant, commercial quantities of the drug may either be synthesised or extracted from plant material, yielding a pure chemical. Extraction can be practical when the compound in question is complex.

Usage

Plant medicines are in wide use around the world. In most of the developing world, especially in rural areas, local traditional medicine, including herbalism, is the only source of health care for people, while in the developed world, alternative medicine including use of dietary supplements is marketed aggressively using the claims of traditional medicine. As of 2015, most products made from medicinal plants had not been tested for their safety and efficacy, and products that were marketed in developed economies and provided in the undeveloped world by traditional healers were of uneven quality, sometimes containing dangerous contaminants. Traditional Chinese medicine makes use of a wide variety of plants, among other materials and techniques. Researchers from Kew Gardens found 104 species used for diabetes in Central America, of which seven had been identified in at least three separate studies. The Yanomami of the Brazilian Amazon, assisted by researchers, have described 101 plant species used for traditional medicines.

Drugs derived from plants including opiates, cocaine and cannabis have both medical and recreational uses. Different countries have at various times made use of illegal drugs, partly on the basis of the risks involved in taking psychoactive drugs.

REFERENCES

Alcohol and Nutrition: The Calorie and Carb Breakdown!. The Catholic University of America.

NHANES (2014): What We Eat in America, NHANES 2013-2014".

Mitchell, Dakota; Haroun, Lee (2012). Introduction to Health Care (3 ed.). Delmar Cengage. p. 279. ISBN 978-1-4354-8755-0.

Nelson, D.L.; Cox, M.M. (2000). Lehninger Principles of Biochemistry (3rd ed.). New York: Worth Publishing. ISBN 978-1-57259-153-0.

Corbridge, D.E.C. (1995). Phosphorus: An Outline of its Chemistry, Biochemistry, and Technology (5th ed.). Amsterdam: Elsevier. ISBN 978-0-444-89307-9.

"Chapter 14. Magnesium". Food and Agriculture Organization of the United States.

Lippard, S.J.; Berg, J.M. (1994). Principles of Bioinorganic Chemistry. Mill Valley, CA: University Science Books. ISBN 978-0-935702-72-9.

Shils, M.S.; *et al.*, eds. (2005). Modern Nutrition in Health and Disease. Lippincott Williams and Wilkins. ISBN 978-0-7817-4133-0.

https://www.downtoearth.org.in/blog/health/food-for-nutrition-nature-livelihood-50396

https://www.nature.com/subjects/nutrition

https://en.wikipedia.org/wiki/Nutrition

https://www.resurgence.org/magazine/article3130-medicines-from-nature.html

https://www.sciencedirect.com/science/article/abs/pii/S0165614799013462

https://en.wikipedia.org/wiki/Medicinal_plants

Section I:
Nutrition

Pages: 3-22

Nutrition and Medicines in Nature
Edited by: **Dr. Jairam Singh and Dr. Pawan Kumar 'Bharti'**
ISBN: 978-93-88854-39-9
Edition: **2020**
Published by: **Discovery Publishing House Pvt. Ltd., New Delhi (India)**

1

Spirulina - Nutrition of the Future

M.R.A. Manimala

INTRODUCTION

Spirulina are multicellular and filamentous blue-green algae that has gained considerable popularity in the health food industry and increasingly as a protein and vitamin supplement to aquaculture diets. It grows in water, can be harvested and processed easily and has very high macro- and micro-nutrient contents.. In many countries of Africa, it is still used as human food as a major source of protein and is collected from natural water, dried and eaten. It has gained considerable popularity in the human health food industry and in many countries of Asia it is used as protein supplement and as health food. Spirulina has been used as a complementary dietary ingredient of feed for fish, shrimp and poultry, and increasingly as a protein and vitamin supplement to aquafeeds. China is using this micro-alga as a partial substitute of imported forage to promote the growth, immunity and viability of shrimp. There has also been comprehensive research on the use of spirulina as aquaculture feed additives in Japan.

Species: Various spirulina species are:

- *Spirulina maxima*
- *Spirulina platensis*
- *Spirulina pacifica*
- *Arthrospira platensis* is the predominant species and commercially cultivated worldwide.
- *Arthrospira maxima* are produced in the South and Central American regions.

Mother Terasa College of Agriculture, (Affiliated to Tamil Nadu Agricultural University) Mettusalai, Illuppur, Pudukkottai – 622 102, (Tamilnadu) (India)

SPIRULINA: NUTRIENT VALUE

Spirulina is one of the natural sources containing the highest amount of protein - five times that of meat. Spirulina provides the majority of essential and nonessential amino acids. It has a fairly well-balanced amino acid pattern and contains the highest amount of beta-carotene, a precursor of vitamin A. It is the only vegetable source of vitamin B12 having two and half times the amount in liver. It is also the source of the essential fatty acid γ-linolenic acid which is the precursor of hormones involved in regulation of body functions. The constituents of spirulina include protein (50-70%) including all essential amino-acids, essential fatty acids, polysaccharides, B vitamins particularly vitamin B12, beta-carotene and minerals particularly iron [Khan *et al.*, 2005].

Spirulina has been demonstrated to be an effective dietary source of vitamin A. An investigation in India on preschool children with vitamin A deficiency demonstrated that the bioavailability of carotenes from spirulina was comparable to that from other sources such as carrots and green leafy vegetables thereby suggesting the potential use of spirulina as a dietary source of vitamin A [Annapurna *et al.*, 1991]. Spirulina has a positive impact on weight and other parameters like arm circumference, height, albumin, prealbumin, protein and hemoglobin improved after spirulina supplementation [Azabji-Kenfack *et al.*, 2011]. Improvement in nutritional status of malnourished HIV-infected patients has also been shown by supplementing the diet with spirulina. Moreover spirulina can be safely administered to children without any risk and is considered a very suitable food (United Nations World Health Organization, Geneva, Switzerland June 8th, 1993).

Biochemical composition of *Spirulina platensis* The basic biochemical composition of *Spirulina* can be summarized as follows,

Protein: *Spirulina* contains unusually high amounts of protein between 55 and 70 per cent by dry weight. It is a complete protein, containing all essential amino acids. (Table 1.1).

Table 1.1: General Composition of Spirulina [Thomas, 2010]

Nutrient Composition	Percentage (%)
Protein	60-69%
Carbohydrates	16-20%
Lipids	5-7%
Minerals	6-9%
Moisture	2.5-6%

Essential fatty acids: Ishikawa *et al.* studied that, GLA has mainly respect to its therapeutic properties such as its ability to decrease blood cholesterol levels. *Spirulina* has a high amount of polyunsaturated fatty acids, 1.5-2.0 per cent of 5-6 per cent total lipid. *Spirulina* is rich in linolenic acid, stearidonic acid, eicosapentaenoic acid, docosahexaenoic acid and arachidonic acid

Vitamins: *Spirulina* contains vitamin B1, B2, B3, B6, B12, vitamin C, vitamin D and vitamin E. (Table 1.3).

Minerals: *Spirulina* is a rich source of potassium, calcium, chromium, copper, iron, magnesium, manganese, phosphorous, selenium, sodium and zinc.

Photosynthetic pigments: *Spirulina* contains many pigments including chlorophyll-a, xanthophylls, β-carotene, echinenone, myxoxanthophyll, etc. and the phycobiliproteins C-phycocyanin and allophycocyanin. (Table 1.2)

Table 1.2: Phytopigments (mg / 100g) [Thomas, 2010]

Pigments	Quantity
Total Carotenoids	400-650
Beta Carotene	150-250
Xanthophylls	250-470
Zeaxanthin	125-200
Chlorophyll	1300-1700
Phycocyanin	15000-19000

Table 1.3: Vitamins (mg/100g) [Thomas, 2010]

Vitamins	Composition
Vitamin B1 (Thiamine)	0.1.5-0.30
Vitamin B2 (Riboflavin)	4.0-7.0
Vitamin B3 (Niacin)	10.0-25.0
Vitamin B6 (Pyridoxine)	0.5-1.5
Vitamin B12	0.10-0.30
Folic acid	0.05-0.30
Inositol	70-90
Vitamin K	0.90-1.05

Nutrient profile of Spirulina vs other foods

- It contains 180% more calcium than whole milk
- It contains 670% more protein than tofu
- It contains 3100% more beta carotene than carrots
- It contains 5100% more iron than spinach

- It have more antioxidant and anti-inflammatory activity in 3g of *Spiurlina* than in five servings of fruits and vegetables [Moorhead *et al.*, 2005]

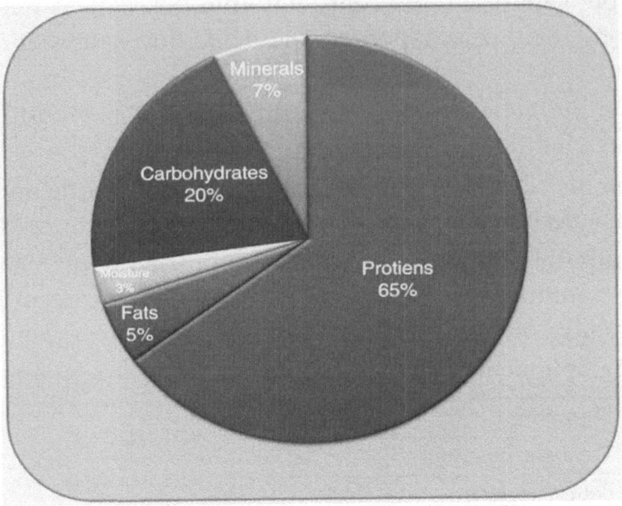

Fig. 1.1: Nutrient composition of *Spirulina*

Mechanism of Action

Sprirulina can be used simply as a protein supplement but it is also considered to have specific effects on the immune system. Preliminary studies in healthy humans suggest that spirulina increases the production of the cytokines, tumour necrosis factor, interleukin (IL)-2, and interferon, and causes CD4+ Thelper cell proliferation [Lobner *et al.*, 2008]. It also appears to increase the activity and cytotoxicity of natural killer cells [Nielsen *et al.*, 2011]. Animal studies have demonstrated chemoprotective effects when spirulina is given with various cytotoxic drugs. Several animal studies have investigated the potential of spirulina to have a protective effect against toxicity related to various cytotoxic agents such as cardiotoxity, nephrotoxicity & hepatotoxicity.

Health Benefits of Spirulina

Research on Spirulina's health benefits has been far-ranging. In addition to antioxidant and anti-inflammatory effects other potential health applications are:

- Protection of the liver and kidneys
- Improvement of blood quality and prevention of anaemia
- Benefits for diabetes
- Reduction in Blood Pressure
- Removal of heavy metals from the body

- Radioprotection
- Prevention of liver and renal toxicity
- Antioxidant action
- Immune protection
- Relief in allergic reactions [Capelli *et al.*,2010]

HISTORICAL BACKGROUND ON THE USE OF SPIRULINA AS HUMAN FOOD AND ANIMAL FEED

Spirulina is a primitive organism originating some 3.5 billion years ago that has established the ability to utilize carbon dioxide dissolved in seawater as a nutrient source for their reproduction. Spirulina is a photosynthesizing cyanophyte (blue-green algae) that grows vigorously in strong sunshine under high temperatures and highly alkaline conditions.

Historical use

In the sixteenth century, when the Spanish invaders conquered Mexico, they discovered that the Aztecs living in the Valley of Mexico in the capital Tenochtitlan were collecting a "new food" from the lake (Sasson, 1997). Spanish chroniclers described fishermen with fine nets collecting this blue coloured "techuitlatl" from the lagoons and making a blue-green cake from it. Other legends say Aztec messenger runners took spirulina on their marathons. Techuitlatl was mentioned by naturalists until the end of the sixteenth century, but not after that, probably reflecting the loss of the lakes as they were drained for urban and agricultural development. The only remnant today, Lake Texcoco, still has a living algae spirulina population.

The Kanembu population living along the shores of Lake Chad collects the wet algae in clay pots, drain out the water through bags of cloth and spread out the algae in the sandy shore of the lake for sun drying. The semi-dried algae is then cut into small squares and taken to the villages, where the drying is completed on mats in the sun (Abdulqader, Barsanti and Tredici, 2000). When dry, women take these algae cakes for sale in the local market. Dihé is crumbled and mixed with a sauce of tomatoes and peppers, and poured over millet, beans, fish or meat and is eaten by the Kanembu in 70 percent of their meals (www.spirulinasource.com). Pregnant women eat dihé cakes directly because they believe its dark colour will screen their unborn baby from the eyes of sorcerers. Spirulina is also applied externally as a poultice for treating certain diseases. Abdulqader, Barsanti and Tredici (2000) further noted that the local trading value of the dihé annually harvested from Lake Kossorom in Chad (about 40 tonnes) amounts to more than US $100,000, which represents an important contribution to the economy of the area.

Fig. 1.2: Ganimou people eat Blue green algae (*Spirulina*) found floating on the lake surface

Rediscovery of spirulina

In 1940, a French phycologist Dangeard published a report on the consumption of dihé by the Kanembu people near Lake Chad. Dangeard also noted these same algae populated a number of lakes in the Rift Valley of East Africa, and was the main food for the flamingos living around those lakes. Twenty-five years later during 1964-65, a botanist on a Belgian Trans-Saharan expedition, Jean Léonard, reported finding a curious greenish, edible cakes being sold in native markets of Fort-Lamy (now N'Djamena) in Chad. When locals said these cakes came from areas near Lake Chad, Léonard recognized the connection between the algal blooms and dried cakes sold in the market.

In 1967 spirulina was established as a "wonderful future food source" in the International Association of Applied Microbiology (Sasson, 1997). Analysis of the nutritional properties of spirulina showed first and foremost an exceptionally high protein content, of the order of 60-70 percent of its dry weight; it also showed the excellent quality of its proteins (balanced essential amino acid content). This first data was enough to launch many research projects for industrial purposes in the 1970s, because micro-organisms (yeast, chlorella, spirulina, some bacteria and moulds) seemed at that time to be the most direct route to inexpensive proteins – the iconic "single cell proteins".

At the same time when Léonard rediscovered spirulina in Africa, a request was received from a company named Sosa-Texcoco Ltd by the "Institut français du pétrole" to study a bloom of algae occurring in the evaporation ponds of their sodium bicarbonate production facility in a lake near Mexico City. While finally no micro-organism fulfilled its promise of cheap protein, spirulina continued to give rise to research and increasing production, reflecting its perceived nutritional assets (Falquet, 2000).

MORPHOLOGY AND TAXANOMIC STATUS

Holmgren *et al.* observed cross walls in *Spirulina* major under electron microscope and suggested the transfer of *Spirulina* major into the genus

Athrospira on the criterion of the presence of cellular septation. *Spirulina* and *Athrospira,* the non heterocyst unbranched filamentous genera of order *Nostacles* and family Osillatoriaceae wear identified. Presence of two filament in a single unit and absence of cellular septation under light microscope wear the main point which differentiated *Spirulina* from *Athrospira* . Hintak described a *Spirulina fusiformis* from the Kenya with a fusiform trichome construction. He mentioned that a relatively small, inconspicuous, broadly rounded calyptra was occasionally formed with or without an accompanying tapering of the trichome. *Spirulina* consisted multicellular, filamentous, unbranched and helicoidel trichomes wear formed by a single spirally twisted cell. Motile structure like flagella and heterocysts which are generally present in many blue green algae wear absent .The filaments wear called 'trichome'. The cells wear cylindrical and the spiral wear loose. The cells exhibited active rotary movements. The helical shape of the trichome was characteristic of the genus but the helical parameters varied with the species even within the same species (Somasekaran, 1987). *Spirulina platensis* is a filamentous, photoautotrophic, alkaliphilic cyanobacterium that belongs to the Family Oscillatoriaceae, Division Cyanophyta. This cyanobacterium blooms in bicarbonate-rich environments and has gained a significant position in recent years as a source of proteins and pigments in the food, pharmaceutical, and cosmetic industries.

Desikachary and Jeeji Bai isolated four strains in India and described taxanomicaly. One of strains had a fusiforms structure with erect end portion. Another strain had a basic spindle shaped condition. The third type had a loosely coiled 'S' condition. The fourth type which had been described as an "I" form was essentially not a straight filament. Even through minor variations wear found between these isolates, they were conceded to belong to the same taxon and described as a new species. Deore studied the taxanomy of *Spirulina gigantea* var. *Schmidle* and *Spirulina platensis* var. *tenius.* The alga *Spirulina gigntea var schmidle* showed trichome with regular spiral, 4-6 numbers per trichome and deep blue green in colour. Trichome was 3 ìm broud, 14.4 ìm long and the distance between two spiral was 31 - 33 ìm. *Spirulina platensis* had pale blue-green and it showed distinct separation. Trichome was 6 ìm broad, 14.4 ìm long, regularly coiled. The breadth of spiral was 26 ìm and distance between two spiral was 31ìm. Pelizer *et al.* reported that *Spirulina platensis* is generally produced in open ponds in liquid culture but there is recent production possible also In solid-state cultivation system but the estimation of cell growth is made difficult in separating cells from the cultivated medium incase of solid-state cultivation systems.

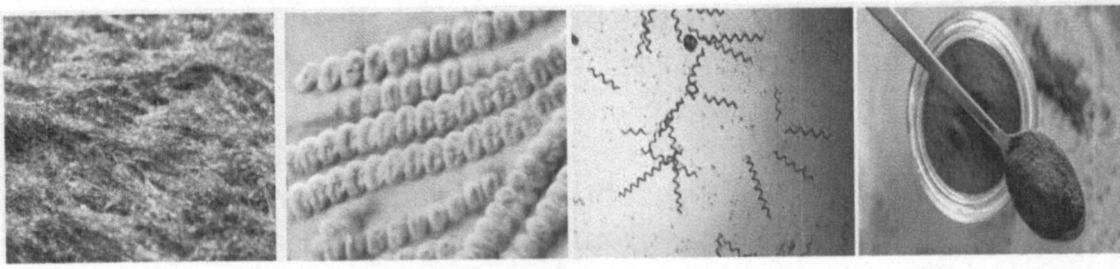

Fig. 1.3: Images of *Spirulina*

Nutrient medium Spirulina required high nutrient inputs and salt concentrations compared to *Scenedesmus* and *Chlorella*. This might be the reason for *Spirulina* was naturally grown in salt lakes exclusively (Ogawa and Teuri,1970). The difficult media currently in use in various centers of production were small alternations of the medium first developed by Zarrouk's for *Spirulina* culture. *Spirulina* required a medium of high alkalinity and a steady supply of bicarbonates ions (Cifferi, 1983).

Carbon source: Ogawa and Terui reported that *Spirulina* did not grow in organic compounds as the sole carbon source. To increase the productions of cyanobacteria, during mass culture, the minimal medium without sodium chloride fertilized with extracts of different organic manures were used. The dry matter production of *Spirulina subsalsa* and *Spirulina platensis* was increased by 5 to 30 per cent. Nasima *et al.* reported that the Rice Husk Ash (RHA) and $NaHCO_3$ l^{-1} were used as a source of carbon in *Spirulina* culture. Addition of 2g of $NaHCO_3$ l^{-1} every other day supported better growth than 1 g RHA l^{-1}everyday. However, from an economic point of view RHA was preferred.

Gardillo *et al.* studied the effect of increased atmospheric CO_2 on photosynthesis and growth of *Spirulina*. The increase of CO_2 did not cause any change in maximum growth rate while it decreased maximum biomass yield as it affected the pigment content of the algae.Vieira Costa *et al.* reported that, the influence of nutrient for biomass production of *Spirulina platensis*, in open raceway ponds in addition of (carbon as sodium bicarbonate, nitrogen as urea, phosphate, sulfate, ferric iron, magnesium and potassium) on the growth rate of the cyanobacteria *Spirulina platensis*. In unsupplemented lagoon water production of *S. platensis* was 0.78 ± 0.01 g/l (dry weight basis) while the addition of 2.88 g/l of sodium bicarbonate resulted in 0.82 ± 0.01 g/l after 40 hours of culture.

Temperature: Temperature in the range of 30-35°C even if the outside temperature as 38°C was most ideally suited for getting maximum yield of *Spirulina*. Temperature above 35°C leads to bleaching of cultures. Partial shading provided a culture temperature of about 30°C even if the outside temperature was 38°C. Rafiqul Islam *et al.* [60] reported that, the maximum specific growth rate of 0.141 was found at 32°C for *Spirulina platensis* and that of 0.144 was found at 37°C for *Spirulina fusiformis*. Maximum biomass production of 2.4 g l-1 and chlorophyll *a* production of 16.6 mg l^{-1} were observed at 32°C for *Spirulina platensis.* Maximum biomass production of 2.3 g l^{-1} and chlorophyll - *a* production of 14.2 mg l^{-1} were observed at 37° C for *Spirulina fusiformis.* Luciane Maria Colla *et al.* found that, temperature was the most important factor and that the greatest amount of gamma-linolenic acid (GLA) was obtained at 30 °C, the fatty acid profile of the *Spirulina* cultivated showing that (in order of abundance) palmitic, linolenic and linoleic olenic and linoleic acids were most prevalent.

Water quality: The characteristics of water quality contributed in the algal mass production. It had dual influence, firstly by affecting the solubility of nutrients added in the medium and also selective accumulation of certain heavy metals by algae during the growth phase. *Spirulina* required light intensities during its growth phase. The optimal light intensity was between 20 and 30 K lux. Subramanian and Jeejibai reported on the effect of different light quality on growth, protein and pigment synthesis of *Spirulina fusiformis.* The light was provided for 10 hours at 2 K lux intensity, with coloured cellophane paper covering the fluorescent bulbs. Blue light yielded highest protein content followed by yellow, white, red and green light. It was evident that white fluorescent light with a red-orange component provided higher energy for better protein and pigment synthesis. Watanable and Hall investigated the photosynthetic productivity of the filamentous cyanobacaterium *Spirulina platensis* in a cone-shaped helical tubular photobioreactor. It was constructed with 0.255 m^2 basal area and conical shape. The inner surface of the photostage was illuminated with compact fluorescent cool white lamps and the input radiation energy was 1249 kj d^{-1}. The maximum photosynthetic efficiency obtained was 6.83 per cent which is corresponded to a production rate of 15.9 g dry biomass $m^{-2}d^{-1}$.

Dubey had reported moderate light intensity in the cultivation of *Spirulina,* suggesting low light intensity at the beginning to avoid photolysis. He also noted that exposing *Spirulina* to high light intensity photolysis them. Pandey *et al.* found that, the influence of light intensity for *Spirulina platensis* growth at 5 Klux light intensity the dry weight of *Spirulina platensis* was 0.85g/500ml while protein content and Chlorophyll *a* were 64.3% and 9.8mg/gm respectively. *Spirulina platensis* is an important source of pharmaceuticals and nutraceuticals such as g-linolenic acid (GLnA). GLnA yield of the culture medium (32 mg/L) were obtained at the highest light intensity of 5.0 klx

pH: Vincent and Silvester reported that the pH had a direct effect on the physiological properties of algae and the availability of nutrient. pH determined the solubility of carbon source and minerals in the culture directly or indirectly. *Spirulina* grew well at pH values between 9 and 11. The optimal pH of the *Spirulina* nutrient medium was shifted from 8.4 to

9.5 during the mass cultivation, due to the consumption of bicarbonate and sodium ions. The influence of pH for *Spirulina platensis* growth, protein and Chlorophyll a content were examined and the dry weight of *Spirulina platensis* was 0.91g/500ml and protein and Chlorophyll *a* content were 64.3% and 13.2mg/gm respectively at pH 9.

Inoculum size: Tasneem Fatma reported that synchronous growth of *Spirulina platensis* was failed to grow both in liquid and solid media at its higher dilution. It was observed that minimum cell population is necessary to initiate and sustain *Spirulina* cultures. The culture filtrate had an absorbance of 0.96 on ninth day increased 50 per cent growth against control (0.63 absorbance).

Agitation: Agitation of algal cultures had the advantages of uniform distribution of CO_2 and prevention of thermal stratification. Many agitational devices had been reported which range from motor driven paddles, pumps, gravity flow, air light systems and manual agitation. Dubey found that, aeration, which could be achieved by rotators, and which provides agitation of growing cells to maintain the cells in suspension, has been described as very necessary in getting good quality and better yields of *Spirulina* species.

Contamination: Venkatraman and Sindhukanya reported the insect contamination in mass culture of *Spirulina platensis*. The mosquito larvae fed on the algal biomass for 2-3 days before entering into pupal stage and the decrease in algal yield was upto 10 per cent. The use of fine wire mesh frame removed all extraneous materials. The presence of bacterial contaminants in outdoor cultivation of *Spirulina platensis*. The bacterial forms occurred in cultures were identified as aerobic spore formers. No the pathogenic forms affecting the products safety were identified.

Other growth factors: Hofner *et al.* reported that the hexavalent chromium was most toxic and the zinc had little effect on the growth of *Chlorella fusce*. All elements tested arrest growth of *Spirulina maxima* at 10^{-4} M and smaller doses had no effect. The effect of mercuric chloride, cadmium chloride, nickel sulpahte and zinc chloride on the growth of *Spirulina platensis*. Among the metals, mercury had been most toxic and the algal growth was reduced even at 0.01 ppm. It was followed by cadmium (0.1 ppm). Higher doses resulted in fragmentation, lysis and death of the algae.

A variety of *Spirulina* products for human consumption were analysed for mercury and lead content, using cold vapour atomic absorption and graphite furnace atomic absorption detection. No *Spirulina* product tested contained Hg or Pb concentrations high enough to approach the WHO/FAO caution guidelines for daily intake of those elements. Nanda and Padhi studied the effect of sodium salt to 2,4-Dichlorophenoxyacetic acid (2,4-D), on the growth and pigmentation of *Spirulina platensis*. It was found to be very sensitive towards 2,4-D and the growth of algae inhibited at 5 mg ml^{-1}.

Ken Sasaki *et al.* reported that the growth of *Spirulina platensis* was stimulated by adding 5-Aminolevulinic acid (ALA, 500 mg l^{-1}). The photosynthetic activity was enhanced by rapid stimulation and accumulation of phycocyanin and chlorophyll II.

Mass Cultivation of *Spirulina* sp.

Spirulina is an economically important filamentous cyanobacterium. The annual production of the algae is about 10,000 tons which makes it the largest microalgal cultivation industry in the world. Due to its richness in protein, phycocyanin, essential amino acids, polysaccharides, carotenoids, minerals, vitamins and essential fatty acids has been regarded as an ideal bio-resource and has drawn increasing attention in recent decades (Chen *et al.*, 2006). *Spirulina platensis* is a cyanobacterium that has been largely studied due to its commercial importance as a source of protein, vitamins, essential amino acids, and fatty acids. More recently, special attention has been given to *Spirulina platensis* as a potential source of pharmaceuticals, and other high value products such as chlorophyll. The utilization of chlorophyll from *Spirulina platensis* is an attractive alternative that should be considered due to its high content of this pigment, and ease of cultivation. The Cyanobacteria *Spirulina platensis* possesses a high tolerance to alkaline pH, for ease of cultivation; a large size for its cell aggregates for ease of harvest; and an easily digestible cell wall. The utilization of chlorophyll from *Spirulina platensis* is an attractive alternative that should be considered due to its high content of this pigment, and ease of cultivation. The Cyanobacteria *Spirulina platensis* possesses a high tolerance to alkaline pH, for ease of cultivation; a large size for its cell aggregates for ease of harvest; and an easily digestible cell wall.

Stanca and Popovici demonstrated that the utilization of urea as a nitrogen source in *Spirulina platensis* cultivation leads to an increase in both the total biomass and the biomass chlorophyll content. Urea is easily assimilated by *Spirulina platensis*, probably due to its spontaneous hydrolysis to ammonia under alkaline cultivation. Rice husk ash (RHA) and $NaHCO_3$ were use as a source of carbon in *Spirulina* culture. They reported that the addition of 2.0 g $NaHCO_3$/litre every two days supported better growth of *Spirulina* than 1.0 g RHA/litre every day, although this might not be supported on economic ground. Zhang *et al.* investigated the effects of initial glucose concentration and light intensity on specific growth rate; phycocyanin concentration and cell dry weight concentration in mixotrophic batch cultivation of *Spirulina platensis* using both shake flask and fermentor. Based on experimental results in shake flask culture, a number of mathematical models were constructed, and the optimal initial glucose concentration and the optimal light intensity were calculated. Finally, a time-dependent kinetic model for mixotrophic batch cultivation of *Spirulina platensis* in fermentor was also proposed. This was in good agreement with the experimental results and could be employed to predict the production of biomass and phycocyanin, and the consumption of glucose in fermentor culture.

Tri-Panji *et al.* attempted to grow *Spirulina platensis* using optimization media from low-cost nutrient sources. Optimum medium composition consisting of mineral salt and organic complex derived from low-cost nutrient sources. *Spirulina platensis* grown on complex media containing latex serum from concentrated latex factory, supplemented with salt minerals might produce high yielding carotenoids. Among eleven media composition containing latex serum examined, best growth on a formulated medium with a ratio of C: N: P: Mg = 1:3:0.3:0.2 yielding 0.350 g biomass/ L This amount was slightly lesser than those on synthetic Aiba & Ogawa medium that yields 0.407 g biomass/L, after eight-week incubation. Elias *et al.* documented improvement for the mass-scale culture of microalgae with the use of sophisticated closed systems. The proposed photo-bioreactor in this study is a combination of helical parts receiving strong light with a main culture vessel mixed and degassed by airlift. A first experimental trial was carried out with the filamentous cyanobacterium *Spirulina platensis* achieving maximal volumetric productivity of 1.2 $gl^{-1}d^{-1}$comparable with the maximal reported values by other closed culture designs for the same organism. The proposed system is under optimization of its engineering elements in order to comprise a sound modular solution for commercial production of microalgae of economic interest.

Dansei *et al.* cultivated the microalgae using urea as the nitrogen source by a fed-batch process. The addition of urea was done in four different modes: intermittent addition every 24 or 48 h, continuous addition by exponentially increasing the added mass, and continuous addition by using a constant mass rate. The experiments were carried out at three different temperatures: 27°C; 30°C and 33°C and at a constant light intensity. The results showed a positive influence of urea in the growth of *Spirulina* but no effect on the chlorophyll content of the cultures. Best results were obtained by continuous urea addition in exponentially increasing amount, at 30°C. Jorge *et al.* [99] studied the influence of nutrient on the growth rate of the Cyanobacteria *Spirulina platensis* using a 22 factorial design. In unsupplemented lagoon water production of *Spirulina platensis* was 0.78 ± 0.01 g/l (dry weight basis) while the addition of 2.88 g/l of sodium bicarbonate (without added urea, phosphate, sulfate or metal ions) resulted in 0.82 ± 0.01 g/l after 400 hours of culture. The further addition of phosphate and metal ions resulted in growth for up to 750 h and a final *Spirulina platensis* biomass of 1.23 ± 0.04 to 1.34 ± 0.03 g/l.

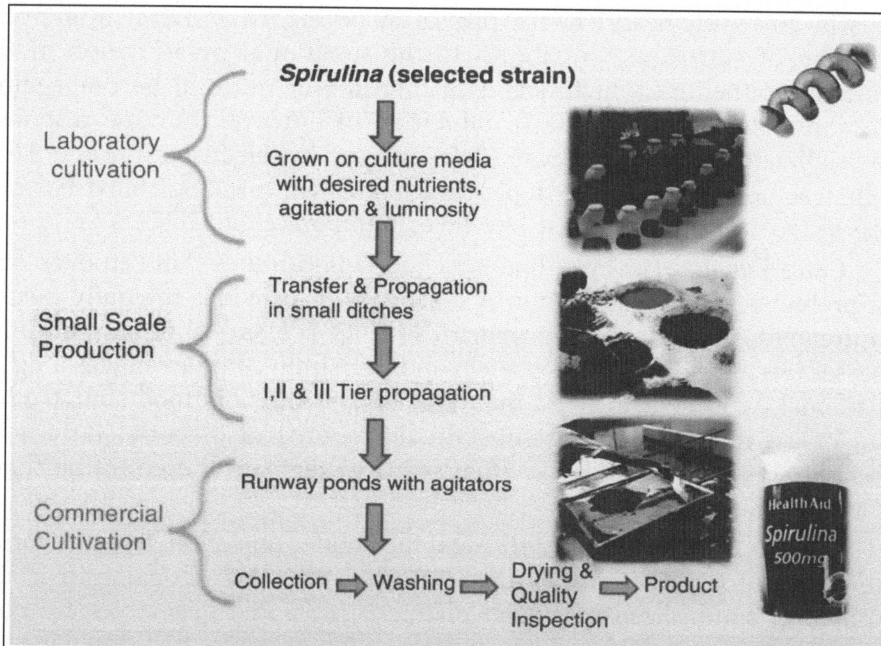

Fig. 1.4: Overview of flowchart for *Spirulina* production from lab to commercial production

THERAPEUTIC USES OF SPIRULINA

Protein source for Malnutrition: Spirulina has no cellulose in its cell walls, being composed of soft mucopolysaccharides. This makes it easily digested and assimilated. It is 85 to 95% digestible making it important for people suffering from intestinal malabsorption, typically, older people. They find spirulina's protein easy to digest. Spirulina is effective for victims of malnutrition diseases like kwashiorkor, where the ability of intestinal absorption has been damaged. For malnourished children, it is more effective than milk powders because milk's lactic acid can be difficult to absorb Kelly *et al.* (2011). Spirulina is 65% protein which is extremely high for a plant, and one of the reasons it is becoming more popular. It also contains sources of all 8 essential amino acids. It's an easy, healthy way to boost your protein intake, and a great source of protein for vegetarians. Furthermore, this protein is highly absorbable (Sharoba, 2014)

Antiviral Activity: There is a strong therapeutic research involving spirulina, its strong antibacterial and antimycotic substance which is isolated from *S.platensis*.These results demonstrate excellent in vitro inhibition of HIV-1 virus both in human T-cell lines and in human monocytes. Thetherapeutic index of the extract is reported to be over 100 and concentrations as low as 5-10 µg/ml evidently reduce the production of virus in any system and hence proves to be highly antiviral in activity. Ingestion of spirulina contributes to the functional preservation of the intestinal epithelium which acts as a first line of mucosal barrier against infections (Sheahan *et al.*, 2003). Inhibition of humoral immune response, cell mediated immune response (delayed type hypersensitivity) and TNF-alpha was noticed in a dose-dependent manner in mice. Spirulina has also been found to protect against hay fever (Simpore *et al.*, 2005).

Cures Eye disease: Spirulina is rich in beta-carotene that can overcome eye problems caused by vitamin A deficiency. It provides the daily dietary requirement of beta-carotene which can help prevent blindness and eye diseases (Seshadri, 1993). The protein and B-vitamin complex makes a major nutritional improvement in an infant's diet. It is the only food source other than breast milk containing substantial amounts of essential fatty acid, essential amino acids and GLA that helps to regulate the entire hormone system (Ramesh *et al.*, 2013).

Substitute for Animal meat: Algal foods offer one of the few vegetarian alternatives for cobalamin (vitamin B12) in the diet. Cobalamin is not required or synthesized by higher plants so fruits and vegetables are poor sources of vitamin B12, which explains why vitamin B12-deficiency is common among people following strict vegetarian or vegan diets.Of all the vitamins, vitamin B12 is the largest and most complex; it represents all of the biologically active cobalamins. The fact that Spirulina has an exceptionally high content of vitamin B12 –as other sea weed do- is of great importance because such vitamin is contained only in animal origin foods. Thus it is considered as a good source for vegans for B12 vitamins.

Effects against Nephrotoxicity: The hepatoprotective action of Spirulina fusiformis is against GalN induced hepatotoxicity in mice. The protective efficacy of Spirulina fusiformis is very promising as evidenced by the reversal of the altered values following administration probably by promoting regeneration of hepatocytes that restore integrity and it was confirmed by the histopathological studies. The hepatoprotective property of the extract may be attributed to the presence of various constituents which are present in Spirulina fusiformis (Mathew *et al.*, 1995).

Still extensive research is required for understanding of the mechanism of action of Spirulina fusiformis for providing protection against galactosamine induced hepatotoxicity (Sharma and Dunkwal, 2012).

Anti-Inflammatory Effects: Recent research reveals that free bilirubin functions physiologically as a potent inhibitor of NADPH oxidase activity. The chromophore phycocyanobilin (PCB), found in blue-green algae and cyanobacteria such as Spirulina, also has been found to be a potent inhibitor of this enzyme complex, likely because in mammalian cells it is rapidly reduced to phycocyanorubin, a close homolog of bilirubin (Helliwell, 2011).

Orally administered Spirulina or phycocyanin (the Spirulina holoprotein that contains PCB) can exert a wide range of anti-inflammatory effects. Until PCB enriched Spirulina extracts or synthetically produced PCB are commercially available, the most feasible and least expensive way to administer PCB is by ingestion of whole Spirulina.

Role of Spirulina in Immunity: Spirulina helps in building immunity and improving resistance to viral infections, enhance components of the mucosal and systemic immune system as it activates the cells of innate immune system. Spirulina has also been shown to activate macrophages, T and B cells (Swartz *et al.*, 1987). Sulfolipids derived from spirulina have also proved effective against HIV. Extracts from Spirulina biomass have also been found active against herpes virus, cytomegalovirus, influenza virus, etc. Spirulina extracts have also been shown capable of inhibiting carcinogenesis. Spirulina use leads to higher levels of natural killer cells, interferon gamma and more potent production of interleukins. Immune system strengthening: Several experiments have shown that spirulina has a favorable regulatory effect on the immune system. It stimulates the activation of macrophages, as well as the activity of T cells and NK cells. This process induces the release of interferon-gamma (IFN-ã), which can eventually lead to virus inactivation. These actions are thought to be mediated by polysaccharides. (Borchers, 2009).

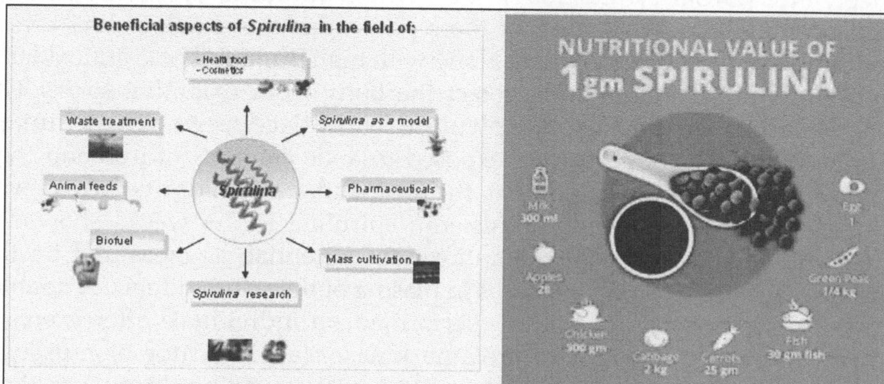

Fig. 1.5: Beneficial uses and nutritional value of *Spirulina*

Spirulina in Anaemia: Spirulina possibly enhances red cell production and function. Over a 12-week study period, there was a steady increase in average values of mean corpuscular haemoglobin with spirulina intake. Older women benefitted more rapidly from Spirulina supplements (Mohan *et al.*, 2014). Levels of anaemia also decreased in children when their diet was supplemented with *Spirulina.* It is a fantastic source of Iron, meaning it is excellent for women during pregnancy. In fact, 100g of Spirulina contains 158% of your daily Iron requirements.

Anticancer Effects: Many researchers find phycocyanin to be a truly potent antioxidant, anti-inflammatory and anti-cancer properties pigment found only in Spirulina and other species of blue green algae. (Subbashini *et al.*, 2004). It has been argued that the combined antioxidant and immune modulation characteristics of Spirulina may have a possible mechanism of tumor destruction and hence play a role in cancer prevention. The effects of Spirulina on oral carcinogenesis, in particular leukoplakia showed tumor regression after topical application or enteral intake of Spirulina extract. Jalaja *et al.*, 2011 studied the effect of Spirulina on chemoprevention of cancer in tobacco chewers in Kerala, India.

It was found supplementation with Spirulina at 1 g/day for 1 year resulted in complete regression. If *Spirulina* proves to have such effect, it can easily be incorporated in the daily diet as a therapeutic agent.

***Spirulina* as Antioxidant:** One of most important characteristics of Spirulina is its antioxidant property. Antioxidants are the substances which neutralize the free radicals generated due to oxidative stress. Free radicals are not only nuisance molecules in the atmosphere but can cause havoc inside the body. They are the unstable products of normal cell processes. Free radicals can damage the concerned cell & lead to the death of these cells. Oxidative stress directly or indirectly leads to various disorders like diabetes, atherosclerosis, rheumatoid arthritis, recurrent aphthous stomatitis, cancer, etc. [Desai *et al.*, 2004]. Very high amounts of beta-carotene, tocopherol and combined form of these antioxidants make Spirulina a very good source of natural antioxidant along with high protein. These antioxidants can become pro-oxidants and protect the body from oxidative stress. The iron chelating properties of spirulina was discovered when human neuroblastoma cells *in vitro* were exposed to toxic amounts of iron and then to spirulina, which revealed that the iron induced oxidative stress was reduced. Geriatric patients administered spirulina for 16 weeks showed a remarkable improvement in the antioxidant potential, as measured by the increased levels of antioxidant status in plasma of these individuals. A double-blinded, placebo controlled study performed on individuals after exercise, showed decreased amount of creatine kinase, (an indicator of muscular breakdown) when they we supplemented with spirulina. Moreover their exhaustion time in the treadmill exercise increased by 52 seconds. This could be explained by the antioxidant potential of spirulina [Trushina *et al.*, 2007]

Fig. 1.6: Commercially available products of *Spirulina*

CONCLUSION

Preventive healthcare says "let your food be your medicine." *Spirulina* truly comes in such category of food supplement. Spirulina has emerged as the wonder food supplement. The highly diverse nutritive nature of spirulina together with its antioxidant and protective health benefits have been utilized in various health related problems. Spirulina shows potent immune stimulating effects, shows antiviral activity against a variety of harmful viruses. It shows promise as a cancer preventative agent and in the treatment of tumors. The effectiveness of spirulina is being very rapidly recognized and being made use of in the treatment and management of various life threatening diseases. World production of consumable algae and algae products to be used as dietary supplements, food additives, functional foods, and medicines has reached thousands of tons per year after research which has proved its importance. The potential health benefits of spirulina must be adequately recognized and implemented thus making full use of this nature's gift.

REFERENCES

Abdulqader, G., Barsanti, L. and Tredici, M.R. 2000. Harvest of *Arthrospira platensis* from LakeKossorom (Chad) and its Household usage among the Kanembu. *Journal of Applied Phycology*, 12: 493-498.

Annapurna V, Shah N, Bhaskaram P, Bamji M, Reddy V; Bioavailability of spirulina carotenes in pre-school Children. J Clin Biochem Nutr., 1991; 10: 145-151.

Azabji-Kenfack M, Edie Dikosso S, Loni EG,Onana EA, Sobngwi E, Gbaguidi E *et al.*; Potential of *Spirulina platensis* as a Nutritional Supplement in Malnourished hiv-infected Adults insub-Saharan Africa: A randomised, Single-blindstudy. Nutr Metab Insights., 2011; 4: 29-37.

BIOTEC Publication 1/2542. pp. 11-31. Place de Fontenoy, Paris. France. United Nations Educational Scientific and Cultural Organization (UNESCO).

Borchers, A.T., Selmi, C., Meyers, F.J. , Keen, C.L. and Gershwin, M.E. (2009) Probioteic and Immunity, *J. Gastroenterol.*, 44 (1), 26-46.

Capelli B, Cysewski GR; Potential Health Benefits of Spirulina Microalgae: A Review of Existing Literature. Nutra Foods, 2010, 9(2) 19-26.

Chen, T., W. Zheng, G.F. Yang, Y. Bai and Y. Wong. 2006. Mixotrophic Culture of High Selenium Enriched *Spirulina platensis* on Acetate and the Enhanced Production of Photosynthetic Pigments. *Enzyme Microbial Technology*, 139: 103-107.

Cifferi, O. 1983. *Spirulina*.The Edible Microorganism. *Microbial Reviews*, 47(4): 551-578.

Danesi, E.D.G., C.O. Rangel Yagui, J.C.M. Carvalho and S. Sato. 2002. An Investigation of the Effect of Replacing Nitrate by Urea in the Growth and Production of Chlorophyll by *Spirulina platensis*. *Biomass Bioenergy*, 23: 261-269.

Desai K, Sivakami S; Spirulina the Wonder Food of the 21st century. Asia Pacific Biotech News, 2004; 8(23): 1298-1302.

Desikachary, T.V and N. JeejiBai. 1992. Taxonomic Studies in *Spirulina* 1.In: Proc. *Spirulina* ETTA National Symposium. MCRC, Madras. pp. 12-20.

Dubey, R.C. 2006. A Textbook of Biotechnology. Fourth Revised and Enlarge edition, S. Chand and Company Limited. 419-421.

Dubey, R.C. 2006. A Textbook of Biotechnology. Fourth Revised and Enlarge Edition, S. Chand and Company Limited. 419-421.

Elias Nerantzis, Ioannis Tzovenis, Stamatis Stamatiadis, Elina Giannakopoulou and Lydia Maniatis.2002. Continuous Production of Arthrospira *Spirulina platensis* in a Helical Photobioreactor. *Microbial Resources*, 6(2): 34-39.

Falquet, J. 2000. A Sustainable Response to Malnutrition in Hot Regions: The Local Production of Spirulina, Geneva, Antenna Technologies.

Gardillo. F.J.L., C. Jimenez, F.L.Figuero and X. Nlell. 1998. Effects of Increased Atmospheric CO2 and Supply on Photosynthesis, Growth and Cell Composition of the Cyanobacterium *Spirulina platensis*. *Journal of Applied Phycology*, 10 (5): 461-469.

Helliwell, K.E., Wheeler, G.L., Leptos, K.C., Goldstein, R.E. and Smith, A.G. 2011. Insights into the Evolution of Vitamin B12 Auxotrophy from Sequenced Algal Genomes. *Mol Biol Evol.*, 28: 2921-2933.

Hintak, F.1985, Morphology of Trichomes in *Spirulina fusiformis* Voronichin from Lake Begoria, Kenya. *Arch. Hydrobial. Supp.*, 71:23.

Hofner.W., M.I, Naguib, I.A. Kobbia and Zeinab K.Ibrahim. 1987. Use of Laboratory Culture of some Algae to Prediet Heavy Metal Toxicity, *Egypt Journal of Microbiology*, 22 (2): 213 -226.

Homlgren, R.P., H.D. Hostetter and V.E. Seholes. 1971. Structural Observation of Cross Walls in the Blue Green Algae, *Spirulina* Major. *Journal of Phycology*, 79 (4): 309-311.

Ishikawa T., Fujiyama Y.,Igarashi C.,Morino M., Fada N., Kagami A., Sakamoto T., Nagano M., and Nakamura H. 1989. Clinical Features of Familial Hypercholesterolemia. *Atherosclerosis*,75: 95-103.

Jalaja Kumari, D., Babitha, S.K., Jaffar, Guru Prasad, M., Ibrahim, M.D. and Siddque Ahmed Khan, M.D. 2011. Potential Health Benefits of Spirulina Platensis, *IJAPR.*, 2: 2-3.

Kelly, M., Capelli., B., Cysewski, R. and Gerald. 2011. Spirulina Nature's Superfood. 3rd Edition. Cyanotech Corporation., 73: 4460.

Ken Sasaki, F.J Marquez, Naomichi Nishio and Shiro Nagai.1995. Promative Effect of Five Amino Levulinic Acid on the Growth and Photosynthesis of *Spirulina platensis*. *Journal of Fermentation and Bioengineering*, 79 (5): 453-457.

Khan Z, Bhadouria P and Bisen PS; Nutritional and Therapeutic Potential of Spirulina. Curr Pharm Biotechnol., 2005; 6(5): 373-379.

Lobner M, Walsted A, Larsen R, Bendtzen K, Nielsen CH; Enhancement of Human Adaptive Immune Responses by Administration of a Highmolecular - Weight Polysaccharide Extract from the Cyanobacterium Arthrospira Platensis. J Med Food., 2008; 11(2): 313-322.

Luciane Maria Colla, Telma Elita Berto Lin and Jorge Alberto Vieira Costa. 2004. Fatty Acids Profile of *Spirulina platensis* Grown Under Different Temperatures and Nitrogen Concentrations. *Z. Natur forsch.*, 59: 55-59.

Mathew, B., Sankaranarayanan, R., Nair, P., Varghese, C., Somanathan, T., Amma, P., Amma, N. and Nair, M. 1995. Evaluation of Chemoprevention of Oral Cancer with *Spirulina fusiformis*. *Nutr. Cancer.*, 24: 197-202.

Mohammad-Taghi, Golmakani, Karamatollah Rezaei, Sara Mazidi and Seyyed Hadi Razavi, 2012. *g*-Linolenic Acid Production by *Arthrospira platensis* using Different Carbon Sources. *European Journal of Lipid Science Technology*,114: 306-314.

Mohan, A., Misra, N., Srivasata, D.,Umapathy, D. and Kumar, S. 2014, Spirulina - the Nature's Wonder: A Review, *Journal of Applied Medical Sciences,* 2 (4), 1334-1339. ISSN: 2320-6691.

Moorhead K, Capelli B, Cysewski G; Nature's Superfood: Spirulina. 2005.

Nantha, B and S. Padhi. 1992. Effect of 2, 4-D on Growth and Pigmentation of *Spirulina platensis.* In: proc. Spirulina ETTA National Symposium, MCRC, Madras. pp. 73.

Nasima Akhtar, M.A., A. Partin Noor Jahan and Md. M.Hossain. 1996. An Integrated Culture System for Outdoor Production of Microalgae and Cyanobacteria. *Bangladesh Journal of Science and Industrial Research,* 31(1): 137-146.

Nielsen CH, Balachandran P, Christensen O, Pugh ND, Tamta H, Sufka KJ *et al.*; Enhancement of Natural Killer Cell Activity in Healthy Subjects by Immulina(R), a Spirulina Extract Enriched for Braun-type Lipoproteins. Planta Med., 2010; 76(16): 1802-1808.

Ogawa, T and G. Teuri. 1970. Blue Green Algae *Spirulina. Journal of Fermentation Technology,* 48: 361.

Ogawa, T and G. Teuri. 1972. Blue Green Algae *Spirulina.* In: Proc. IV IFS. *Fermentation Technology Today,* pp. 543.

Pandey, J.P., Neeraj Pathak and Amit Tiwari. 2010. Standardization of pH and Light Intensity for the Biomass Production of *Spirulina platensis. Journal of Algal Biomass Utilization,* 1(2): 93-102.

Pelizer, L.H., Danesh. E.D.G, Rangel, C.O, Sassano, C.E.N, Carvalho, J.C, Sato, S and Maraes, I.O. 2002. Influence of Inoculum Age and Concentration of *Spirulina platensis* Cultivation. *Journal of Food Engineering.* Elsevier Science Ltd. Oxford England. In Press (Paper 02/1397).

Pitan., 2007; 76(2): 21-25.

Ramesh, S., Manivasgam, M., Sethupathy, S. and Shantha, K. 2013. Effect of Spirulina on Anthropometry and Bio-Chemical Parameters in School Children. *IOSR-JDMS.,* 7(5): 11-15.

Sasson, A. 1997. *Micro Biotechnologies: Recent Developments and Prospects for Developing Countries.*

Schwartz, J. and Shklar, G. 1987. Regression of Experimental Hamster Cancer by Beta Carotene and Algae Extracts. *J Oral Maxillofac Surg.,* 45(6): 510-515.

Seshadri, C.V. 1993. Large Scale Nutritional Supplementation with Spirulina Alga. All India Company., Coordinated Project on Spirulina. Shri Amma Murugappa Chettiar Research Center (MCRC), India.

Sharma, V. and Dunkwal, V. 2012. Development of Spirulina based 'Biscuits': A Potential method of Value Addition. *Ethno Med.,* 6(1): 31-34.

Sharoba, M.A. 2014. Nutritional Value of Spirulina and its use in the Preparation of some Complementary Baby Food Formulas. *J. Agroaliment. Proc. Technol.,* 20(4): 330-350.

Sheahan, S., Bellamy, C.O., Harland, S.N., Harrison, D.J. and Prost, S. 2008. TGF beta Induces Apoptosis and EMT in Primary Mouse Hepatocytes Independently of p 53, p 21 Cip 1 or Rb status. *BMC Cancer.,* 8: 191-201.

Simpore J, Zongo F, Kabore F, Dansou D, Bere A, Nikiema JB; Nutrition Rehabilitation of HIV Infected and HIV-Negative Undernourished Children Utilizing Spirulina. *Annal Nut Metabolism.,* 2005; 49(6): 373-380.

Somasekaran, T. 1987. Technology of Production of B.G.A. *Spirulina platensis* and its Application. Ph.D., CFTRI, Mysore, pp: 150-170.

Stanca, D and E. Popovici. 1996. Urea as Nitrogen Source in Modified Zarrouk Medium. *Reviews in Biology*, 41: 25-31.

Subbashini, J., Mahipal, S.V., Reddy, M.C., Mallikarjuna Reddy, M., Rachamallu, A. and Reddanna, P. 2004. Molecular Mechanisms in C-Phycocyanin induced Apoptosis in Human Chronic Myeloid Leukemia Cell Line K-562. *Biochem Pharmacol.*, 68(3): 453-462.

Subramaniyan, S.K and N. Jeeji Bai. 1992. Effect of Different Nitrogen Levels and Light Quality on Growth, Protein and Synthesis in *Spirulina fusiformis*. In. Proc. *Spirulina* ETTA National Symposium, MCRC, Madras. pp. 97-99.

Tanseem Fatma. 1990. Effect of Culture Filtrate on Growth of *Spirulina platensis*. *Curent Sciences*, 59(6): 797-798.

Thomas SS; The Role of Parry Organic Spirulina in Health Management. 2010.

Tri-Panji and Suharyanto. 2001. Optimization Media from Low-cost Nutrient Sources for Growing *Spirulina platensis* and Carotenoid Production. *Menara Perkebunan*, 69(1): 18-28.

Trushina EN, Gladkikh O, Gadzhieva ZM, Mustafina OK, Pozdniakov AL; The Influence of Spirulina and Selen-spirulina on some Indexes of Rat's Immune Status (Article in Russian). Vopr.

Venkataraman, L.V and T.C. Sindukanya. 1981. Insect Contamination (*Ephydra californa*) in the Mass Outdoor Culture of Green Alga *Spirulina platensis* Proc., *Indian Academy of Sciences*, 90: 665-672.

Vieira Costa, J.A, Luciane Maria Colla and Paulo Duarte Filho. 2003. *Spirulina platensis* Growth in Open Raceway Ponds Using Fresh Water Supplemented with Carbon, Nitrogen and Metal Ions. *Z. Naturforsch*. 58c: 76-80.

Watanable, Y and D.O. Hall. 1996. Photosynthetic Production of Filamentous Cyanobacterium *Spirulina platensis* in a Cone Shaped Helicaltubular Photo Bioreactor. *Applied Microbial Biotechnology*, 44: 693-698.

Zhang, X.W., Y.M. Zhang and F. Chen. 1999. Application of Mathematical Models to the Determination Optimal Glucose Concentration and Light Intensity for Mixotrophic Culture of *Spirulina platensis*. Process Biochemistry, 34: 477-481.

Pages: 23-32

Nutrition and Medicines in Nature
Edited by: Dr. Jairam Singh and Dr. Pawan Kumar 'Bharti'
ISBN: 978-93-88854-39-9
Edition: **2020**
Published by: **Discovery Publishing House Pvt. Ltd., New Delhi (India)**

2

Nutrient Deficiency in Plants

Prasann Kumar[1,2*], Shipa Rani Dey[1]

GRAPHICAL ABSTRACT

Keywords: Crop, Deficiency, Nutrient, Plant

INTRODUCTION

- An element is a pure chemical that contains only one type of atom.
- A compound is a molecule that contains one or more elements.

[1] **Department of Agronomy, School of Agriculture, Lovely Professional University, Jalandhar - 144 411 (Punjab) (India)**

[2] **Divison of Research and Development, Lovely Professional University, Jalandhar - 144 411 (Punjab) (India)**

- The 16 elements required by plants are obtained from the soil, water and air.
- Thirteen of these elements must be supplied by the soil.
- Six of the soil elements required by plants are needed in relatively large amounts and are usually added to the soil through fertilizer or lime. These are called macronutrients.
- The remaining 7 elements supplied by soil are required in very small amounts and are termed micronutrients.

Micronutrients

- Macronutrients are needed in relatively large amounts by plants

Element	Symbol	Source
Oxygen	O	Air/Water
Hydrogen	H	Air/Water
Carbon	C	Air/Water
Nitrogen	N	Soil
Phosphorus	P	Soil
Sulfur	S	Soil
Potassium	K	Soil
Calcium	Ca	Soil
Magnesium	Mg	Soil

Fig. 2.1: Macronutrients

Source: Based on review of literature

Macronutrients – Form Used By Plants

Nutrient	Form Used
Carbon	CO_2
Oxygen	H_2O
Hydrogen	H_2O
Nitrogen	NO_3^-, NH_4^+ (Charge on the molecule)
Phosphorus	H_2PO_4 & HPO_4^{2-}
Potassium	K^+
Calcium	Ca_2^+
Magnesium	Mg^{2+}
Sulfur	SO_4^-

Fig. 2.2: Form used by plants

Source: Based on review of literature

Micronutrients

- Macronutrients are needed in relatively small amounts by plants.
- They are usually supplied by fertilizers.

Element	*Symbol*	*Source*
Iron	Fe	Soil
Manganese	Mn	Soil
Boron	B	Soil
Molybdenum	Mo	Soil
Copper	Cu	Soil
Zinc	Zn	Soil
Chlorine	Cl	Soil

Fig. 2.3: Micronutrients

Source: Based on review of literature

Micronutrients – Form Used By Plants

Nutrient	*Form Used*
Iron	Fe^{2+}
Manganese	Mn^{2+} Charge on the molecule
Boron	$H_2BO_3^-$
Molybdenum	MoO_4^{2-}
Copper	Cu^{2+}
Zinc	Zn^{2+}
Chlorine	Cl^-

Fig. 2.4: Form used by plants

Source: Based on review of literature

Nutrient Deficiency Symptoms

- Nutrient deficiency symptoms usually appear on the plant when one or more nutrients are in short supply.
- In many cases, deficiency may occur because an added nutrient is not in the form the plant can use.
- Deficiency symptoms for specific elements are included on the "Key to Nutrient Disorders".

Nutrient Deficiencies

- Every soil is not susceptible to the same nutrient deficiencies.

- For example, coarse-textured soils low in organic matter are susceptible to sulfur deficiencies whereas sulfur is usually in adequate supply in clayey soils or soils high in organic matter.

Macronutrient Deficiencies & Soils

Element	***Soil Factor Causing Deficiency***
N & K	Excessive leaching on coarse-texture low organic matter soils
P	Acid low organic matter soils
	Cold wet soils such as occurs during darly spring
	Newly cleared soils
S	Excessive leaching on coarse-textured low organic matter soils in areas where air pollution is low (minimal levels of SO_2 in the air)
Ca & Mg	Excessive leaching on coarse-textured low organic matter soils
	Soils where large amounts of K have beem applied

Fig. 2.5: Macronutrient deficiencies & soils

Source: Based on review of literature

Micronutrient Deficiencies & Soils

Element	***Soil Factor Causing Deficiency***
Fe	Poorly drained soils, Low organic matter soils, pH>7.0, Soils high in P
Zn	Cold wet soils low in organic matter and highly leached, High pH soils (pH>7.0), Soils high in P, Exposed subsoils
Cu	Peat and muck soils, High pH, sandy soils, Soils heavily fertilized with N
B	Excessive leaching on coarse-textured low organic matter soils, Soilswith pH>7.0
Mn	Excessive leaching on coarse-texture low organic matter soils, Soil with pH>6.5
Mo	Soils high in Fe oxides, high adsorption of molybdenum, Soil cropped for a long time.

Fig. 2.6: Micronutrient deficiencies & soils

Source: Based on review of literature

Deficiency Symptoms - N

- General Chlorosis
- Chlorosis progresses from light green to yellow.
- Entire plant becomes yellow under prolonged stress.
- Growth is immediately restricted and plants soon become spindly and drop older leaves.

Fig. 2.7: Nitrogen deficiency

Source: Based on review of literature

Deficiency Symptoms - P

- Leaves appear dull dark green, or red-purple, especially on the underside and especially at the midrib and vein.
- Petioles may also exhibit purpling. Restriction in growth may be noticed.

Fig. 2.8: P deficiency

Source: based on review of literature

Deficiency Symptoms - K

- Leaf margins tanned, scorched, or have necrotic spots (may be small black) spots which later coalesce).
- Margins become brown and cup downward.
- Growth is restricted and die back may occur.
- Mild symptoms appear first on recently matured leaves.

Fig. 2.9: K deficiency

Source: Based on review of literature

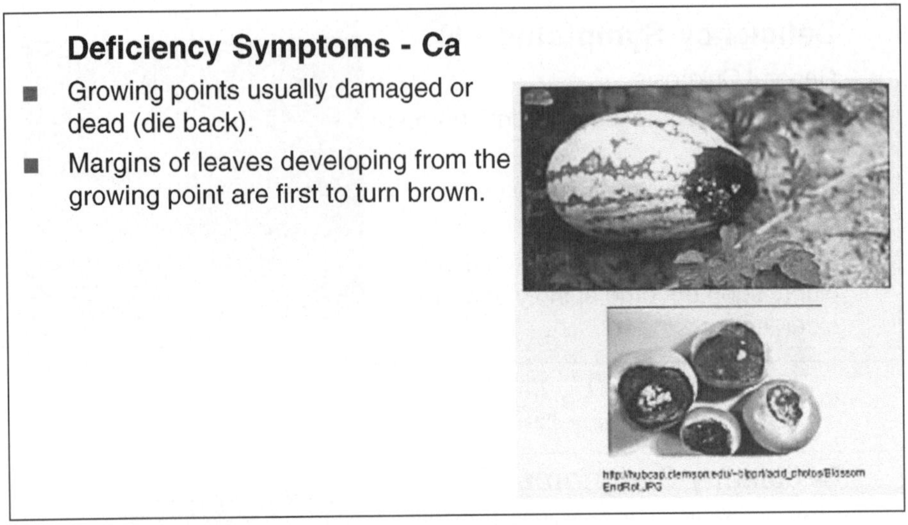

Fig. 2.10: Ca deficiency

Source: Based on review of literature

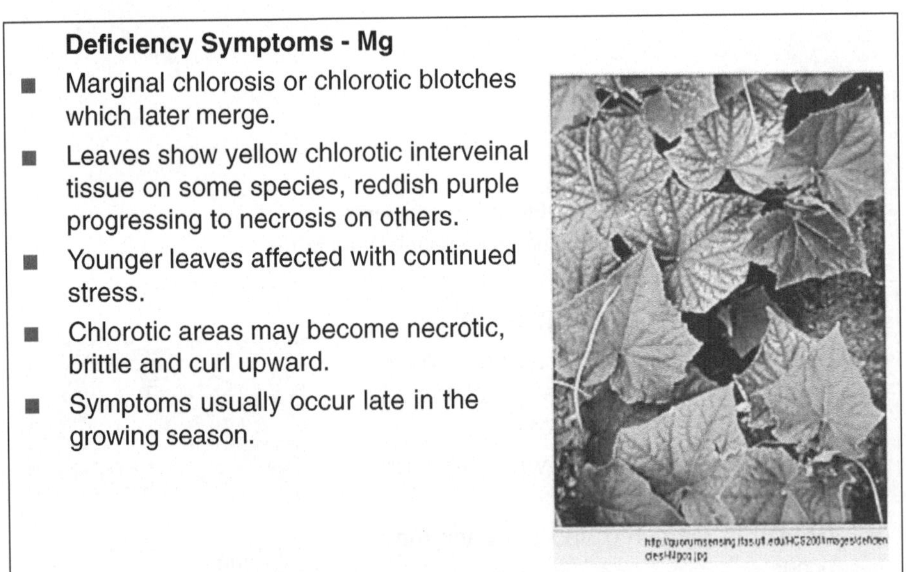

Fig. 2.11: Mg Deficiency

Source: Based on review of literature

Deficiency Symptoms - S

- Leaves uniformly light green, followed by yellowing and poor spindly growth.
- Uniform chlorosis does not occur.

Fig. 2.12: S deficiency

Source: Based on review of literature

Deficiency Symptoms - Cu

- Leaves wilt, become chlorotic, then necrotic.
- Wilting and necrosis are not dominant symptoms.

Fig. 2.13: Cu deficiency

Source: Based on review of literature

Deficiency Symptoms - Fe

- Distinct yellow or white areas appear between veins and veins eventually become chlorotic.
- Symptoms are rare on mature leaves.

Fig. 2.14: Fe deficiency
Source: Based on review of literature

Deficiency Symptoms - Mn

- Chlorosis is less marked near veins.
- Some mottling occurs in interveinal areas.
- Chlorotic areas eventually become brown, transparent, or necrotic.
- Symptoms may appear later on older leaves.

Fig. 2.15: Mn deficiency
Source: Based on review of literature

Deficiency Symptoms - Zn

- Leaves may be abnormally small and necrotic.
- Internodes are shortened.

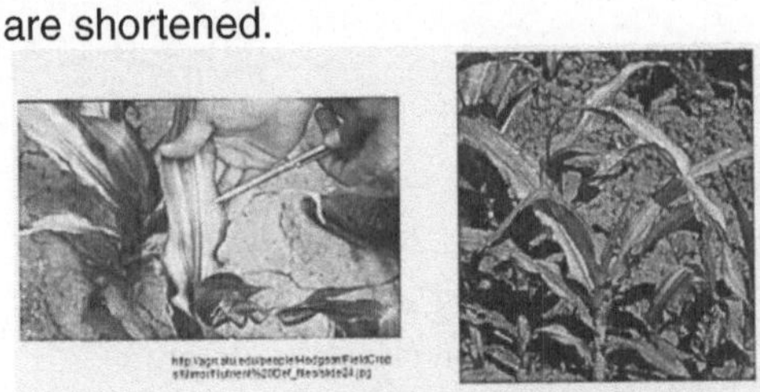

Fig. 2.16: Zn deficiency symptom
Source: Based on review of literature

Deficiency Symptoms - B

- Young, expanding leaves may be necrotic or distorted followed by death of growing point.
- Internodes may be short, especially at shoot terminals.
- Stems, may be rough, checked, or split along the vascular bundles.

Fig. 2.17: B deficiency

Source: based on review of literature

Crops Highly Susceptible to Deficiencies

Element	*Crops*
Mn	Soybean, small Grain & Peanuts
Cu	Wheat & Corn
Zn	Corn
Mo	Soybeans & Cauliflower
B	Alfalfa, Apples, Peanuts, Tobacco & Tomatoes
Fe	Ornamentals, Fruit Trees, Soyabeans, Grain Sorghum & Some Grassses

Fig. 2.18: Highly Susceptible to deficiencies

Source: Based on review of literature

CONCLUSION

Micronutrients are present in plant tissue in quantities measured in parts per million, ranging from 0.1 to 200 ppm, or less than 0.02% dry weight.These elements stay beneath soil as salts, so plants consume these elements as ions. Most soil conditions across the world can provide plants adapted to that climate and soil with sufficient nutrition for a complete life cycle, without the addition of nutrients as fertilizer.The macronutrients are consumed in larger quantities; hydrogen, oxygen, nitrogen and carbon contribute to over 95% of a plant's entire biomass on a dry matter weight basis. This is done because, even with adequate water and light, nutrient deficiency can limit growth and crop yield.However, if the soil is cropped it is necessary to artificially modify soil fertility through the addition of fertilizer to promote vigorous growth and increase or sustain yield.

REFERENCES

https://en.wikipedia.org/wiki/Plant_nutrition
ncert.nic.in/textbook/pdf/kebo112.pdf
https://www.toppr.com/guides/biology/mineral-nutrition/
https://byjus.com › Biology › Biology Article
https://link.springer.com/chapter/10.1007/978-81-322-2286-6_20
https://www.askiitians.com › Revision Notes › Biology
www.agritech.tnau.ac.in/agriculture/agri_min_nutri_essentialelements.html
https://www.sciencedirect.com/book/.../mineral-nutrition-of-higher-plants
https://www.annualreviews.org/doi/abs/10.../annurev.pp.01.060150.000245

Pages: 33-53

Nutrition and Medicines in Nature
Edited by: **Dr. Jairam Singh and Dr. Pawan Kumar 'Bharti'**
ISBN: 978-93-88854-39-9
Edition: **2020**
Published by: **Discovery Publishing House Pvt. Ltd., New Delhi (India)**

3

Nutritive Value and Importance of Probiotics

M.R.A. Manimala

ABSTRACT

Consumption of probiotic products help in maintaining good health. It is generally recognized that an optimum 'balance' in microbial population in our digestive tract is associated with good nutrition and health. Continuous development of new functional foods is the response of science and industry to the increased consumer awareness regarding health and role of foods for improving quality of life. In the present changing scenario, consumer awareness has increased towards the health driven foods, hence recent advances in functional foods demonstrate much promise in new product development using probiotics to derive health benefits. Probiotic foods come under functional foods which, in addition to their basic nutritive value and natural being, will contain the proper balance of ingredients, which will help as functional, therapeutic and nutraceutical agents enabling the human population to prevent the risk of illness and diseases.

INTRODUCTION

Probiotics are "living microorganisms" which aid the existing flora or help to repopulate the colon when bacteria levels are reduced by antibiotics, chemotherapy or disease. They favorably alter the intestinal microflora balance, inhibit the growth of harmful bacteria, promote good digestion, boost immune function and increase resistance to infection [Abd El-Salam, 2012]. Lactic acid bacteria (LAB) can produce a huge amount of bioactive compounds. Alpha and beta-caseins, albumin and globulin from milk and dairy products, rubisco from spinach, beta-conglycinin from soy and gluten

Mother Terasa College of Agriculture, (Affiliated to Tamil Nadu Agricultural University) Mettusalai, Illuppur, Pudukkottai - 622 102, (Tamilnadu) (India)

from cereals constitute a good source of important bioactive compounds. Many experimental evidences demonstrate that some LAB strains also produce anti-hypertensive, anti-thrombotic, cholesterol-lowering, metal-chelating, antimicrobial, anti-oxidant, immune-modulating, chaperone-like and opioid/opioid antagonist peptides from food proteins (Pessione, 2012).

Today there are more than 70 lactic acid bacteria-containing products worldwide, including sour cream, yogurt, powdered milk, buttermilk, and frozen deserts. Probiotics are increasingly being marketed as dietary supplements in tablet, capsule, and freeze-dried preparations. Recent clinical trials have demonstrated the beneficial health effects of probiotic bacteria that have been incorporated in foods and animal feed. These effects include the prevention of diarrhea, balancing of intestinal microflora, stimulation of the immune system, modulation of systemic immune homeostasis, antitumor properties, and lactose intolerance. Probiotic foods have emerged as the major nutritional factor impacting and influencing gastrointestinal physiology and function. At present it is generally recognized that an optimum 'balance' in microbial population in our digestive tract is associated with good nutrition and health. In addition to these beneficial health effects, researchers have demonstrated that probiotic bacteria produce bacteriocins and organic acids that act as antimicrobials to inhibit the growth of pathogens as well as improve functions of intestinal epithelial cells (Modi, 2014)

PROBIOTICS: DEFINITION AND HISTORICAL PERSPECTIVE

Probiotics are dietary supplements containing potentially beneficial bacteria or yeasts. According to the currently adopted definition by FAO/ WHO, 2001, probiotics are: 'Live microorganisms which when administered in adequate amounts confer a health benefit on the host'. The term 'probiotics' was first coined by Parker (1974) to describe the use of microbes in animal health and nutrition. Probiotics have emerged as the major nutritional factor impacting and influencing gastrointestinal physiology and function. Probiotic in Greek means 'for life' and was first used by Lilley and Stillwell (1965) to describe "substances secreted by one micro-organism to stimulate the growth of another – as an antonym to 'antibiotic'. Parker (1974) went a step further and defined probiotic as an organisms and substances, which contribute to intestinal microbial balancer. Fuller (1989) further refined this description and redefined probiotic as 'a live microbial feed supplement which beneficially affects the host animal by improving its intestinal microbial balance'.

Naidu *et al.*, (1999) defined Probiotic as microbial dietary adjuvant that beneficially affects the host physiology by modulating mucosal and systemic immunity, as well as improving nutritional and microbial balance in the intestinal tract". Probiotic active substance is a cellular complex of lactic acid bacteria (LAB) that has a capacity to interact with host mucosa and may beneficially modulate the immune system independent of LAB's viability (Naidu *et al.*, 1999). The concept of probiotics was first propounded by the Nobel Prize winning Russian scientist Elie Metchnikoff (1908) who ascribed the long, healthy life of Bulgarian peasants to their consumption of fermented milk products (Bibel, 1988). Metchnikoff believed that the fermenting bacteria (*Lactobacillus*) present in yoghurt positively influenced the microflora of the colon of these peasants by decreasing toxic microbial activities (metabolites) and thereby improving the balance of microbes living in the digestive tract to foster immunity (Fig.3.1).

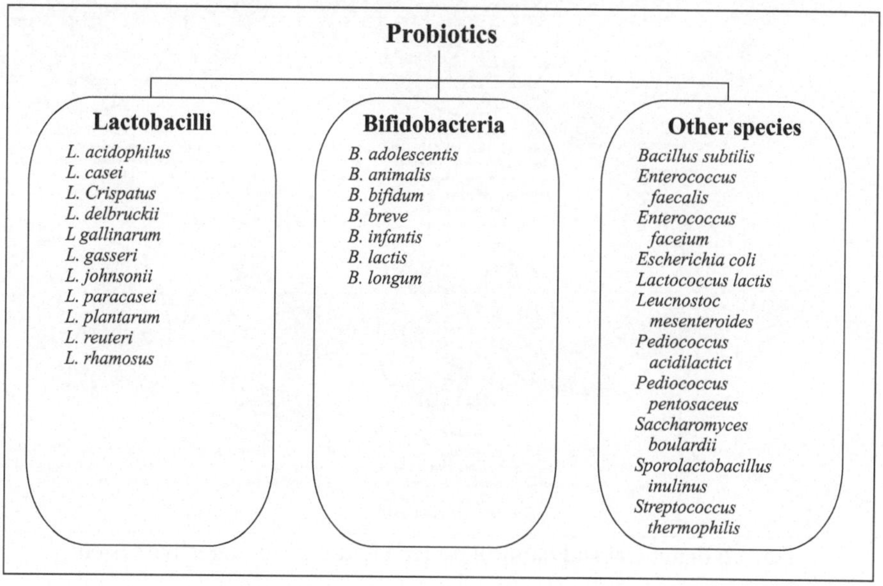

Fig. 3.1: Different types of probiotics

Concept of Probiotics

Sperti (1971) described probiotics as organisms and substance, which contribute to intestinal microbial balance. The following criteria must be met before a probiotic can be described as useful (Fuller, 1992):

- The probiotic must be capable of being prepared in a viable manner and on a large scale (e.g., for industrial purposes).
- During use, and under storage, the probiotic should remain viable and stable.
- It should be able to survive in the intestinal ecosystem (Fig. 3.2)

The host animal should gain benefit from harbouring the probiotic. Lactic acid bacteria (LAB) are the most common type of microbes used. LABS have been used in the food industry for many years, because they are able to convert sugars (including lactose) and other carbohydrates into lactic acid. This not only provides the characteristic sour taste of fermented dairy foods such as yogurt, but also by lowering the pH may create fewer opportunities for spoilage organisms to grow, hence creating possible health benefits on preventing gastrointestinal infections. Nichols (2007). Strains of the genera *Lactobacillus* and *Bifidobacterium*, are the most widely used probiotic bacteria (Tannock G, 2005).

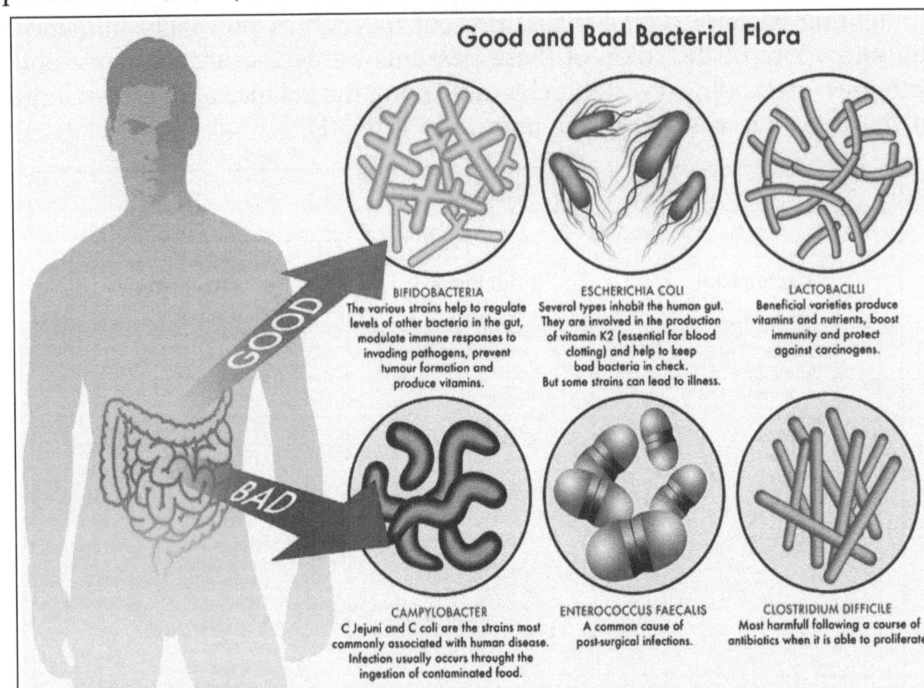

Fig. 3.2: Beneficial and harmful bacteria found in our digestive system

Health Benefits of Probiotics

The consumption of probiotic products is helpful in maintaining good health, restoring body vigour, and in combating intestinal and other disease disorders. Several probiotics have reportedly shown various special therapeutic or prophylactic properties (Table 3.1)

Maintenance of Normal Micro Flora

Yoghurt with specific strains of live active cultures has been demonstrated to help maintain the normal intestinal microbiota balance and suppress harmful bacteria in intestine. A particular strain of bacteria used in yoghurt, *Lactobacillus* strain GG, aids in treatment and prevention of antibiotic associated diarrhoea, traveller's diarrhoea, and acute diarrhoea in children. In adults, this particular strain of *Lactobacillus* has been shown to stimulate bowel function by altering the microflora and suppressing fermentation in the intestine. Yoghurt with *Lactobacillus gasseri* may be beneficial for older adults with "atopic gastritis" a condition that predisposes to intestinal infections and constipation (Salminen, 1996).

Table 3.1: Various therapeutic or prophylactic properties of probiotic (Parvez *et al.*, 2006)

S.No.	Microflora	Mechanism
1.	*Bifidobacteria* species, *Enterococcus faedum* and *Lactobacillus* strains	Reduced incidence of neonatal necrotizing enterocolitis. Decreased duration of acute diarrhoea from gastroenteritis. Administration of multiple organisms, predominantly *Lactobacillus* strains shown to be effective in ameliorating pouchitis Lactose digestion improved, decreased diarrhoea and symptoms of intolerant individuals with short bowel syndrome microbial interference therapy – the use of non-pathogenic bacteria to eliminate pathogens and as an adjunct to antibiotics – improved mucosal immune function, mucin secretion and prevention of disease.
2.	*Lactobacillus acidophilus*	Significant decrease of diarrhoea in patients receiving pelvic irradiation, decreased polyps, adenomas and colon cancer in experimental animals, prevented urogenital infection with subsequent exposure to three pathogens *Escherichia coli, Klebsiella pneumoniae, Pseudomonas aeruginosa.*
3.	*Lactobacillus plantarum*	Lowered serum cholesterol levels, reduced incidence of diarrhoea in daycare centres when administered to only half of the children. Especially effective in reducing inflammation in inflammatory bowel; e.g., enterocolitis in rats, small bowel bacterial overgrowth in children, pouchitis. Reduced pain and constipation of irritable bowel syndrome. Reduced bloating, flatulence, and pain in irritable bowel syndrome in controlled trial. Positive effect on immunity in HIV+ children. Shortened the duration of acute gastroenteritis. Shortened acute diarrhoea.
4.	*Lactobacillus rhanosus, Lactobacillus Salivarius and Bacteriodes species*	Enhanced cellular immunity in healthy adults in controlled trial. Suppressed and eradicated *Helicobacter pylori* in tissue cultures and animal. Models by lactic acid secretion Chronic colitis, gastritis, arthritis (increased bacterial urease activity in chronic juvenile arthritis)
5.	*Saccharomyces boulardii*	Reduced recurrence of *Clostridium difficle* diarrhoea, effects on *C difficle* and *Klebsiella oxytoca* resulted in decreased risk and/or shortened duration of antibiotic-associated diarrhoea. Shortened the duration of acute gastroenteritis. Decreased only functional diarrhoea, but not any other symptoms of irritablebowel syndrome.

Probiotic hypothesis precludes that the addition of certain exogenous microorganisms to the intestinal tract will have a positive health benefits. It is therefore, imperative and important that probiotic strains are of human origin since some health promoting effects may be species dependent. Probiotic bacteria consumed even in high numbers are not known to become permanent colonizers of human gut and rarely detectable in faecal or intestinal samples beyond a couple of weeks after ingestion (Sanders, 1999). Only regular ingestion of probiotic supplemented foods can, therefore, lead to nutritional and health benefits. Short-term benefits of consuming probiotics include improved lactose digestion and alleviation of GI disturbances or vaginal infections. optimal health benefits a daily dose of 100 million to 10 billion probiotic bacteria is a good target. (Girdhari Sharma and Bikash, 2006)

Several health points have been attributed to probiotics, which increased the commercial attention in development of different applications leading to the rapid augment of this market segment. Of these characteristics, the most agreed-upon are modulation of intestinal microflora, immune response enhancement, improved gastrointestinal health, and protection against infectious illness and inflammatory bowel disease (IBD). Selecting and incorporating a probiotic strain to produce a safe and biological active final product in both food and pharmaceutical formulation contain different steps that are programmed in figure 3.3.

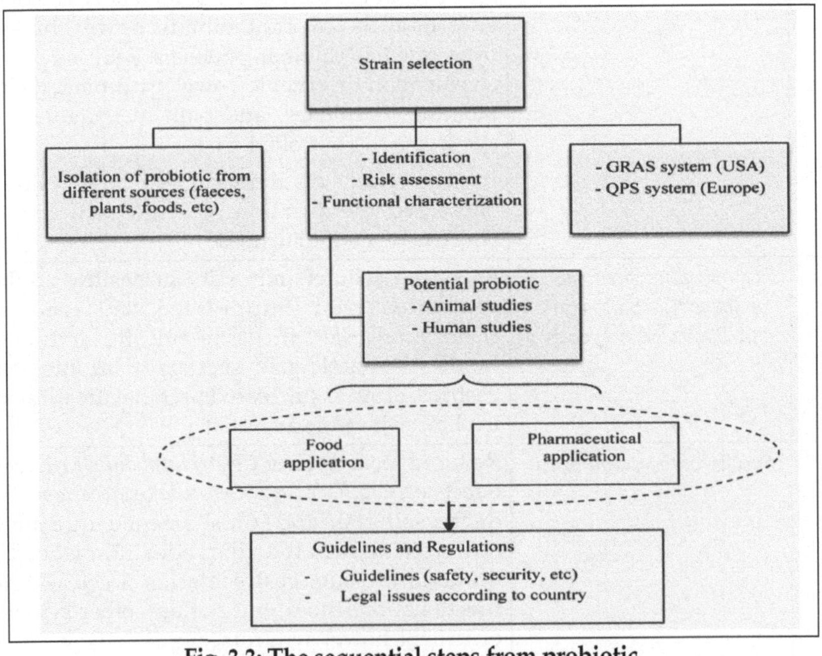

Fig. 3.3: The sequential steps from probiotic selection to their application in final products

Therapeutic Applications

Enhancement of the Immune System

Intake of yoghurt may improve some of the body's immune defence responses. When adults consumed 1 cup of yoghurt with live cultures per day for one year, allergic symptoms decreased (Water *et al.*, 1999). The probiotics can enhance both specific and nonspecific immune responses. These effects are believed to be mediated through activating macrophages, increasing levels of cytokines, increasing natural killer cell activity and/or increasing levels of immunoglobulins (Perdigon and Alvarez 1992). The use of probiotics in immune compromised patients appears promising. Children with HIV infections have episodes of diarrhoea and frequently experience malabsorption associated with possible bacterial overgrowth. Administration of *L.plantarum* 299v (can be safely administered to immuno compromised hosts) may have a positive effect on immune response and has the potential to improve growth and development. Clinical testing has focused mostly on immune cell levels and not on actual incidence of disease (Parvez *et al.*, 2006). The immune enhancing effects have been reported in several studies for two *Lactobacillus* strains, namely, *Lactobacillus acidophilus* LC1 and *Lactobacillus* GG with both strains appearing to enhance natural immunity and also act as immunoadjuvants (Lee and Salminen, 1995). The use of lactic acid bacteria in foods is age old, and *Lactobacilli* have a 'generally regarded as safe' (GRAS) status. A probiotic mixture of *L.acidiphilus, B.bifidum, Streptococcus thermophilus* and *Lactobacillus bulgaricus* has been found to successfully prevent traveller's diarrhoea.

Reduction of Lactose Intolerance

It is well established that intake of yoghurt enhances lactose digestion in individuals with low intestinal levels of lactase, the enzyme necessary to digest lactose or milk sugar, i.e. a condition called lactose non-persistence. The lower lactose content of some dairy foods compared to milk my attribute to the beneficial effect of these foods for individuals who have difficulty in digesting lactose. The beneficial effects may also be explained by the ability of the starter cultures used in the manufacture of yoghurt with live, active cultures to produce the enzyme lactase, which digests the lactose in yoghurt. Yoghurt without live cultures, unfermented or sweet acidophilus milk, and cultured buttermilk are tolerated about the same as milk by individuals with lactase nonpersistence. In take of cultured dairy products such as yoghurt may also improve tolerance to milk in individuals with cow's milk allergy/sensitivity (Kolars *et al.*, 1984).The beneficial effect appears to be a consequence of the lactic acid bacteria in fermented milk increasing lactase activity in the small intestine (Marteau *et al.*, 1990);

Reduction of Serum Cholesterol Levels

Different strains of lactic acid in cultured dairy foods appear to have different effects on blood cholesterol levels. Studies have shown that feeding of fermented milks containing very large number of probiotic bacteria (app. 109/g) to hypocholesterolemic patients has lowered cholesterol level from 3g/l to 1.5 (Homma,1988). In a study of older adults, intake of about 1 cup of yoghurt with live cultures per day for one year prevented an increase in blood total and low density lipoprotein (LDL) cholesterol levels (Pearce, 1996). The preliminary studies of Nakamura *et al.*, (1996) indicated that probiotic bacteria or their fermented products may also play a role in blood pressure control, with animal and clinical studies documenting antihypertensive effects of probiotic ingestion. Elderly hypertensive patients who consumed fermented milk with a starter containing *Lactobacillus helveticus* and *Saccharomyces cerevisiae* experienced reductions on systolic and diastolic blood pressure. Parvez *et al.*, (2006) felt that there is a critical need for long-term, well-controlled human studies to evaluate the benefit of probiotic consumption on heart disease risk through their effects on hypertension and blood lipid levels.

Anticarcinogenic Activity

Among the many potentially risky exposures are chemical exposures. Cancer-causing chemicals (carcinogens) can be ingested or generated by metabolic activity of microbes that live in the GI system. It has been hypothesized that probiotic cultures might decrease the exposure to chemical carcinogens by: (i) ingested carcinogens; (ii) altering the environment of the intestine and thereby populations or metabolic activities of bacteria that may generate carcinogenic compounds; (iii) producing metabolic products (e.g. butyrate) which improve a cell's ability to die when it should die (a process known as apotosis or programmed cell death); (iv) producing compounds that inhibit the growth of tumour cells; or (v) stimulating the immune system to better defend against cancer cell proliferation (Parvez *et al.*, 2006). The possible reason for the preventive effect of probiotics on carcinogens may be their effect on other bacteria in the intestine. Probiotics might suppress the growth of bacteria that convert procarcinogens, thereby reducing the amount of carcinogens in the intestine. The activity of the enzymes that convert procarcinogens is often used as an indicator of the effect of probiotics on the intestinal micro-flora and experimental results suggested that consumption of L.casei might delay the recurrence of bladder tumours (Aso *et al.*, 1995).

The possibility that lactic acid bacteria in cultured dairy foods may protect against certain cancers such as colorectal cancer, and possibly breast cancer has been investigated. Studies indicate that specific bacterial strains of Lactobacillus reduce the growth of cancer cells and the activity of faecal carcinogenic enzymes implicated in the development of colon cancer. In laboratory, intake of yoghurt has been shown to reduce colorectal tumors (Wollowski *et al.*, 1999). A review of cancer suppressant role of probiotics and probiotic products is presented in (Table 3.2). As most of these studies have carried out on experimental animals and mice to the exclusion of human subjects, more conclusive studies are required on humans to prove the efficacy of probiotics and probiotic containing foods against malignancy problems.

Protection against Ulcers

MaccFarlane and Cummings (2002) observed some preliminary evidence that probiotic bacteria may inhibit the gastric colonization and activity of H.pylori, which is associated with gastritis, peptic ulcers, and gastric cancer. Several workers (Filippo *et al.*, 2001) proposed the use of probiotics in the field of *Helicobacter pylori*, infection for improving eradication rate and tolerability and for compliance of multiple antibiotic regimens used for the infection. An inhibition of *Helicobacter pylori* infection was also in humans consuming *Lactobacillus johnsonii* (Michetti *et al.*, 1999).

Protection against Allergies/Eczema

Probiotic bacteria are known to alleviate intestinal inflammation in infants with atopic eczema/dermatitis syndrome (AEDS). Probiotics may also be helpful in alleviating some of the symptoms of food allergies such as those associated with milk protein. Possibly by degrading these proteins to smaller peptides and amino acids, added to the diet of infants on a hydrolysed whey formula, decreased the symptoms of atopic dermatitis (Majamaa and Isolauri 1997). Probiotics have also been observed to up regulate anti-inflammatory cytokines, such as interleukin-10, in atopic children (Pessi *et al.*, 2000). Probiotic therapy has been reported to be successful in the management of inflammatory bowel disease and in controlling severe food allergy problems manifesting as severe atopic eczema and hypersensitivity of milk in adults (Pessi *et al.*, 2000)). (Fig. 3.4)

Application of Probiotics in Food Industry

Fermented products represent a rich source of nutrients and may improve lactose digestion through the breaking down of lactose into glucose and galactose by bacterial enzymes. Fermented milk products also help to enhance the immune system with modulation of the cellular immune response through bioactive peptides, whose activity may extend beyond the immune function through some unknown mechanisms. Thus, the fermented milk and probiotics used for fermentative purposes may contribute towards variety of health benefits, viz. the modulation of intestinal health and the immune system, as well as anticarcinogenic, antidiarrheal and hypo-cholesterolaemic effects (Arora, 2006). The therapeutic effects of probiotics are widely known and are being used in many fermented dairy products throughout the world.

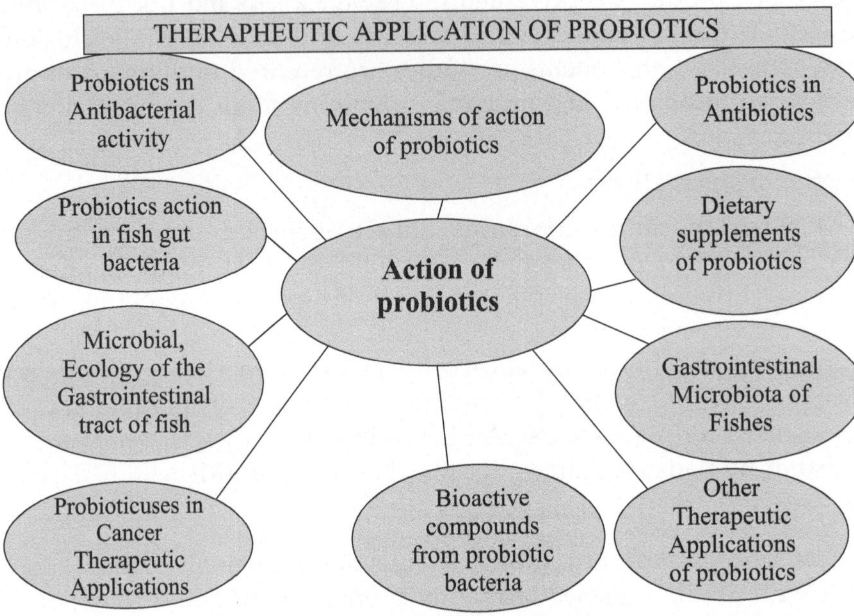

Fig. 3.4: Applications of probiotics

Salminen *et al.*, 1998b has detailed therapeutic applications as follows:

- Prevention of urogentital infections
- Alleviation of constipation
- Protection against traveller's diarrhoea
- Reduction of antibiotic induced diarrhoea
- Prevention of hypercholesterolaemia
- Prevention of osteoporosis

In humans, *lactobacilli* (e.g., *Lactobacillus acidophilus, L. casei, L. delbruekii*) are commonly used as probiotic, either as single species or in mixed culture with other bacteria. Other genera that have been used as probiotics are *bifidobacteria (Bifidobacterium bifidum, B. adolescentis, B. longum, B. infantis*) and *streptococci* (e.g. *Streptococcus salivarius ss. Thermophilus, S. lactis*) (Gibson and Roberfroid, 1995).

Various scientists reported the mechanism of probiotic organisms and summarized (Fedorak and Madsen, 2004)

- Production of inhibitory substances.
- Blocking of Adhesion sites by competitive inhibition

- Competition for nutrients otherwise consumed by pathogenic microorganisms
- Stimulation of immunity

Probiotic Dairy Products

Oral consumption of probiotics could be occurred via drug products, namely supplements, and food products. They have their own characteristics and functions which are discussed below and are shown concisely in Table 3.2.

Table 3.2: Parameters determined the ability of commercial probiotic cultures to survive stress conditions in food/drug preparation or in the gastrointestinal tract (GIT)

Stage	Parameter	Basis of effect
(1)	(2)	(3)
Cultures selection	Strain	Variation in the nature and quantity of genetically determined cell components
Fermentation	Above optimal growth condition Sub-optimal growth temperature	Strains structure determined by fermentation condition in a way that mentioned parameters are able to enhance exopolysaccharides production by some species and also change their lipid composition of cell membranes
	Sub-optimal pH	
	Presence of oxygen	
Concentration	Pumping during ultrafiltration	The damages induced during ultrafiltration and centrifugation is able to decrease the ability of probiotic bacteria toresist the stress.
	Pressure during centrifugation	
Stabilization	Freezing or drying	Freezing and drying condition damage the cell wall, membranes and intracellular components of probiotic bacteria. Consequently those exposed to freeze-dried condition are more prone to be damaged during food/drug or GIT stress.

(Table Contd...)

(1)	(2)	(3)
Encapsulation	–	Free cells are exposed to stressful condition more rapidly compared to encapsulated ones.
Shipping	Temperature	Increasing the temperature enhance the cells damage.

Probiotic Dietary Supplements

A dietary supplement (also might be called 'food supplement') is an orally administered substance designed to deliver a certain dietary ingredient, to complement the diet [20-22]. In other words, they are not substantially applied to treat or cure a specific human disease. They are usually packaged in different forms of capsules, tablets, powders (in sachets), or liquids in measured doses [23,24]. In order to produce a beneficial supplement, probiotic must be able to toleratethe severe conditions of gastrointestinal tract and arrive viable to the site of action [25-27]. This fact must be considered during supplement formulation, production and storage. The manufacturing process of a dietary supplement is similar to medicines however the severe courses of action used in medicinal products are not necessary to pursue. Probiotic formulations comprise selecting microorganisms able to subsist throughout the technological process and remain viable subsequently with unaffected properties for long periods of storage [28,29]. The active element of a probiotic supplement is the resistant probiotic microorganism(s) in a highly enough amount to guarantee precise dosing and good stability [30].

Fermented Milk Products

In fermented probiotic products it is important that the probiotic culture used contributes to good sensory properties. For milk based products the probiotic strains are often mixed with *S. thermophilus* and *L. delbrueckii* to achieve the desired flavor and texture. The stability of food as a substrate for probiotic can be improved by adding energy sources (e.g glucose), growth factors (e.g. yeast extract and protein hydrolysates) or suitable antioxidants, minerals or vitamins (Gomes *et al.*, 1998). Today a broad variety of fermented and non-fermented dairy products containing microorganisms with probiotic function is available in the market.

Probiotic Cheese

A few studies have evaluated cheese as a carrier of probiotic organism. Dinakar and Mistry (1994) incorporated *Bifidobacterium bifidum* into cheddar cheese as starter adjunct. This strain survived well and retained a viability of 2×10^7 cfu/gm of cheese even after six months of ripening, without adversely affecting cheese flavour, texture or appearance. This suggested that cheddar cheese could provide suitable environment for probiotic organisms. Stanton *et al.*, 1998 observed that two *Lactobacillus paracasei* strain grow and sustain high viability in cheddar cheese while *Lactobacillus salivarius* strain die during the ripening period. All the *Lactobacilli* strains were isolated from human upper gastrointestinal tract (GIT). The researchers were in the opinion that probiotic cheddar cheese can be manufactured containing high levels of *L. paracasei* strains (10^8 cfu/gm cheese) at a relatively low cost without any negative impact on cheese quality, flavour and texture. Attempts have been made (Mc Brearty *et al.*, 2001) to manufacture probiotic cheddar cheese by incorporating two commercially available *bifidobacteria* strains as starter adjuncts in cheese milk. It was observed that between this two strains of *Bifidobacterium*, *B. lactis* Bb-12 survived at high number (>10^8 cfu/gm cheese) than *B. longum* BB 536 (10^5 cfu/gm cheese) after six months of ripening. High viability of *Bifidobacteria* and *B.bifidum* not sustained in cottage cheese after 15 days of storage at 4°C and white brined cheese (Ghoddusi and Robinson, 1996) following 60 days of ripening.

Probiotic Ice-cream

Probiotic ice-cream is a suitable vehicle for delivering beneficial probiotic organisms to the consumers. Probiotic ice-cream can be made by fermenting a standard mix with *L. aciophilus* and *B. bifidum* cultures and then freezing the mix in a batch freezer. Direct culture addition for producing probiotic ice-cream as an additional advantage as compared to conventional frozen yoghurt that it saves time and capital required or culture fermentation. The initial freezing and churning stage of converting mix into ice-cream have the greatest effect on viability in most cases (Haynes and Playne, 2002). Good textured fermented ice-cream can be made by heat treatment at 62°C for 30 min releases some free amino acids and other stimulating substances which would allow the culture to begin acid production more quickly. It also provides a semi sterile environment for the growth of culture bacteria; therefore, competition for nutrients from other non-lactic acid bacteria is reduced. The preferred pH of probiotic ice-cream based on overall acceptance was pH 5.5 (Hekmat and McMahon, 1992). Such an ice-cream contains high levels of viable organisms, even after 17 weeks of frozen storage.

Nondairy Products

However dairy products are still the favored product to be used to incorporate probiotic bacteria, their high lactose and cholesterol content, their necessity to be stored at refrigerator temperature, the consumers demand for vegetarian based probiotic bacteria and even new taste and flavor are the motivation factors to produce nondairy products [46,47]. Accordingly, different types of probiotic contained non-dairy products have been produced during past two decades including juices and nondairy beverages, vegetable, cereal based products, chocolate based products, processed meats and etc. [32,33,48,49]. Production of a new non-dairy probiotic product should accomplish the consumer's demand for the products which are pleasant and healthy. So the development process of a new non-dairy probiotic product would be challenging either scientific or applied research [50,51]. In fact to design a new food, it is necessary to optimize the best formulation

Fig. 3.5: Probiotics food products

Prebiotics

The concept of prebiotic is relatively new. According to Gibson and Roberfroid (1995), a prebiotic is defined as "a non digestible food ingredient that beneficially affects the host by selectively stimulating the growth and/or activity of one or a limited number of bacteria in the colon that can improve the host health". These are termed as "colonic foods" as these upon entering the colon and serving as substrates for the endogenous colonic bacteria, indirectly provide the host with energy, metabolic substrate and essential micronutrients.

A food ingredient may be classified as a Prebiotic if it meets the following criteria:

- It should not be hydrolysed or absorbed in the upper GIT.
- It should selectively induce the growth of beneficial bacteria in colon.
- It should be able to repress the growth of pathogenic bacteria.
- It should induce luminal or systemic effects beneficial to host.
- It should decrease the colonic pH.
- It should have a known structure, which can be documented.
- It should be palatable as food ingredient and large scale processing must be easy.

Milk sugar lactose can be modified to derive products such as galactooligosaccharides, lactitol, lactosucrose and lactulose, all possessing prebiotic properties. The beneficial effects of prebiotics are:

- Non-digestable and low energy value (<9 kJ/g)
- Increase in stool volume.

- Modulation of the colonic floraby stimulation of beneficial bacteria and inhibition of undesirable bacteria.
- Prevention of intestinal infection.

Probiotic Challenges

Commercially, viable probiotic strains are incorporated into fermented food products or are supplied as freeze-dried supplements or pharmaceutical preparations (Holzapfel & Schillinger, 2002). The basic requirement for probiotics is that products should contain sufficient numbers of microorganisms up to the expiry date (Fasoli *et al.*, 2003). Thus, probiotics must contain specific strains and maintain certain numbers of live cells for them to produce health benefits in the host. Different countries have decided on the minimum number of viable cells required in the probiotic product for it to be beneficial. In Australia, a minimum viable count of 106 organisms per gram should be available in fermented milk products at the end of the shelf life. However, according to Krasaekoopt *et al.* (2003), there are no specifications as to how many probiotics should be available in Australian fermented products. The same minimum count (10 organisms per gram) was approved by countries of MERCOSUR which includes Argentina, Paraguay, Brazil and Uruguay. In products containing multiple probiotic organisms, at least a million of each of them per gram should be present to produce required beneficial effects.

In Japan, a minimum of 107 viable cells per millilitre of fresh dairy product is required. The South African legislation states that functional foods containing probiotic bacteria must deliver 1 × 108 bacterial cells per day. A daily intake of 109 to 1010 cfu viable cells is considered the minimum dose shown to have positive effects on host health. This could be achieved by consuming 100 g of a product containing between 106 and 107 viable cells g-1 daily (Fasoli *et al.*, 2003). Retention of viability of the probiotic bacteria presents a major marketing and technological challenge for application of probiotic cultures in functional foods. Many active cultures die during manufacturing, storage or transport of the finished product and also during the passage to the intestine. Thus, the majority die even before the consumer receives any of the health benefits (Siuta-Cruce & Goulet, 2001). A serious problem of shelf instability had been encountered with dried cultures. Refrigerated products also have short lives due to negative effects of low temperature and formation of crystals on bacterial cells. The numbers of viable bacteria continually decrease with time during refrigerated storage. Market surveys have revealed much lower counts in the products even before the expiry date (Talwalkar *et al.*, 2001). Shelf life for probiotics is thus unpredictable; hence, the industry has had difficulty backing up label claims (Siuta-Cruce & Goulet, 2001). Excesses of 50 to 200% cells have been incorporated into products in an attempt to make-up for cells that die during storage. For example, in tablets containing dry cells, where the tablets are labelled as containing a certain minimum count of active cells per tablet, to be safe, the manufacturer must incorporate an excess of cells at the time the tablets are manufactured, thereby assuring that the labelling will remain accurate while the product is in stock by the retailers. This practice increases the cost and makes the use instructions inaccurate.

Probiotics, after surviving food processing, are upon consumption then exposed to conditions prevailing in the stomach and small intestine before they reach their site which is the colon (Siuta-Cruce & Goulet, 2001). The microbes may die during their transit through the upper intestinal tract to the colon and therefore they may not be able to colonize the colon (Talwakar *et al.*, 2001). They must therefore survive gastric acidity and bile salts which they encounter during their passage through the GIT (Siuta-Cruce & Goulet, 2001;). Their survival in the GI T depends on the strain and species-specific resistance to low pH (pH values ranging from 1.3 to 3.0) in gastric juice and to bile salts found in the small intestine. Probiotic bacteria can only perform when they find adequate environmental conditions and when they are protected against stresses (e.g extreme temperatures, high pressure, shear forces) they encounter during their production at the industry level or in the GIT (gastric www.intechopen.com 30 New Advances in the Basic and Clinical Gastroenterology acids and bile salts) (Siuta-Cruce & Goulet, 2001). Factors affecting viability during storage such as temperature, moisture, light and air should also be taken into consideration. Oxygen toxicity is another major problem in the survival of probiotic bacteria in dairy foods. High levels of oxygen in the product are detrimental to the viability of these anaerobic bacteria. Manufacturers of probiotics are facing the challenge that they should produce probiotic cultures that can survive for long periods, and are resistant to acidity in the upper intestinal tract so that they can reach the colon in high numbers to colonize the epithelium.

Probiotic cultures should therefore be produced in a way that will protect these sensitive bacteria from unfavourable interactions with detrimental factors (Siuta-Cruce & Goulet, 2001). In view of the health benefits associated with probiotics, it is not surprising that there is increasing interest in their viability. Probiotics do not have a long shelf life in their active form. Refrigeration is required in most cases to maintain shelf life as high temperatures can destroy probiotic cultures. However, most probiotics still have a short shelf-life even under low temperature storage. There is low recovery of viable bacteria in products claiming to contain probiotic bacteria. The preservation of these probiotic microorganisms presents a challenge because they are affected by exposure to temperature, oxygen and light (Chen *et al.*, 2006). Survival of most bifidobacteria in most dairy products is poor due to low pH and/or exposure to oxygen. Naturally many LAB may excrete exopolysaccharides to protect themselves from harsh conditions but this is usually not enough to give them full protection (Shah, 2000)

Methods for Improving Probiotic Viability

In view of the health benefits associated with probiotics, it is not surprising that there is an increasing interest in their viability. The common practice is storage at refrigerated temperatures to prolong their shelf life. Nevertheless, most of them still have a short shelf-life. There is low recovery of viable bacteria in products claiming to contain probiotic bacteria. Viability of probiotics is reduced as a result of their exposure to high temperature, oxygen, low pH and light (Chen *et al.*, 2006). Naturally many LAB may excrete exo-polysaccharides (EPS) to protect themselves from harsh conditions. However, protection afforded by these EPS is not sufficient (Shah, 2002). As a result, researchers are continuously searching for ways to improve survival of probiotic cultures during processing, storage and GIT transit. Different approaches are used in an attempt to preserve viability of probiotic cultures. These include among others, pre-exposure of probiotic cultures to sub-lethal stresses (Desmond *et al.*, 2002) and incorporation of micronutrients such as peptides and amino acids.

The disadvantage of pre-exposure to sublethal stresses is that it may result in significant decreases in cellular activity, cell yield and process volumetric productivity. Other alternative methods for improving probiotic viability are genetic modification (Sheehan *et al.*, 2007) immobilization, two-step fermentations, use of oxygen-impermeable containers and microencapsulation. Of these techniques, microencapsulation is relatively new and has been investigated by various researchers. Microencapsulation is a process by which solids, liquids or gases are packaged into miniature, sealed microcapsules that can release their contents at controlled rates under influences of specified conditions. It stabilizes the probiotics, increases their survival during processing and storage, controls the oxidative reaction, ensures sustained or controlled release at a specific target site (both temporal and time-controlled release) and improves shelf life (Anal & Singh, 2007)

The encapsulated probiotics are released from the microparticles as a result of many factors such as changes in pH and/or temperature. These changes may cause microcapsule walls to swell and rupture or dissolve. Microparticles reduce loss of probiotic cell viability by blocking reactive components such as atmospheric moisture, oxygen, high temperature, pressure, bacteriophage attack and cryoeffects. Studies have indicated that probiotic cultures enclosed within solid fat microcapsules retain both their activity and vitality (Krasaekoopt *et al.*, 2003). Methods of microencapsulation used in pharmaceutical and food industries are classified as either physical or chemical. Physical methods include pan coating, air-suspension coating, centrifugal extrusion, vibrational nozzle and spray drying (Anal & Singh, 2007), spray coating, annular jet, spinning disk, spray cooling, spray drying and spray chilling, extrusion coating, fluidized bed coating, liposome entrapment, coarcervation, inclusion complexation, centrifugal extrusion and rotational suspension separation. Chemical methods include interfacial polymerization, in-situ polymerization, matrix polymerization and extrusion. Extrusion and emulsion techniques are the mostly commonly used methods. There is a diversity of materials used for encapsulation of probiotics. These include among others, alginate, κ-carrageenan, locust bean gum, cellulose acetate phthalate, chitosan, gelatin, cellulose, pectin, whey protein and rennet. These materials are used either as supporting materials or gelling agents by different investigators. Although generally there are positive effects of microencapsulation, this method is not without disadvantages. Some types of the resulting microparticles may shrink and lose mechanical strength due to their sensitivity to acids, may present problems for large scale production, others require use of potassium ions that should not be taken in large amounts in diet, some of the polysaccharides used are prohibited in specific foods in other countries (Picot & Lacroix, 2004). Additionally and possibly the key disadvantage, is that the mentioned microencapsulation methods use water and other organic solvents whose use is less favoured due to their high costs and concerns about their negative environmental impacts.

Progress towards elimination of use of organic solvents has been made with development of microencapsulation technique using supercritical technology (Moolman *et al.*, 2006). This microencapsulation technique is based on the formation of an interpolymer complex between poly (vinyl pyrrolidone) (PVP) and poly (vinyl acetate-co-crotonic acid) (pVA-CA) in supercritical carbon dioxide (scCO2). A supercritical substance is neither a gas nor a liquid but possesses properties of both, making it unique. Since supercritical fluids have a wide spectrum of solvent characteristics, they can be used as solvents in different techniques. Microparticles produced using this method have suitable morphological characteristics, encapsulation efficiency and affords encapsulated probiotic cultures protection in simulated gastrointestinal fluids (Mamvura *et al.*, 2011)

CONCLUSION

Probiotic foods have emerged as the major nutritional factor impacting and influencing gastrointestinal physiology and function. At present it is generally recognized that an optimum 'balance' in microbial population in our digestive tract is associated with good nutrition and health. In addition to these beneficial health effects, researchers have demonstrated that probiotic bacteria produce bacteriocins and organic acids that act as antimicrobials to inhibit the growth of pathogens as well as improve functions of intestinal epithelial cells. Recent clinical trials have demonstrated the beneficial health effects of probiotic bacteria that have been incorporated in foods and animal feed. These effects include the prevention of diarrhea, balancing of intestinal microflora, stimulation of the immune system, modulation of systemic immune homeostasis, antitumor properties and lactose intolerance.

REFERENCES

AbdEl-Salam, M.H, Hippen, A.R., Salem, M.M., Assem, F.M. and El-Aassar, M. 2012 Survival of Probiotic Lactobacillus casei and Enterococcus fecium in Domiati Cheese of High Linoleic Acid Content. Emir. J. Food Agric., 24(2): 98-104.

Anal A.K. & Singh H. 2007. Recent Advances in Microencapsulation of Probiotics for Industrial and Applications and Targeted Delivery. Trends in Food Science & Technology 18, 240-251.

Arora B 2006 Health Related Properties of Fermented Milk Products – A Review. Indian Journal of Dairy Science 59(2): 57-63.

Aso Y, Akajan H, Kotake T, Tsuka-moto T and Imaik 1995 Preventive Effect of a Lactobacillus casei Preparation on the Recurrence of Superficial Bladder Cancer in a Double-blind Trial. Eur Ural 27: 104-109.

Boylston, T.D., Vinderola, C.G., Ghoddusi, H.B. & Reinheimer, J.A., 2004. Incorporation of Bifidobacteria into Cheeses: Challenges and Rewards. International Dairy Journal 14, 375-387.

Cheddar Cheese Quality. International Dairy Journal 11:599-610. Ghoddusi H B and Robinson R K 1996 The Test of Time. Dairy Industries International 61(7): 25-26, 28.

Chen, B.H. & Yao, Y.Q., 2002. Beneficial Microbe Composition, New Protective Material for Techniques of Probiotics for Yoghurt. Int Dairy J 13: 3-13. The Microbes, method to Prepare the same and uses thereof. US Patent 6368591.

Dinakar P and Mistry V V 1994 Growth and Viability of *Bifibacterium bifidum* in Cheddar Cheese. Journal of Dairy Science 77: 2854-2864.

Fasoli, S., Marzotto, M., Rizzotti, L., Rossi, F., Dellaglio, F. & Torriani, S., 2003. Bacterial Composition of Commercial Probiotic Products as Evaluated by PCR-DGGE Analysis. International Journal of Food Microbiology 82, 59-70.

Fedorak R N, Madsen K L 2004 Probiotics and Prebiotics in Gastrointestinal Disorders. Current Opinion Gastroenterology 20: 149-155.

Filippo C, Dicaro S, Santarell L, Armuizzi A, Gasbarrini and Gasbarrini A 2001. Heticobacter Pyroli Treatment : A Role for Probiotics, Pig Dis 19: 144-147.

Food Technology 55, 36-42.

Fuller R 1989 Probiotics in Man and Animals. Journal of Applied Bacteriology 66: 365-378.

Gibson G R and Roberfroid M B 1995 Dietary Modulation of the Human Colonic Microbiota: Introducting the Concept of Prebiotics. Journal of Nutrition 125: 1401-1412.

Gibson G R and Roberfroid M B 1995 Dietary Modulation of the Human Colonic Microbiota: Introducting the Concept of Prebiotics. Journal of Nutrition 125: 1401-1412.

Girdhari Sharma and Bikash C Ghosh 2006 Probiotic Dairy Foods and Prebiotics for Health Benefit. Indian Food Industry 25(1): 68-73.

Gomes Am, Malcata F X and Klaver F A (1998) Growth Enhancement of *Bifidobacterium lactis* Bo and Lactobacillus Acidphilus by Milk Hydrolysates. Journal of Dairy Science 81: 2817-2825.

Haynes I N and Playne M J 2002 Survival of Probiotic Cultures in Low Fat Icecream. Australian Journal of Dairy Technology 57(2): 10-14.

Hekmat S and McMohan D J 1992 Survival of *Lactobacillus acidophilus* and *Bifidobacterium bifidum* in Icecream for use as a Probiotic Food. Journal of Dairy Science 75(6): 1415-1420.

Homma N 1988 Bifidobacteria as a Resistant Factor in Human beings. Bifidobacteria Microflora 7: 35-43. Journal of Food Microbiology 71, 245-248.

Kolars J C, Levitt M D, Aouji and Salvaiano D A 1984 Yoghurt – an Autodigesting Source of Lactose, Northern English Journal of Medicine 310: 1.

Lee, Yuan-Kun and Salminen S 1995 The Coming of Age of Probiotics. Trends in Food Science and Technology 6: 241-245.

Lilley D M and Stillwell R H 1965 Probiotics: Growth Promoting Factors Produced by Microorganisms Science 147: 747-748.

MacFarlane G T and Cummings J H 2002 Probiotics, Infection and Immunity. Current Opinion of Infectious Disease 15: 501-506.

Majamaa H and Isolauri E 1997 Probiotics : A Novel Approach in the Management of Food Allergy. Journal of Allergy Clinical Immunology 99: 179-185.

Mamvura, C.I., Moolman, F.S., Kalombo,L., Hall, A.N. & Thantsha, M.S, Characterisation of the Poly-vinylpyrrolidone)-Poly-(vinylacetate-Co-Crotonic Acid) (PVP:PVAc- CA) Interpolymer Complex Matrix Microparticles Encapsulating a *Bifidobacterium lactis* Bb12 Probiotic Strain. Probiotics & Antimicrobial Proteins (2011) 3: 97-102.

Marteau P, Flourie B, Pachart F, Chastang C, Desjeux J F and Rambaud J C 1990. Effect of the Microbial Lactose (EC 3.2/23) Activity in Yoghurt on the Intestinal Absorption of Lactose. An in vivo Study in Lactose Deficient Humans. British Journal of Nutrition 64: 71-79.

McBrearty S, Ross R P, Fitzgerald B F, Collins J K, Wallace J M and Staton C. 2001. Influence of Two Commercially Available Bifidobacteria Cultures.

Michetti P, Dorta P H, Wiesel D, Brassart E, Verdu M, Herranz C, Felley N, Porta, M 1999 Effect of whey-based Culture Supernatant of *Lactobacillus acidophilus* (johnsonii) La 1 on Helicobacter pyroli Infection in Humans, Digestion 60: 203-209.

Modi, N. 2014. Probiotics and Necrotisingenterocolitis: The Devil (as always) is in the Detail. Neonatology 105: 71-73.

Moolman F.S., Labuschagne P.W., Thantsha M.S., Rolfes H., Cloete T.E. 2006. Encapsulating.

Naidu A S, Bidlack W R and Clemens R A 1999 Probiotic Spectra of Lactic Acid Bacteria (LAB). Critical Reviews of Food Science & Nutrition 38(1): 13-126.

Nakamura Y, Masuda O and Takano T 1996 Decrease of Tissue Angiotensin-1- Converting Enzyme Activity upon Feeding Sour Milk in Spontaneously Hypertensive Rats. Bioscience, Biotechnology and Biochemistry 60: 488-489.

Nichols, Andrew W 2007 "Probiotics and Athletic Performance: A Systematic Review". Current Sports Medicine Reports 6(4): 269-273. Current Medicine Group LLC. Doi: 10.1007.

Parker R B 1974 Probiotics, the Other Half of the Antibiotic Story. Animal Nutrition Health 29: 4-8.

Parvez S, Malik K A, AhKang S and Kim H Y 2006 Probiotics and their Fermented Food Products are Beneficial for Health. Journal of Applied Microbiology 100: 1171-1185.

Pearce J 1996 Effect of Milk and Fermented Dairy Products on the Blood Cholesterol Content and Profile of Mammals in Relation to Coronary Heart Disease. International Dairy Journal 6: 661.

Perdigon G and Alvarez S 1992 Probiotics and the Immune State, in Probiotics: The Scientific Basis (Ed. Fuller R). London : Chapman and Hall pp. 146-180.

Pessi T, Sutas Y, Hurme M and Isolauri E 2000 Interleukin to Generation in Atopic Children Following Oral *Lactobacillus rhamnosus* G G, Clinical Experimental Allergy 36: 1804-1808.

Pessione, E. (2012). Lactic Acid Bacteria Contribution to Gut Microbiota Complexity: Lights and Shadows. Front. Cell Infect. Microbiol. 2:86.

Picot A., Lacroix C., 2004. Encapsulation of Bifidobacteria in whey Protein-based Microcapsules and Survival in Simulated Gastrointestinal Conditions and in Yoghurt. International Dairy Journal, 14, 505-515.

Saleminon S 1996 Functional Dairy Foods with Lactobacillus Strain G G, Nutrition Review 54 (Suppl.): 99.

Salminen S, Ouwchand A C and Isolawi E 1998b Clinical Applications of Probiotic Bacteria. International Dairy Journal 8: 563-907.

Sanders M E 1999 Probiotics. Food Technology 53(11): 67-77.

Shah N.P. 2000. Some Beneficial Effects of Probiotic Bacteria. Bioscience Microflora 19, 99-106.

Sheehan V.M., Ross P., and Fitzgerald G.F. 2007. Assessing the Acid Tolerance and Technological Robustness of Probiotic Cultures for Fortification in Fruit Juices. Innovative Food Science and Emerging Technologies 8, 279-284 Simple Way for Screening of Oxygen Tolerance in Probiotic Bacteria.

Siuta-Cruce, P. & Goulet, J., 2001. Improving Probiotic Microorganisms in Food Systems.

Sperti G S 1971 Prebiotics, Avi Publishing Co., West Port, U.K.

Talwalkar, A., Kailasapathy, K., Peirs, P. & Arumugaswamy, R., 2001. Application of Probiotics with an Interpolymer Complex in Supercritical Carbon Dioxide. South African Journal of Science 102, 349-354.

Tannock G (editor) 2005 Probiotics and Prebiotics: Scientific Aspects, 1st ed., Caister Academic Press. ISBN 978-1-904455-01-8.

Water V J, Keen C L and Gershwin H E 1999 The Influence of Chronic Yoghurt Consumption on Immunity. Journal of Nutrition 129 (Suppl.): 1492S.

Wollowski I, Jist, Bakalinsky A T, Neudecker and Pool-Zohel B L 1999 Bacteria used for the Production of Yoghurt Inactivate Careinogens and Prevent DNA Damage in the Colon of Rats. Journal of Nutrition 129:77.

Pages: 54-81

Nutrition and Medicines in Nature
Edited by: **Dr. Jairam Singh and Dr. Pawan Kumar 'Bharti'**
ISBN: 978-93-88854-39-9
Edition: **2020**
Published by: **Discovery Publishing House Pvt. Ltd., New Delhi (India)**

4

Foliar Nutrition in Green Gram (*Vigna radiata* L.)

V. Aravinth

ABSTRACT

Field experiment was conducted during January - April, 2019 at Thanthai Roever Institute of Agriculture and Rural Development to study the effect of foliar nutrition on green gram. The experiment was laid out in Randomized Block Design with twelve treatments replicated thrice. The growth and yield components of green gram viz., dry matter production and number of pods per plant were favourably influenced by 2% DAP + 3% Panchagavya. It was followed by application of 3% Panchagavya alone. 2% DAP + 3% Panchagavya recorded the highest seed yield of 751.55 kg ha^{-1} as compared to other treatments.

INTRODUCTION

Pulse crop plays an important role in Indian agriculture and India is the largest producer and consumer of pulses in the world. Pulses contain high percentage of quality protein nearly three times as much as cereals (Upadhayay *et al.*, 1999). Thus, they are the source to overcome protein malnutrition among human being. For vegetarian diet, pulses form the major source of protein. Pulses are wonderful gift of nature with unique ability of biological nitrogen fixation, deep root system, mobilization of insoluble soil nutrients and bringing qualitative changes in soil properties which make them known as soil fertility restorers.

Green gram (*Vigna radiata* L.) is the one of the most important pulses of rain fed areas grown through out the country. This crop is grown in different cropping systems as a mixed crop, catch crop and sequential crop

Assistant Professor of Agronomy, Thanthai Roever Institute of Agriculture and Rural Development, Perambalur - 621 115 (Tamil Nadu) (India)

in the country. Green gram seed contains 23.86 per cent protein, 62.62 per cent carbohydrates, 1.15 per cent fat and minerals combinations, amino acid and essential vitamins. It is used as nutritive fodder specially for milch cattle. It is also used as a green manuring crop. Green gram is a native of India and in India the total green gram production was estimated as 1.5 to 2.0 million tonnes from about 3 to 4 million hectare area with an average productivity of 500 $kgha^{-1}$, whereas in Tamil Nadu it occupies an area of about 43.05 lakh hectares with a production of about 20.70 lakh tonnes and productivity of 481 kg ha^{-1}.

The yield potential of green gram is very low because of the fact that the crop is mainly grown in rain fed condition with poor management practices and also due to the various physiological, biochemical as well as inherent factors associated with the crop. Apart from the genetic makeup, the physiological factors viz., insufficient partitioning assimilates, poor pod setting due to the flower abscission and lack of nutrients during critical stages of crop growth, coupled with a number of disease and pest (Mahala *et al.*, 2001) constitute the major constraints for the poor yield. The productivity of green gram in our country is very low. Hence, there is a need for enhancement of the productivity of green gram by proper agronomic practices.

One among them is foliar application of organic and inorganic sources of nutrients for exploiting genetic potential of the crop. This is considered to be an efficient and economic method of supplementing part of nutrient requirements at critical stages. Foliar application is credited with the advantages of quick and efficient utilization of nutrients, elimination of losses through leaching, fixation and regulating the uptake of nutrients by plant (Manonmani and srimathi, 2009).

Foliar nutrition facilitates easy and rapid utilisation of nutrients. Foliar spray of Cow urine, Panchagavya and DAP was found to be beneficial in enhancing the yield of pulses.

Keeping the above in view the present investigation was undertaken with the following objectives:

- To study the effect of foliar nutrition on the growth of green gram.
- To assess the effect of foliar nutrition on yield parameters and yield of green gram.
- To workout the economics.

REVIEW OF LITERATURE

System approach to plant nutrition is gaining importance as evidenced by the recent research findings. Improved management of organic matter is considered to be a pre- requisite for sustaining soil health and crop productivity. Application of organic and inorganic nutrients maintains the soil nutrient supply in an optimum amount for sustaining soil health and crop productivity through optimization of benefits from all possible sources of plant nutrients.

The literature pertaining to influence of foliar nutrition on the growth, yield parameter, yield and economics in green gram are presented in this chapter.

Effect of Foliar Nutrition on the Growth of Green Gram

Experiment conducted by Chandrasekhar and Bangarusamy (2003) at the Collage of Agriculture, Tamil Nadu indicated that foliar application of DAP 2% along with KCl 1% and NAA 40 ppm significantly increased total dry matter production (24.08 g plant-1) over control (20.24 g plant-1) in greengram. Shinde and Bhilare (2003) revealed that, application of 2 per cent DAP at 65 DAS through foliar spray recorded higher plant height (55.72 cm), number of branches (29.15/plant) and dry matter/plant (33.15 g). Krishnaveni *et al.* (2004) observed that foliar application of DAP (2%) + ZnSO4 (0.5%) at 15, 30 and 45 DAS recorded the maximum plant height and chlorophyll content in green gram on clay loam soils at Agricultural College and Research Institute, Madurai.

Mahobia *et al.* (2006) revealed that the maximum plant height and dry matter production of pigeonpea were recorded at harvest with 2% DAP spray at 50% flowering compared with 1% DAP during *kharif* season at the Indira Gandhi Agriculture University, Raipur. Experiment conducted by Thakare *et al.*(2006) at the College of Agriculture, Nagpur indicated that soil application of 50% RDF along with foliar application of 2% DAP or urea with 50 ppm IAA or NAA at 20 and 35 DAS significantly increased leaf chlorophyll in soybean over recommended dose of fertilizer. Jayakumar *et al.*, (2008) stated that application of 2% DAP at pre flowering stage significantly increased the growth parameters like plant height (30.1cm), number of branches (3-4) and higher leaf area index in green gram.

Yadav *et al.* (2008) revealed that, in fieldpea maximum plant height (77.30 cm) and number of branches (5.00) was obtained by foliar application of NAA 50 ppm treated plants compared to control (62.50 and 4.40, respectively). Deotale *et al.* (2011) reported that foliar spray of 6% cow urine in soybean significantly increased plant height (34.83 cm), dry matter (17.02 g) when compared with water spray (29.88 cm, 14.07 g). Medhi and Roy (2011) revealed that foliar application of 2%DAP significantly influenced the plant height (55.88c), leaf area index (3.05), and leaf chlorophyll content of green gram. Doss *et al.* (2013) reported that application of 2%DAP significantly increased the growth and grain yield of green gram. Sashikumar *et al.* (2013) reported in blackgram that significantly higher growth components such as plant height (37.11 cm), number of branches (8.27 plant-1) were recorded with RDF + foliar spray of 40ppm NAA + 0.5% chelated micronutrient + 2% DAP over rest of the treatments.

Dwivedi *et al.*(2014) reported that plant height (cm), dry matter accumulation (g/plant), no. of branches (plant-1) and pods plant-1 were significantly higher (i.e. 70.88 cm, 17.09 g, 3.8 and 34.3 respectively) in green gram under foliar spray of 15% K Sap + RDF than other treatments. Rajesh *et al.* (2014)reported that the morphological traits viz., plant height, number of branches per plant, number of trifoliates per plant and days to 50% flowering, total dry matter and maturity were significantly increased by NAA @ 20 ppm in green gram.

Effect of Foliar Nutrition on yield Parameter and yield of Green Gram

Sashikumar *et al.* (2013)reported in blackgram that significantly higher significantly higher grain yield (1298kg ha-1) and number of pods/plant (38.73) were recorded with (RDF + foliar spray of 40ppm NAA + 0.5% chelated micronutrient + 2% DAP) over rest of the treatments. Doss *et al.* reported the results of the experiment conducted during 2012 indicated that, significantly higher grain yield of greengram was recorded with foliar spray of Panchagavya (597.3 Kg ha-1) as compared to other treatments. Subrahmaniyan *et al.* (2000) reported that application of combined nutrients (Diammonium phosphate 2.5 kg + ammonium sulphate 1.0 kg + borax 0.5 kg + NAA (naphthalene acetic acid) @ 40 ppm) on 25th and 35th day after sowing (DAS), followed by foliar spray of NAA @ 40 ppm alone on 45th and 55th DAS significantly gave the highest values of growth and yield attributes and pod yield of groundnut.

Yakadri and Thatikunta (2002) reported that application of lower dose (25 kg ha-1) of potash in combination with DAP two per cent at pre-flowering + pod developing stage recorded higher seed yield (13.80 q ha-1) and 1000-seed weight (33.80 g) over no spray (8.25 q ha-1 and 27.2 g respectively) in green gram.

Experiment conducted by Chandrasekhar and Bangarusamy (2003) at the College of Agriculture, Tamil Nadu indicated that foliar application of DAP (2%) + KCl (1%) + NAA (40 ppm) significantly increased the number of pods per plant (19.45) and seed yield (1443.38 kg ha-1). However, these treatments were on par with DAP two per cent (13.2, 1162.41 kg ha-1, respectively) in green gram. Seeds of green gram [*Vigna radiata* (L.) Wilczek cv. K-851] were selected for Petriplate and pot studies. In pot study, 3% Panchagavya spray at 10 DAS significantly increased the growth of green gram plants. The total leaf area of the plant also increased by 2 and 3% Panchagavya spray. An experiment conducted in Allahabad Agricultural Institute by Dixit and Elamathi (2007) revealed that, foliar application with DAP two per cent + NAA 40 ppm + B 0.2 per cent + Mo 0.05 per cent at 30 DAS in green gram increased the seeds per pod (25.86), 1000 seed weight (30.33 g), grain yield (10.16 q ha-1) and haulm yield (30.33 q ha-1) over no spray.

Ghosh and Joseph (2008) reported that 2% DAP recorded significantly higher number of pods per plant (21.77) number of seeds per pod (8.77) and 1000 grain test weight (31.7g) gram in green gram. Manonmani and shrimathi (2009) concluded that application of 2% DAP recorded higher 100 seed weight and seed yield in green gram. Choudhary and yadhav (2011) reported that application of 2% DAP recorded the highest dry matter accumulation per meter row length (114.9 g) in green gram.

Economics

Shyamrao Kulkarni (2012) reported that higher grain yield of greengram was recorded with foliar spray of Panchagavya which registered higher gross returns, net returns and B:C ratio due to higher productivity in terms of yield in green gram.

MATERIALS AND METHODS

Field experiment was conducted at Thanthai Roever Institute of Agriculture and Rural Development, Perambalur, Tamil Nadu, during January to April 2019 to study the effect of foliar nutrition on green gram. The materials and the methods followed are presented in this chapter.

Materials

Location of the Experiment Farm

The field experiment was conducted at Thanthai Roever Institute of Agriculture and Rural Development, Perambalur. The experimental farm is geographically situated at 11.8° N latitude, 78.8° E longitude and an altitude of 150 m above mean sea level.

Weather and Climate

The average rainfall of Perambalur is 908mm per annum. The weather data during cropping period are presented in Table 4.1.

Soil Characteristics

The soil is clay loam with low in available nitrogen, medium in available phosphorus and high in available potassium. The details of soil analysis are furnished in Table 4.2.

Crop and Variety

Green gram variety VBN 3 was chosen for the study. The morphological characteristics of VBN 3 are furnished in Table 4.3.

Methods

Experimental Design

The experiment was laid out in Randomized Block Design with three replications. The layout of the experimental field is shown in Figure 4.1.

Table 4.1: Weather data during cropping period (January-April, 2019)

Month & days	Standard week	Mean temperature °c		Relative humidity (%)	Rainfall (mm)	No. of rainy days
		Max	Min			
January 2019						
04-10	5	31.30	22.44	90	-	-
11-17	6	32.92	23.67	92	-	-
18-24	7	33.66	21.67	93	-	-
25-03	8	31.48	19.16	94	-	-
February 2019						
04-10	9	37.18	21.50	92	-	-
11-17	10	35.25	21.10	93	-	-
18-24	11	34.68	20.67	94	-	-
25-31	12	37.42	25.24	93	-	-
March 2019						
01-07	13	38.98	26.86	89	-	-
08-14	14	36.83	21.32	91	-	-
15-21	15	32.11	19.89	93	-	-
22-28	16	34.43	20.78	92	-	-
29-04	17	30.97	19.65	94	-	-
April 2019						
05-11	18	33.54	20.98	92	-	-

Table 4.2: Physico-chemical properties of the experimental soil

Sl.No.	Particulars	
A.	**Mechanical Analysis (International pipette method-Piper, 1966)**	
1.	Coarse sand (%)	36.62
2.	Fine sand (%)	14.11
3.	Silt (%)	12.37
4.	Clay (%)	36.47
5.	Textural class	Clay loam
B.	**Chemical Analysis**	
1.	Available nitrogen (kg ha-1)(Subbiah and Asija,1956)	198
2.	Available phosphorus (kg ha-1) (Olsen *et al.*, 1954)	18.6
3.	Available potassium (kg ha-1) (Jackson,1973)	287.84
4.	Organic carbon (%) (Walkely and Black, 1934)	0.26
5.	Soil reaction (pH) (Jackson, 1973)	7.38
6.	Electrical conductivity (dSm-1) (Jackson, 1973)	0.32

Table 4.3: Varietal characteristics of green gram

Particulars	**Green gram VBN 3**
Parentage	CO 1 * Vellore local
Duration (days)	65-75
Height (cm)	35-55cm
Average yield (kg ha^{-1})	878
100 grain weight (g)	2.8-3.5
Special features	Moderately resistant to powdery mildew and yellow mosaic, Intermediate flowering.

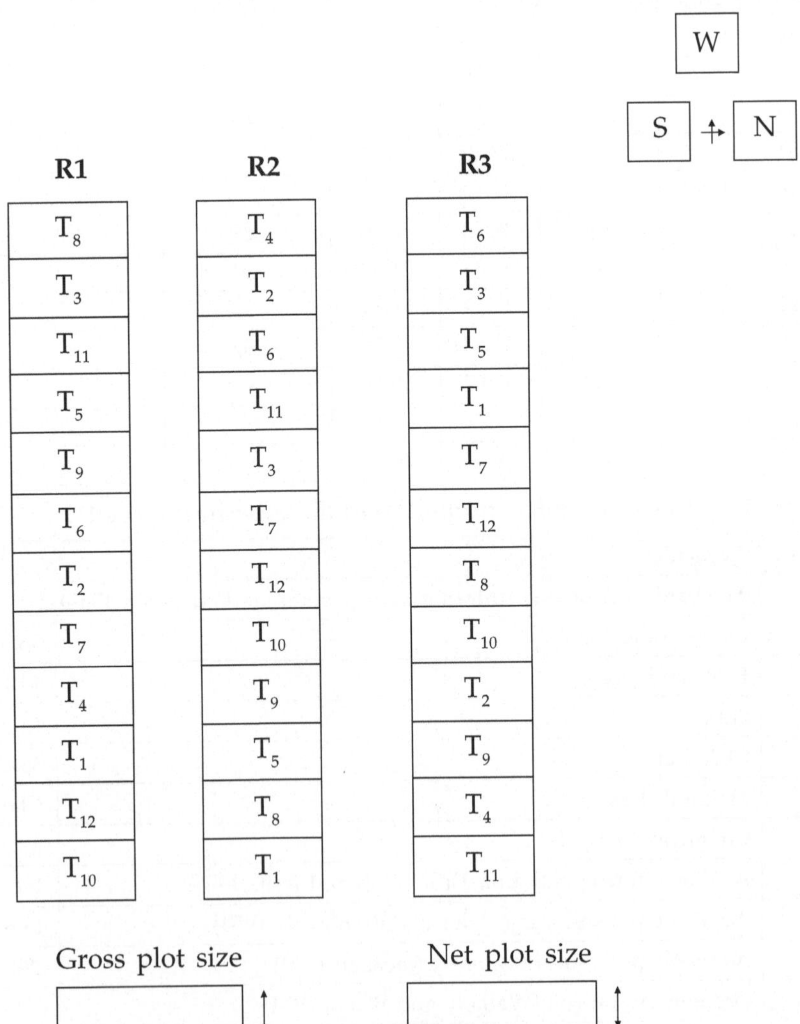

Fig. 4.1: Layout of the experimental field

Experimental Details

Particulars	Green gram
Season	January - April
Variety	VBN 3
Field number	B6
Experimental design	RBD
Gross plot size	4*3m
Net plot size	3.75*2.75m
Replication	3
Date of sowing	10.01.2019
Date of harvesting	01 .04.2019

Treatment details

T_1 : Control
T_2 : 2% DAP alone
T_3 : 4% Cow urine
T_4 : 6% Cow urine
T_5 : 3% Panchagavya
T_6 : 2% DAP + 4% Cow urine
T_7 : 2% DAP + 6% Cow urine
T_8 : 2% DAP + 3% Panchagavya
T_9 : 4% Cow urine + 3% Panchagavya
T_{10} : 6% Cow urine + 3% Panchagavya
T_{11} : 2% DAP + 4% Cow urine +3% Panchagavya
T_{12} : 2% DAP + 6% Cow urine +3% Panchagavya

Crop Management

Field Preparation

The experimental field was ploughed with tractor drawn cultivator and rotavator in criss-cross manner so as to obtain tilth.

Fertilizer Application

Recommended FYM was applied to the field before sowing. Fertilizers were applied plot wise as per the treatment schedule. Nitrogen was applied as urea, phosphorus as Di ammonium phosphate. Full dose of recommended N and full dose of p_2o_5 was applied basally.

Foliar Application of Nutrients

Preparation of 2% DAP

2% DAP was prepared by dissolving 20 g of DAP in 1000 ml of water. For this, 10 kg of DAP was dissolved in 25 litres of water and kept overnight. The supernatant liquid was dissolved in 475 litres of water to make 500 litres required to 1 hectare.

Preparation of 3% Panchagavya

3% Panchgavya was prepared by dissolving 30 ml in 1000 ml of water. For 1 ha, 15 litres of panchagavya was dissolved in 485 litres of water.

Preparation of 4% Cow Urine

4% cow urine was prepared by dissolving 4 ml of cow urine in 96 ml of water.

Preparation of 6% Cow Urine

6% cow urine was prepared by dissolving 6 ml of cow urine in 94 ml of water.

Seeds and Sowing

Green gram seeds @20 kg/ha was sown. Irrigation was given at critical stages depending upon the climatic conditions.

Gap Filling

Gap filling was done at 10 DAS so as to maintain uniform plant population.

Water Management

Irrigation was given immediately after sowing with due care to avoid excess flooding of water and subsequent irrigations were given as and necessary.

After Care

Need based plant protection measures were taken to protect the crop from the damage of insects and diseases.

Harvesting

The pods were harvested from the net plot area separately after observing the symptom of pod

Biometric Observations

Five plants in each replication of individual treatment were selected at random and labelled for recording biometric observations. The observations were recorded at harvest.

Growth Components of Green Gram

Plant Height

The plant height was measured from ground level to the tip of terminal leaves at harvest and recorded in cm.

Leaf Area Index

Leaf area index was calculated at flowering stage by adopting the procedure suggested by pattuswamy *et al.* (1976).

LAI was calculated by using the following formula

$$\text{Leaf area index} = \frac{L \times B \times K \times \text{number of leaves/plants}}{\text{Spacing (cm}^2)}$$

Where,

L= Maximum length of the leaf in cm.

B=Maximum breadth of the leaf in cm.

K= Constant factor (0.7)

Dry Matter Production (DMP)

From each plot five plants were selected at random from outside the net plot area and then oven dried at 65 ± 5°C till it reached a constant weight. The DMP was recorded at harvest stage and expressed in kg ha^{-1}.

Yield Components of Green Gram

Number of Pods per Plant

Five plants tagged in each plot were used for counting the pod number per plot.

Number of Seeds per Pod

Number of seed per plot was recorded from the sample tagged plants in each plot.

Hundred Seed Weight

After harvest and adequate drying of one hundred seeds from each plot were counted, weighted and expressed in grams.

Yield

Grain yield

The grain yield was recorded from the net plot at 14 per cent moisture basis and expressed in kg ha^{-1}.

Haulm yield

The dry weight of the haulm was recorded by subtracting the grain yield from the total DMP at harvest and expressed in kg ha^{-1}.

Soil Analysis

Pre sowing samples were taken. The soil samples were shade dried and passed through 2mm sieve. The sample was analysed for the nutrient status.

Mechanical Analysis

The mechanical composition of the soil was analysed following International Pipette Method suggested by piper (1996).

Soil Reaction (pH)

The pH of the soil was determined in 1:2:5 soil water suspension using PH meter as per procedure described by Jackson (1973).

Electrical Conductivity (EC)

The electrical conductivity (EC) was measured at1:2 soil water suspension with Elico conductivity bridge (Jackson, 1973).

Organic Carbon

The organic carbon content was determined by the method suggested by Walkley and black (1934).

Available Nitrogen

This was estimated by alkaline permanganate method (Subbiah and Asija, 1956) and expressed in kg ha-1

Available Phosphorus

This was estimated by the method described by Olsen *et al.* (1954) and expressed in kg ha-1.

Available Potassium

This was estimated by neutral ammonium acetate extract method as suggested by Jackson (1973) and expressed in kg ha-1.

Statistical Analysis

The data on observations and characters studied were statistically analysed and whenever the results were found significant, the critical differences were arrived at 5 per cent level to draw statistical conclusions (Panse and Sukhatme, 1978).

Economics

The economic parameters such as gross return, net return and return per rupee invested for all the treatments were worked out based on the prevailing market prices. The net return was worked out for the different treatments by subtracting the cost of cultivation from gross return. The return per rupee was calculated by using the following method.

Return rupee^{-1} invested = gross return (Rs.ha^{-1})/cost of cultivation (Rs.ha^{-1}).

EXPERIMENTAL RESULTS

Field experiment was conducted during January-April, 2019 at Thanthai Roever Institute of Agriculture and Rural Development to study the effect of foliar nutrition on the growth and yield of green gram. The experimental results of the study are presented in this chapter.

Growth Components of Green Gram

Plant Height

The data on plant height recorded at harvest are presented in Table 4.4.

Table 4.4: Effect of foliar spray on plant height in green gram (cm)

Treatment	Treatment schedule	Harvest
T_1	Control	38.00
T_2	2%DAP alone	43.00
T_3	4% Cow urine	37.00
T_4	6% Cow urine	40.00
T_5	3% Panchagavya	46.00
T_6	2% DAP + 4% Cow urine	42.00
T_7	2% DAP + 6% Cow urine	41.00
T_8	2% DAP + 3% Panchagavya	49.00
T_9	4% Cow urine + 3% Panchagavya	42.00
T_{10}	6% Cow urine + 3% Panchagavya	39.00
T_{11}	2% DAP + 4%Cow urine + 3% Panchagavya	40.00
T_{12}	2% DAP + 6%Cow urine + 3% Panchagavya	41.00
SEd		0.23
CD(p=0.05)		0.48

The plant height was significantly influenced by foliar nutrition.

The treatment, T8 (2% DAP + 3% Panchagavya) recorded the highest plant height of 49 cm at harvest. This was followed by T5 (3% Panchagavya). It was followed by 2% DAP alone. The least plant height of 38 cm at harvest was recorded in T1 (Control).

Leaf Area Index

The data pertaining to leaf area index at flowering stage are presented in Table 4.5.

Table 4.5: Effect of foliar spray on leaf area index in green gram

Treatment	Treatment schedule	Flowering stage
T_1	Control	2.30
T_2	2%DAP alone	3.98
T_3	4% Cow urine	3.22
T_4	6% Cow urine	3.24
T_5	3% Panchagavya	4.03
T_6	2% DAP + 4% Cow urine	3.32
T_7	2% DAP + 6% Cow urine	3.11
T_8	2% DAP + 3% Panchagavya	4.17
T_9	4% Cow urine + 3% Panchagavya	3.41
T_{10}	6% Cow urine + 3% Panchagavya	2.40
T_{11}	2% DAP + 4% Cow urine + 3% Panchagavya	3.65
T_{12}	2% DAP + 6% Cow urine + 3% Panchagavya	3.81
SEd		0.01
CD (p=0.05)		0.02

Among the treatments, T8 (2% DAP + 3% Panchagavya) recorded the highest leaf area index of 4.17. It was followed by T5 (3% Panchagavya). The lowest leaf area index of 2.30 was recorded in T1 (control).

Dry matter production

The data recorded on dry matter production at harvest stage are presented in Table 4.6.

Table 4.6: Effect of foliar spray on DMP in green gram (kg ha^{-1})

Treatment	Treatment schedule	Harvest stage
T_1	Control	705
T_2	2%DAP alone	1751
T_3	4% Cow urine	1165
T_4	6% Cow urine	1351
T_5	3% Panchagavya	1975
T_6	2% DAP + 4% Cow urine	1029
T_7	2% DAP + 6% Cow urine	1292
T_8	2% DAP + 3% Panchagavya	2150
T_9	4% Cow urine + 3% Panchagavya	1257
T_{10}	6% Cow urine + 3% Panchagavya	853
T_{11}	2% DAP + 4% Cow urine + 3% Panchagavya	1132
T_{12}	2% DAP + 6% Cow urine + 3% Panchagavya	1235
SEd		0.70
CD (p=0.05)		1.40

The dry matter production was significantly influenced by foliar nutrition.

Among the treatments,T8 (2% DAP + 3% Panchagavya) recorded the highest dry matter production of 2150 kg ha^{-1}. It was followed by the treatment, T5 (3% Panchagavya). The least dry matter production of 705 kg ha^{-1} was recorded in T1 (Control).

Yield Components

Number of Pods per Plant

The data on number of pods per plant are furnished in Table 4.7.

Table 4.7: Effect of foliar spray on number of pods/plant in green gram

Treatment	Treatment schedule	Pods/plant
T_1	Control	20.17
T_2	2%DAP alone	33.56
T_3	4% Cow urine	26.24
T_4	6% Cow urine	26.55
T_5	3% Panchagavya	34.56
T_6	2% DAP + 4% Cow urine	28.36
T_7	2% DAP + 6% Cow urine	25.98
T_8	2% DAP + 3% Panchagavya	40.40
T_9	4% Cow urine + 3% Panchagavya	31.36
T_{10}	6% Cow urine + 3% Panchagavya	24.76
T_{11}	2% DAP + 4% Cow urine + 3% Panchagavya	27.50
T_{12}	2% DAP + 6% Cow urine + 3% Panchagavya	30.65
SEd		0.07
CD (p=0.05)		0.15

The number of pods per plant was significantly influenced by foliar nutrition.

The treatment, T8 (2% DAP + 3% Panchagavya) significantly recorded the highest number of pods per plant of 40.40. This was followed by the treatment, T5 (3% Panchagavya). The least number of pods per plant of 20.17 was recorded in T1(Control).

Pod Length

The data on pod length are represented in Table 4.8.

Table 4.8: Effect of foliar spray on pod length in green gram (cm)

Treatment	Treatment schedule	Pod length
T_1	Control	6.90
T_2	2%DAP alone	7.46
T_3	4% Cow urine	7.20
T_4	6% Cow urine	7.33
T_5	3% Panchagavya	7.48
T_6	2% DAP + 4% Cow urine	7.38
T_7	2% DAP + 6% Cow urine	7.18
T_8	2% DAP + 3% Panchagavya	7.75
T_9	4% Cow urine + 3% Panchagavya	7.41
T_{10}	6% Cow urine + 3% Panchagavya	7.07
T_{11}	2% DAP + 4%Cow urine + 3% Panchagavya	7.22
T_{12}	2% DAP + 6%Cow urine + 3% Panchagavya	7.38
SEd		0.01
CD (p=0.05)		0.02

The pod length was significantly influenced by foliar nutrition.

The treatment, T8 (2% DAP + 3% Panchagavya) numerically recorded the highest pod length of 7.75 cm. This was followed by T5 (3% Panchagavya). The least pod length of 6.90 cm was noticed in T_1 (Control).

Number of Seeds per Pod

The data on number of seeds per pod are presented in Table 4.9.

Table 4.9: Effect of foliar spray on number of seeds/pod in green gram

Treatment	Treatment schedule	Number of seeds/pod
T_1	Control	5.32
T_2	2%DAP alone	6.23
T_3	4% Cow urine	5.95
T_4	6% Cow urine	5.98
T_5	3% Panchagavya	6.50
T_6	2% DAP + 4% Cow urine	6.02
T_7	2% DAP + 6% Cow urine	5.68
T_8	2% DAP + 3% Panchagavya	6.60
T_9	4% Cow urine + 3% Panchagavya	6.19
T_{10}	6% Cow urine + 3% Panchagavya	5.53
T_{11}	2% DAP + 4% Cow urine + 3% Panchagavya	6.29
T_{12}	2% DAP + 6%Cow urine + 3% Panchagavya	6.32
SEd		0.13
CD (p=0.05)		0.27

The number of seeds per pod was significantly influenced by foliar nutrition.

The treatment T8(2% DAP + 3% Panchagavya) numerically the highest number of seeds per pod of 6.6. This was followed by T5 (3% Panchagavya). The least number of seeds per pod of 5.32 was recorded in T_1 (Control).

Hundred Seed Weight

The data on hundred seed weight are presented in Table 4.10.

Table 4.10: Effect of foliar spray on hundred seed weight in green gram (g)

Treatment	Treatment schedule	Hundred seed weight(g)
T_1	Control	5.59
T_2	2% DAP alone	6.18
T_3	4% Cow urine	5.80
T_4	6% Cow urine	5.93
T_5	3% Panchagavya	6.20
T_6	2% DAP + 4% Cow urine	6.01
T_7	2% DAP + 6% Cow urine	5.79
T_8	2% DAP + 3% Panchagavya	6.28
T_9	4% Cow urine + 3% Panchagavya	6.08
T_{10}	6% Cow urine + 3% Panchagavya	5.66
T_{11}	2% DAP + 4%Cow urine + 3% Panchagavya	5.88
T_{12}	2% DAP + 6%Cow urine + 3% Panchagavya	5.98
SEd		0.05
CD (p=0.05)		0.10

The treatment T8(2% DAP + 3% Panchagavya) numerically recorded the highest hundred seed weight of 6.43 g. This was followed by T5 (3% Panchagavya). The least hundred seed weight of 5.29 g was recorded in T_1(Control).

Yield

Grain yield

The data on grain yield are presented in Table 4.11.

The grain yield was significantly influenced by foliar nutrition.

Among the treatments, the highest grain yield of 751kg ha^{-1} was recorded in T8 (2% DAP + 3% Panchagavya). This treatment was followed by T5 (3% Panchagavya). The least grain yield of 511 kg ha^{-1} was recorded in T1(Control).

Table 4.11: Effect of foliar spray on grain yield of green gram (Kg ha^{-1})

Treatment	Treatment schedule	Grain yield
T_1	Control	511
T_2	2% DAP	681
T_3	4% Cow urine	560
T_4	6% Cow urine	573
T_5	3% Panchagavya	720
T_6	2% DAP + 4% Cow urine	589
T_7	2% DAP + 6% Cow urine	542
T_8	2% DAP + 3% Panchagavya	752
T_9	4% Cow urine + 3% Panchagavya	601
T_{10}	6% Cow urine + 3% Panchagavya	618
T_{11}	2% DAP + 4%Cow urine + 3% Panchagavya	644
T_{12}	2% DAP + 6%Cow urine + 3% Panchagavya	660
SEd		10.66
CD (p=0.05)		22.10

Haulm yield

The data on haulm yield are presented in Table 4.12.

Table 4.12: Effect of foliar spray on haulm yield of green gram (Kg ha^{-1})

Treatment	Treatment schedule	Haulm yield
T_1	Control	851
T_2	2% DAP	1043
T_3	4% Cow urine	873
T_4	6% Cow urine	901
T_5	3% Panchagavya	1053
T_6	2% DAP + 4% Cow urine	919
T_7	2% DAP + 6% Cow urine	970
T_8	2% DAP + 3% Panchagavya	1285
T_9	4% Cow urine + 3% Panchagavya	921
T_{10}	6% Cow urine + 3% Panchagavya	957
T_{11}	2% DAP + 4%Cow urine + 3% Panchagavya	920
T_{12}	2% DAP + 6%Cow urine + 3% Panchagavya	922
SEd		0.70
CD (p=0.05)		1.4

The haulm yield was not significantly influenced by the treatments. Among the treatments, T8 (2% DAP + 3% Panchagavya) numerically produced the highest haulm yield of 1285 kg ha^{-1}. This treatment was followed by T5 (3% Panchagavya). The least haulm yield of 851 kg ha^{-1} was recorded in T1(Control).

Economics

The data on economics of different treatments are presented in Table 4.13.

Table 4.13: Effect of treatments on economics in green gram

Treatment	Treatment details	Cost of cultivation (Rs. ha^{-1})	Gross return (Rs. ha^{-1})	Net return (Rs. ha^{-1})	BCR
T_1	Control	11,300	22133	10,833	1.95
T_2	2% DAP	12,420	39066	26,647	3.15
T_3	4% Cow urine	11,740	31200	19,460	2.65
T_4	6% Cow urine	13,320	32800	19,480	2.46
T_5	3% Panchagavya	12,640	36426	23,786	3.30
T_6	2% DAP + 4% Cow urine	12,420	34720	22,300	2.79
T_7	2% DAP + 6% Cow urine	12,640	29066	16,427	2.29
T_8	2% DAP + 3% Panchagavya	12,420	42133.2	29,713	3.39
T_9	4% Cow urine + 3% Panchagavya	12,640	36133.2	23,493	2.85
T_{10}	6% Cow urine + 3% Panchagavya	12,420	26133.2	13,713	2.10
T_{11}	2% DAP + 4% Cow urine + 3% Panchagavya	14,830	32713.90	22,865	2.20
T_{12}	2% DAP + 6% Cow urine + 3% Panchagavya	14,540	33567.87	22,820	2.30

The highest net return (Rs. 29,713) and return rupee^{-1} invested (3.39) was obtained under T8 (2% DAP + 3% Panchagavya. It was followed by T5 (3% Panchagavya). The least net return (Rs.10,833) and return rupee^{-1}(1.95) was obtained under T_1 (Control).

DISCUSSION

Field experiment was conducted during January to April, 2019 at Thanthai Roever Institute of Agriculture and Rural Development to study the effect of foliar nutrition on green gram. The experiment was laid out with twelve treatments in a Randomized block design replicated thrice. The results of the field experiment are discussed in this chapter.

Growth Components

The integrated nutrient management greatly influenced the dry mater production (Fig. 4.2.) in green gram. The treatment T8(2% DAP + 3% Panchagavya) significantly influenced the dry matter production of crop. This might be due to the favourable effect of integrated use of DAP and Panchagavya which helped the crop in increasing the dry matter yield of crop through optimum supply of nutrients.

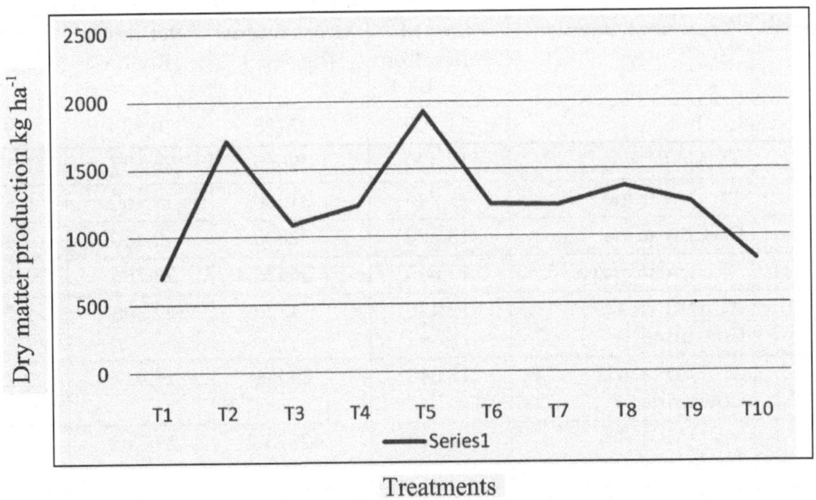

Fig 4.2: Dry matter production kg ha^{-1}

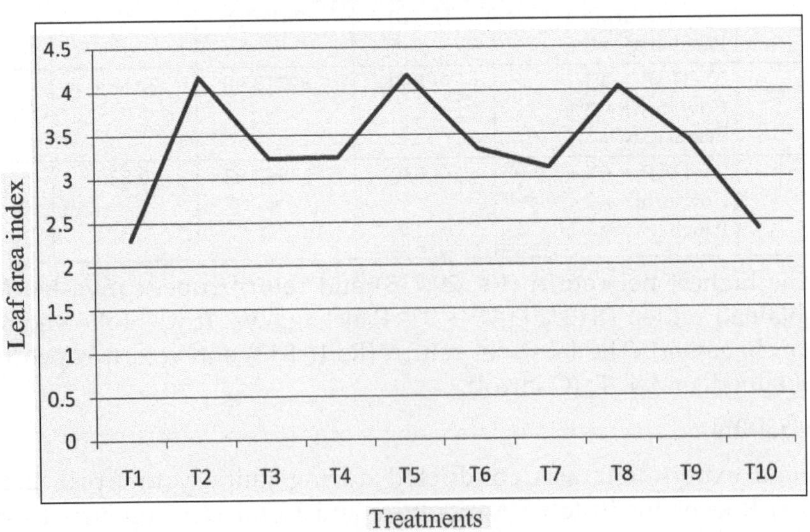

Fig. 4.3: Leaf area index

Yield Components and yield

The yield potential of green gram is determined by resultant value of yield components which are greatly influenced by the growth parameters. Among the treatments 2% DAP + 3% Panchagavya (T8) significantly recorded the highest number of pods per plant (Fig. 4.3.). This might be due to the favourable effect of foliar nutrition in enhancing the dry matter production of crop thereby contributing to higher number of pods per plant.

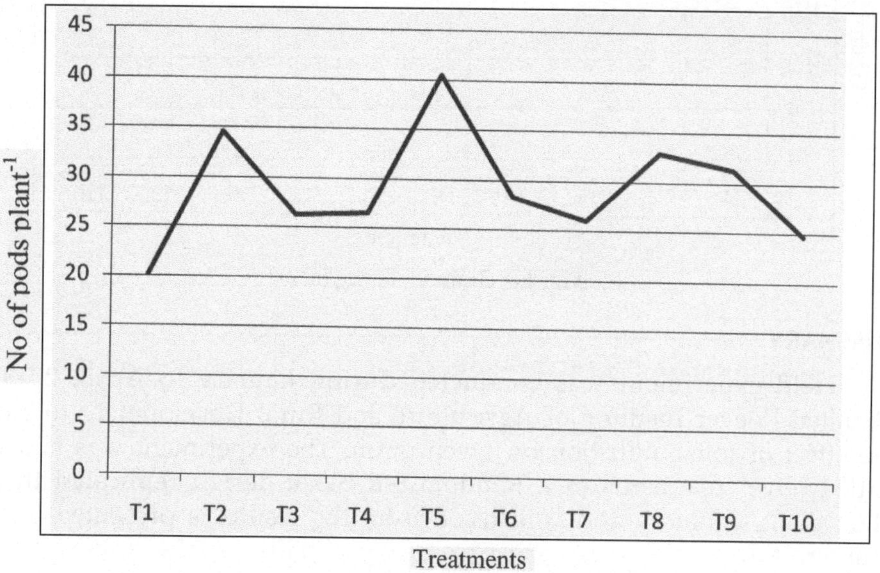

Fig. 4.4: No of pods plant^{-1}

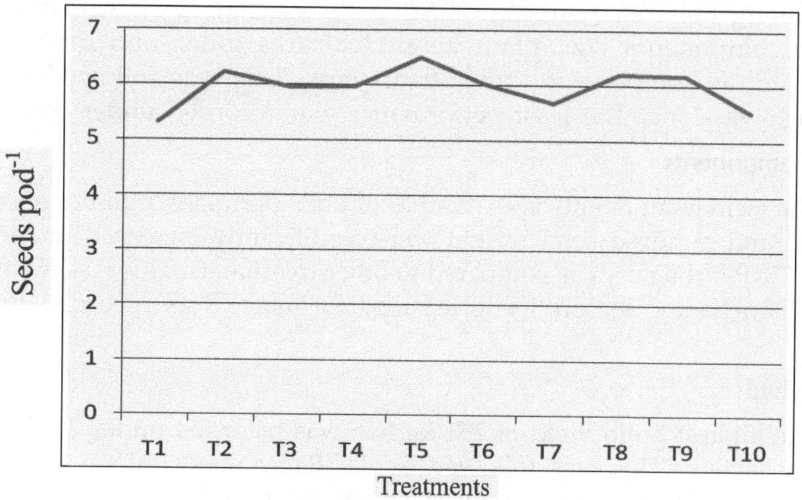

Fig. 4.5: Seeds pod^{-1}

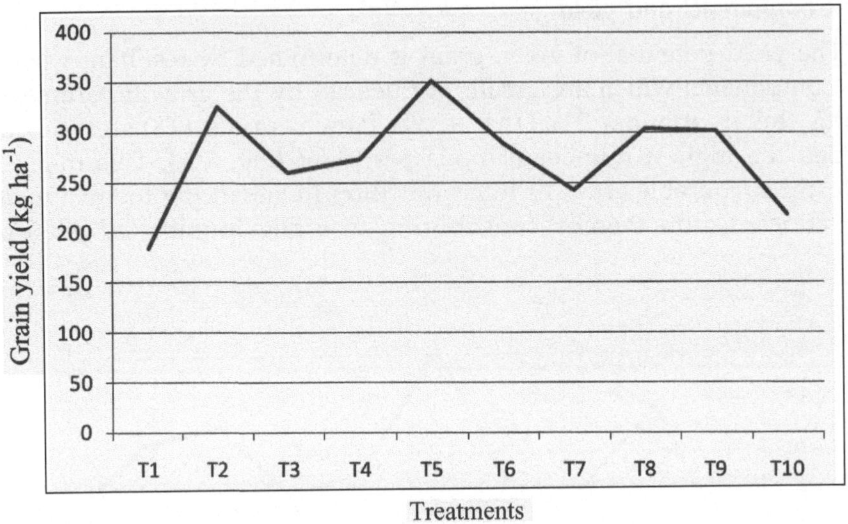

Fig. 4.6: Grain yield (kg ha^{-1})

SUMMARY

Field experiment was conducted during January to April, 2019 at Thanthai Roever Institute of Agriculture and Rural Development to study the effect of foliar nutrition on green gram. The experiment was laid out with twelve treatments in a Randomized block design replicated thrice. The salient summary and conclusion from the results is presented in this chapter.

Growth Components

Among the treatments 2% DAP + 3% Panchagavya increased the growth components viz., plant height,leaf area index and dry matter production as compared to other treatments. This was followed by 3% Panchagavya alone. The least performance was recorded under control.

Yield Components

The yield components viz., number of pods per plant, number of seeds per pod and hundred seed weight were significantly increased under 2% DAP + 3% Panchagavya as compared to other treatments. This was followed by 3% Panchagavya alone. The least performance was recorded under control.

Grain yield

The highest grain yield of 751 kg ha^{-1} was recorded under 2% DAP + 3% Panchagavya.This was followed by 3% Panchagavya alone. The least grain yield of 511 kg ha^{-1} was recorded under control.

Economics

The highest benefit cost ratio of 3.39 was recorded under 2% DAP + 3% Panchagavya. This was followed by 3% Panchagavya alone. The least benefit cost ratio of 1.95 was recorded under control.

CONCLUSION

Based on the result of the experiment, it can be concluded that application of 2% DAP + 3% Panchagavya will be economical in green gram for realizing higher yield and benefit cost ratio. This practice is economically viable, practically applicable and agronomically efficient technology which paves way for the realization of higher returns from green gram besides improvement in soil fertility. Next to this practice, foliar application of 3% Panchagavya recorded higher benefit cost ratio.

GENERAL VIEW OF THE FIELD

SEED SOWING

THINNING

FOUR LEAF STAGE

FLOWERING AND POD FORMATION

WEEDING

BIOMETRIC OBSERVATION

DRYING

WINNOWING

ABBREVIATIONS

T	-	Treatment
R	-	Replication
Ph	-	Potential hydrogen
EC	-	Electrical conductivity
dSm	-	1-deci-Siemen per meter or deci mho per meter
ml	-	milliliter
%	-	percent
g	-	gram
mg/1	-	milligram per literbor ppm
ANOVA	-	Analysis of varience
cm	-	centimeter
ht	-	height
g/plant	-	gram per plant
DAS	-	Days after sowing
Kg/plot	-	kilogram per plot
Mg	-	milligram
RDF	-	Recommended dose of fertilizers
SEd	-	Standard error

CD - Critical difference
BCR - Benefit Cost Ratio
ppm - Parts per million
DAP - Diammonium phosphate

REFERENCES

Amutha.R., Nithila,s., and Siva Kumar. 2012. Management of Source Limitation by Foliar Spray and Growth Regulators in Green Gram. International j.Plant sci.,7(1): 65-68.

Anandhakrishnaveni S., Palchamy, A. and Mahendran S. 2004, Effect of Foliar Spray of Nutrients on Growth and yield of Green Gram (*phaseolus radiatus*). Legume Res., 27(2): 149-150.

Ali MA, Abbas G, Mohy-ud-Din Q, Ullah K, Abbas G, *et al*. (2010) Response of Mungbean (*Vigna radiata* L.) to Phosphatic Fertilizer under Arid Climate. J Animal & Plant Sci 20: 83-86.

Baghel M.S. and Yadhav H.S. 1992. Response of Green Gram to Date of Sowing and Growth Regulators to Physiological Parameters and Seed yield. Bharathiya Krisi Annusandhan Patrika, 9: 38-42.

Balusamy M. and Meyyazhagan N. 2000. Foliar Nutrition to Pulse Crop. Training Manual on Recent Advances in Pulses Production Technology, CASA,Tamil Nadu Agricultural University: 113-115.

Chandrasekar C.N. and Bangarusamy U.2003. Maximizing the yield of Mung Bean by Foliar Application of Growth Regulating Chemicals and Nutrients. Madras agric. J.90:(1-3): 142-145.

Dixit PM, Elamathi S, Kishor KZ, Neeta C (2008) Effect of Foliar Application of Nutrients and NAA in Mungbean. J Food Legume 21: 277-278.

Fazulla Sheriff. A, Ashok S. Sajjan, H.B. Bahalad, L.B. Nagaraj and S. Giresh Palankar. Effect of Organics on Seed yield and Quality of Green Gram (vigna radiate L.) Legume Research 40(2): 388-392.

Ganapathy M., Baradhan G. and Ramesh N (2008). Effect of Foliar Nutrition on Reproductive Efficiency and Grain yield of Rice Fallow Pulses. Legume Res., 31(2): 142-144.

Geetha, P. and Velayutham, A. 2009. Refinement of Nutrient Management Techniques for Growth, yield and Nutrient uptake of Rice Fallow Black Gram. Madras Agricultural Journal; 96(1/6): 163-166.

Govindan, K and Thirumugan, V. 2000. Response of Green Gram to Foliar Nutrition of Potassium. Journals of Maharastra Agricultural Universities, 25: 302-303.

Gomez KA, Gomez AA (2010) Statistical Procedures for Agricultural Research. 2nd edn. Wiley India Pvt. Ltd., India.

Hussain N, Mohammad M, Rehana HK (2011) Response of Nitrogen and Phosphorus on Growth and yield Attributes of Blackgram (*Vigna mungo* L.). Res J Agric Sci 2: 334-336.

Manivannan V, Thanunathan K, Imayavaramban V, Ramanathan N (2003) Growth and Growth Analysis of Rice Fallow Blackgram as Influenced by Foliar Application of Nutrients with and without Rhizobium Seed Inoculation. Legume Res 26: 296-299.

Nawange DD, Yadav AS, Singh RV (2011) Effect of Phosphorus and Sulphur Application on Growth, yield Attributes and yield of Chickpea (*Cicer arietinum* L). Legume Res 34: 48:50.

Pramanik SC (2009) Rainwater Management Techniques for Successful Production of Pulses in Rainfed Areas. Indian Farming 58: 15:18.

Ravisankar N, Chandrasekharan B, Sathiyamoorthi K, Balasubramanian TN (2003) Effect of Agronomic Practices for Multi-blooming in Greengram (*Vigna radiata* L.) (cv. Pusa Bold). Madras Agric J 90: 166-169.

Pages: 82-96

Nutrition and Medicines in Nature
Edited by: Dr. Jairam Singh and Dr. Pawan Kumar 'Bharti'
ISBN: 978-93-88854-39-9
***Edition:* 2020**
***Published by:* Discovery Publishing House Pvt. Ltd., New Delhi (India)**

5

Apple of Tropics
Its Production and Quality Assurance with Special Reference to Nutrition

Prasann Kumar[1*2], Shipa Rani Dey[1]

GRAPHICAL ABSTRACT

Keywords: Apple, Biology, Crop, Dose, Economy.

[1] **Department of Agronomy, School of Agriculture, Lovely Professional University, Jalandhar - 144 411 (Punjab) (India)**
[2] **Divison of Research and Development, Lovely Professional University, Jalandhar - 144 411 (Punjab) (India)**

INTRODUCTION

Guava (*Psidiumguajava* L.) is a tropical fruit belonging to family Myrtaceae. It is a very important fruit crop of the subtropical and tropical regions of the world, commonly known as 'Apple of Tropics'. It is the fourth most important fruit crop after mango, banana, and citrus. It had been cultivated in India since the early 17th century and gradually became a crop of commercial significance. It is the native to tropical America and was introduced in India during the 17th century (Menzal, 1985). Gradually, the area of guava extended in India and considerable genetic diversity of guava is reported in Indo-Gangetic plains (Rajan *et al.*, 2007).

According to the report of FAO (2017), India is the largest producer of guava followed by China, Indonesia, Pakistan, Mexico, Brazil, Bangladesh, Nigeria, Philippines, Vietnam, Kenya, and Egypt. The guava fruit is a berry, bear round or oval in shape fruit. Fruit skin is rough to smooth having a green color and many small, hard or semi-hard seeds embedded in the core of the pulp. It is a highly nutritious fruit and a moderately good source of calcium, iron and a fair source of phosphorus. The ascorbic acid content of guava fruit is 2-5 times more than that of citrus (Singh, 2005). Numerous parts of the plant i.e. fruit, leaf, root, and bark are also used in the treatment of gastroenteritis, diarrhea (Jaiswal and Amin, 1992). In India, Guava is the fifth widely grown fruit crop. In India, the area under guava cultivation is 2,51,000 ha with annual productivity of 4.88 million tonnes. Guava is also the important crop of Punjab and ranks second after citrus. It grows well in almost all the districts of the state. In Punjab, guava fruit covers an area of 2.5 lakh ha yielding 40.5 lakh MT accounted for 3.97% of the area and 4.42% of production. The average productivity of guava is now 15.9mt/ha (Bal 2018). Guava is one of the most delicious and nutritious fruit. The fruit of guava is an excellent source of ascorbic acid. Due to the very high concentration of pectin in guava fruit, it may play an important role in the decrease of cholesterol and thereby decreases the risk of cardiovascular disease.

NATURE AND ITS DURATION FOR STORAGE

Guava is highly perishable in nature and post-harvest loss is estimated to be at 3.4-15.1 percent (Chadha and Pareek, 1993). Under ambient conditions, fruit keeps well for only 2-3 days after harvest. Because of high moisture content and thin and soft skin, guava fruits are subjected to a higher rate of transpiration, respiration, ripening and other biological activities even after harvest which deteriorates the quality of the fruits in a short period and finally makes them unmarketable. Hence it is necessary to reduce rates of these physicochemical changes in order to enhance the shelf life of guava fruits. In Punjab, the fruit grower does not have adequate facilities for extending the life of guava fruits. Hence, often glut in the market and produce does not fetch good prices. To overcome these problems there is a need to find out suitable low-cost post-harvest techniques for extending storability of guava. It is well known that guava is a highly perishable fruit crop, undergoes rapid post-harvest ripening in a few days under ambient conditions (Bashir and Abu-Goukh, 2003). Under ambient storage condition, guava becomes over-ripe within a week however, in cold-storage condition, the shelf life can be extended up to 14 days (Mahajan *et al.*, 2009). The biochemical reactions that occur during ripening to senescence results deterioration of cellular structures mainly the cell membrane which results in a loss of compartmentalization of metabolites and ions in the cells, resulting to the loss of tissue structure and causes homeostasis. Storage of fruit below 10°C may cause severe chilling injury symptoms in the form of surface pitting, skin and flesh browning (Reyes and Paull, 1995). Despite its high nutritive value, world trade of guava fruit is limited due to its perishable nature, short post-harvest life and susceptibility to chilling injury (Rai *et al.*, 2010) and (Mahajan *et al.*, 2009).

STORAGE ATMOSPHERE AND ITS METABOLITES

An inappropriate storage atmosphere may result in accumulation of fermentative metabolites resulting in the development of severe off-flavors, thus rendering the fruit unacceptable to the consumer. Studies have been shown that we can increase the longevity of harvested fruits by using different types of strategies i.e. the application of antitranspirants (Chahal and Bal, 2003), coatings with wax (Mahajan *et al.*, 2005), use of ethylene inhibitor and treatment with irradiation (Pandey *et al.*, 2010). There are many techniques meant for enhancing the post-harvest life of fruits with the aim at reducing the respiration rate and thereby the catabolism. Chitosan having chemical structure close to that of cellulose has long been known to protect perishable produce from deterioration by reducing transpiration, respiration and maintaining the textural quality (Krishna and Rao, 2014). Beneficiary effects of chitosan coating on quality of 'pearl' guava (Hong *et al.*, 2012), quality and shelf life of peeled litchi fruits (Dong *et al.*, 2004) has been reported. tomato (El-Ghouth *et al.*, 1992), litchi (Zhang and Quantick, 1997), peach (Li and Yu, 2001), mango (Kittur *et al.*, 2001), longan fruit (Jiang and Li., 2001), papayas and litchis (Ali *et al.*, 2011) and Lin *et al.*, 2011) has been reported. Aloe vera gel was best known for its therapeutic effect on burned or irritated skin but in future,we could be eating the gel as a healthful additive to our fruits and vegetables. Aloe vera gel has antibacterial and antifungal activities. The gel works as a barrier and act as a moisture barrier and reduced weight loss browning softening and of yeast and molds.

Ascorbic acid is used as additives and an antioxidant to protect the food quality (Bastos *et al.*, 2009). Ascorbic acid has been reported to delay enzymatic browning in many fruits due to its antioxidant activity (Gill *et al.*, 1998). The postharvest application of antioxidants in many cases effectively reduced weight loss and increased the storage period in mangoes (Ahmed, 1998).Therefore, the coating of the fruit at after harvest could be a solution for extending the period of marketing and provide wholesome food to the people. Edible coatings make good oxygen and lipid barriers, barrier for microbes and has to have good eating properties like color, taste, flavor, and texture. The use of coating has gained importance in reducing moisture loss and maintaining firmness (Farooqhi *et al.*, 1988 and Chauhan *et al.*, 2005). The edible coating is being traditionally used to improve fruit and vegetable appearance and its preservation. Last few years the use of various edible bio-materials at the post-harvest stage is becoming popular among growers for the enhancement of shelf-life of fruits. ables for increased shelf-life which has virtually replaced old commercial methods of post-harvest of fruits and vegetables due to its obvious advantage. Like chemically treated fruits were prohibited by quarantine authorities of importing countries due to chemical residues. Therefore the edible coating of fruits is a useful alternative purpose as well as to increase the shelf-life of fruits (Kumar and Sethi, 2018). Nowadays edible coating has opened a new avenue to overcome the problem of keeping quality of fruits because coating slows down the rate of metabolism of the produce and production of ethylene which delays ripening. Since the response of fruits to coating treatments vary with different kinds of fruits and varieties and conditions. Hence keeping the above views, the present investigation on "Effect of different coating materials on the post-harvest shelf life quality of the guava (*Psidiumguajava* L.) fruit" was conducted for the comparative study under the following objective (Table 5.1).

Table 5.1: Effect of edible coating of fruits and vegetables

S.No.	Fruit and vegetables	Used Edible coating
(1)	(2)	(3)
1.	Fresh-cut Apple	Sodium Alginate, Gellan Gum, Sunflower oil. Whey protein concentrate, WPI & WPP
2.	Blueberry	CMC, Chitosan, Monoglycerides, Sodium alginate, Calcium casienate
3.	Tomato	Aloe vera gel
4.	Grapes	Aloe vera gel
5.	Mango	Chitosan, Aloe vera. Tapico flour, Sago flour, Soy protein. Chitosan
6.	Cantaloupe	Aloe vera gel. Pectin, Chitosan

(Table Contd...)

(1)	(2)	(3)
7.	Guava (fresh cut)	Aloe vera juice
8.	Pistachio	Chitosan and Aloe vera gel
9.	Potato	Chitosan, WPC, Coconut oil
10.	Papaya	Aloe vera, Chitosan Papaya leaf extract
11.	Sapota	Aloe vera juice
12.	Pumpkin, Carrot, Radish, Cantaloupe, Cucumber	Chitosan, calcium salt.

Source: Based on review of literature

REVIEW ON CURRENT RESEARCH FOR THE SAKE OF RESEARCH

Srivastava *et al.* (1962) recordedthe storage life of guava fruits by treating with a carnauba-paraffin or carnauba-resin wax by 80 percent at room temperature and by 50 percent at 8-10^{0}C. Similarly, the extended shelf life of banana by about a week has been recorded by Agnihotri and Ram (1971). Waxing of banana fruits was found to reduce the PLW while in non-waxed fruits there was increased loss in weight upto a period of seven days of storage under ambient temperature. Dalal *et al.* (1971) suggested that the use of wax emulsions 4-6% extending the shelf-life without any detrimental effect on the quality of several fruits. Garg *et al.* (1971) evaluated the organoleptic quality of Dashehari mango fruits, under room temperature with different treatments. Combinations of prepackaging and waxolscoredthe highest of 86.6 followed by 77.0, 72.3 and 60.3 under wax treatment, prepackaging and control, respectively, indicating the superiority of repacking of the skin coated fruits over the untreated ones.Muthuswamy *et al.* (1971) reported reduced PLW (%) of banana fruits treated with 6 and 12 percent wax emulsion. Further, they concluded that the application of paraffin wax to cut end surface slightly reduced PLW (%). Garg and Ram (1973) reported that dipping of mango cv. Lucknow Safeda for 30 to 60 sec. in6 percent wax emulsion with sodium ortho-phenyl phenate 0.4% for 30-60 seconds extended the shelf-life of fruits by three days as compared to the control at 30 degree Celsius. Garg *et al.* (1976) reported significantly least weight loss 25.7 and 18.4 percent in guava (cv. Allahabad Safeda) treated with wax emulsion, after 9 days at room and 21 days at low-temperature storage condition respectively. Retention of acidity and ascorbic acid was better in waxed fruits as compared to control. Sheikh *et al.* (1977) found extended shelf-life of mango fruits using fungicidal wax emulsion coating. Pillai and Balakrishnan (1978) showed that W-12 wax emulsion prolonged the storage life by 4 to 5 days in banana cv. Nendran and Dwarf Cavendish. Bhullar and Farmahan (1980) indicated that coating of guava fruits with wax emulsion 6 percent delayed the rate of ripening and prolonged the storage life upto 10 days, with minimum physiological loss in weight (8.2%) and fruit rot (5.0%). Jawanda *et al.* (1980), similarly, also recorded less storage loss (9.32- 9.52) in ber fruit cv. umran and sameur, respectively,when treated with wax emulsion dipped for 30 seconds and stored in polyethylene bags. Roy *et al.* (1980) reported that wax emulsion treatment of Langra and Himsagar mango were most effective in extending storage life to 10 days as compared to 6 days in control. They also reported that weight loss was highest in control (14-15%) and it was lowest (4.2-7.3%) in combined treatment of wax emulsion with Maleic hydrazide. In an experiment to extend the storage life of kinnow fruits, it was found that the wax emulsion (12%) was the best coating material as a treatment to minimize the weight loss of fruit. Wax emulsion (6-12%) with and without 2, 4-D (50-100 ppm) and cytosol (500-1000 ppm) gave better retention of juice during storage. Wax emulsions alone or in combination with 2, 4-D retarded the rate of normal change of TSS (Bhullar *et al.,* 1981).Wild (1981) observed that the wax coating reduced the weight loss from 11.5 to 4.3 percent in oranges stored for 21 days.Passam (1982) noted extended shelf-life of mango when treated with wax 3 percent emulsion of stay-fresh wax at ambient temperature (28-32°C) during the experiment. Singh and Chauhan (1982) reported that taxol- 0-12 coating with pre-cooling increased shelf-life of guava by 2 days. It also reduced fruit rotting and retained higher sugars. They also found that the activities of pectinase and cellulase were lowest in wax treated guava fruits. Thus the fruit with wax treatment can safely be stored up to 4 days at ambient temperature. Wax emulsion applied to guava fruits reduced weight loss and produced a surface shine. Yellow skin color developed normally and respiration rate and ethylene production were not affected (Brown, 1983).Wild and Scott (1983) could maintain lime fruits, green and marketable for 4 months by treating with wax containing GA plus 2,4-D and storing in controlled atmosphere (1% $C0_2$, 12% O_2), with ethylene removed, at 10° C. Rao and Chundawat (1986) recorded a significantly lower percentage of ripened banana cv. Location fruits treated with wax (12%) compared to control on the 12th day of storage. Singhrot *et al.* (1987) recorded enhanced shelf life (up to 35 days) of Baramasi lemon with the treatment of taxol and captan. Banik *et al.* (1988) recorded prolonging storage of ber fruits with wax emulsion. Fruit coated with paraffin wax and then kept at 10 to 12°C temperature could be stored well up to 18 days with minimum spoilage and PLW as against 100 percent spoilage occurred in untreated fruits (held at 28-30°C and 70-75% R.H.) on the ninth day of storage. They also observed that fruits coated with 2 percent paraffin wax emulsion could be retained up to 12 days at room temperature with minimum spoilage. Karibasappa and Gupta (1988) found that packaging with the polythene reduced loss of weight. However the retention of ascorbic acid was recorded maximum in Benlate plus taxoltreated Khasi mandarins fruits, after 7 weeks of storage. Post-harvest treatments with fungicides as well as wax emulsion reduced theweight loss and increased the palatability rating of the fruits of Kinnow mandarin. The palatability rating maximum in the fruits treated with wax emulsion and the effect increased with its increasing concentration. Fungicides and wax emulsion treatments helped in reduction of fruit rotting during storage (Singh *et al.*, 1988).

Desai *et al.* (1989) confirmed that the Tal-prolong treated fruits had significantly higher values of starch, indicating the ripening process in these banana fruits was retarded significantly followed by those banana treated with Topsin plus wax emulsion, benomyl plus wax emulsion and wax emulsion alone. Wax emulsion was as effective as the Tal-prolong and gave the best result when used in combination with benomyl or Topsin. Shivaramareddy and Thimmaraju (1989) observed a reduction in spoilage and weight loss when mango fruits (cv. Alphonso) were coated with wax emulsion (2, 4 and 6%) and stored in perforated polyethylene bags. They found 6 percent wax emulsion as best coating concentration over the 2 and 4% concentration of wax emulsion. El-Ghouth *et al*, (1991) reported that application of chitosan coating had been shown to improve the storability of several perishable fruits such as strawberry. Aworh *et al.* (1991) found that waxing minimized weight loss in oranges and grapefruits. Over 31 days of storage, weight loss in control was 20 percent compared with 13.8 percent in waxed fruits.Paliyath and Droillard (1992) noticed that the process of membrane degradation during ripening is accelerated by Reactive Oxygen Speciesproduced during stress conditions that occur after harvest such as cold conditions of storage, post-harvest handling, etc. under such condition ascorbic acid may have potential to protect food quality. Patel *et al.* (1993) reported that with the coating of 6 and 12% wax emulsions on guava delayed the ripening process, show color development, less physiological loss,extend the shelf life and higher marketable number of fruits.Singh *et al.* (1993) reported that wax coating was best in prolonging the storage life of guava fruits cv. Allahabad Safeda by way of minimizing the physiological loss in weight, improving color development gloss and retaining chemical constituents during storage. Singh *et al*, (1993) reported that wax coating was best in extending the storability of guava fruits Cv. Allahabad Safeda. They found less physiological loss in weight, improving color development gloss and retaining chemical constituents during storage of fruit. Patel *et al.* (1993) reported that wax emulsions 6 and 12 percent are most effective to retard the ripening process, delay the color development of guava fruits and thereby extend the shelf-life of fruits. Physiological weight loss was minimum and marketability of fruits was also higher with 6 and 12 percent of wax emulsion. Jagdeesh (1994) studied showed that post-harvest treatments of with corn starch 6% extended the keeping quality of guava fruits upto 9 days. The treated fruits showed a reduced physiological loss in weight and retained higher content of TSS, ascorbic acid, acidity, total and reducing sugars and organoleptic scores during storage. Baviskar *et al.* (1995) reported that wax emulsion (W-0-12) treatment of 6 per cent coupled with polyethylene bags (150 gauge) with 2 per cent vents and CFB packaging is considered beneficial in the shelf-life improvement of stored ber upto the fifteen days in cool chamber and twenty nine days of cool store, while at room temperature wax treatment with polyethylene packaging was found beneficial. Sarkar *et al.* (1995) concluded that Giant Governor cv. banana could be stored for 14 days after harvest without significant effect on the quality when they were treated with 6 percent waxol. Singh *et al.*, (1997) studied the effect of waxol and corn starch coating on the quality of guava. They reported that the coated guava fruits retain good organoleptic properties up to 12 days of storage at ambient condition.Arvanitoyannis (1999) reported that chitosan has a great potentiality as a biodegradable, edible coating or film in food packing thus making it a potential raw material for edible films or coatings. Baldwin *et al.*, (1999) reported the effect of edible coating on fruit atmospheres and quality factors during simulated commercial storage at 10 or 15°C with 90-99% RH followed by simulated marketing conditions of 20°C with 56% RH. Polysaccharide and carnauba wax was used asthe main ingredient. The carnauba wax coating recorded better for reducing water loss compared to uncoated and polysaccharide-based coating treatments. Chen and Nussinovitch (2000) used Locust bean gum into traditional wax formulations of citrus fruit cultivars: Nova and Michal. Their performance was analyzed and compared to the inclusion of the non-gelling xanthan gum in a similar formulation. Both galactomannans reduced weight loss of the fruit during respiration in a manner similar to a wax-based coating without gum.Jiang and Li (2001) also reported that chitosan coating could extend the post-harvest life of longan fruit and maintain their quality. Yaman and Bayoundurlc (2002) studied the effect of semperfresh TM on sweet cherry storage. They found that Semperfresh TM @ 20 g/was most effective to reduce the weight loss of sweet cherry. They recorded increased shelf life by 21% at ambient condition and by 26% at cold storage condition without noticeable losses in quality. Semperfresh TM coatings were effective in reducing the ascorbic acid loss due to the low oxygen permeability of coating which decreases the activity of the enzymes and prevents oxidation of ascorbic acid. Bai *et al* (2003) reported coating with shellac higher fruit gloss, lowest internal O_2, highest CO_2, and least loss of flesh firmness in apple varieties. They used Zein to prepare coatings by dissolving zein in aqueous alcohol with propylene glycol. Gloss levels on Gala apple surfaces varied due to zein and PG content in coating formulations from that of controls to levels observed for shellac-coated fruit. At least 4 percent (by weight) PG was necessary for adequate gloss.

Lee *et al* (2003) investigated the effect of edible coatings with anti browning agents on minimally processed apple slices. Initial respiration rate showed a decrease by 5% and 20% in carrageenan (0.5 g/100 mL)-coated and whey protein concentrate (5 g/100 mL) coated apples, respectively, at 25° C. Edible coatings in combination with antibrowning agents effectively enhanced the shelf life of minimally processed apple slices by 2 week when stored with packed trays at 3°C. Addition of $CaCl_2$(1g/100 mL) significantly inhibited the loss of firmness.Ayranci and Tunc (2004) applied edible coatings of different composition on fresh fruits of apricots and green peppers. They reported that coating lowers the loss rate of water from green peppers and apricot. Han *et al.*, (2004) used chitosan-based edible coatings to extend the post-harvest life of strawberries and red raspberries stored at either 2°C and 88 percent relative humidity (RH) for 3 weeks or –23°C up to 6 months. Decreased decay and weight loss were noted with coating.Plotto *et al.*, (2004) studied the effect of dipping Mango fruits for 30 seconds in 5 ppm chlorine dioxide, 2% calcium ascorbate and 0.5% N -acetyl- L-cysteine (antioxidants), or coating solutions of 1% carboxymethylcellulose (CMC) or CMC and 0.5% maltodextrin (CMM). Coated fruit and fruit treated with antioxidants stored at 5°C maintained good visual quality after three weeks as compared to controls. When stored at 10°C, the visual quality of the two controls was the lowest, but overall, none of the treatments were acceptable after 14 days. CMC-treated fruit tended to be firmer when stored at 5°C after 11 days, but not at 10 °C. Zhang *et al* (2004) studied the physiological and physical changes in cucumber after treating with edible films coating and ozone water. The study showed that it can also lower the soluble solids content and inhibit the polyphenol oxidases (PPO) activity. Del-Valle *et al* (2005) investigated the effect of prickly pear cactus mucilage as an edible coating to improve the shelf-life of strawberries were tested to determine their effects on color, texture and sensory quality of the fruit. From the results, it was concluded that the use of mucilage coatings leads to increased strawberry shelf life.

Maftoonazad and Ramaswamy (2005) evaluated the effect of a methyl cellulose-based coating on the respiration rate, color, and texture of avocados stored at room temperature. Coated avocados demonstrated lower respiration rates, greener color and higher firmness as compared to the uncoated control during the storage. The appearance of brown spots and mesocarp discoloration normally related to fruit ripening were delayed in the coated fruits. Perez-Gago *et al.* (2005) prepared edible composite coatings from whey protein isolate, whey protein concentrate or hydroxypropyl methylcellulose as the hydrophilic phase, and bees waxor carnauba wax as the lipid phase and coated on apple pieces. Results show that apple pieces coated with whey protein-based coatings had higher L, and lower b, a and

Browning Index values than HPMC-based coated and uncoated apple pieces,which indicate that whey proteins exert an antibrowning effect. Coatings containing BW were more effective in decreasing enzymatic browning than coatings containing Cary.

Tanada-Palmu *et al.* (2005) determined the effect of wheat gluten-based films on strawberry quality under refrigerated condition. Coating of wheat-gluten and bees wax, stearic and palmitic acids had a positive effect on the firmness, weight loss. Martýnez-Romero *et al.* (2006) reported that aloe vera coated fruit showed a reduced loss in firmness, during storage and extend the shelf life of the fruits. The softening process in sweet cherries has been reported to be dependent on the increase in polygalacturonase, ß-galactosidase, and pectin methylesteraseactivities.Vargas *et al.* (2006) studied on strawberries cultivar Camarosa to evaluate the effect of Chitosan (1%, w/v) with oleic acid coating kept under the cold storage at 4°C for 10 days. They found that no significant differences in terms of hue or chroma were found due to coatings. Durango *et al.* (2006) developed an edible antimicrobial coating to evaluate its effect on minimally processed carrot by means of microbiological analyses. Coatings based on 4% yam starch (w/w) + 2% glycerol (w/w) and coatings based on 4% yam starch (w/w) + 2% glycerol (w/w) + chitosan in 0.5% and 1.5% concentrations were prepared. Samples of minimally processed carrot slices were immersed in these coatings. During storage, all the samples had counting <100 CFU/g for Staphylococcus aureusand <3 MPN/g for Escherichia coli. Starch + 0.5% chitosan coating controlled the growth of mesophilic aerobes, yeasts and molds, and psychrotrophic during the first five days of storage, compared to the control. Starch + 1.5% chitosan-coated samples showed reductions in mesophilic aerobes, mold and yeast and psychrotrophic counting of 1.34, 2.50 and 1.30 log cycles, respectively, compared to the control. The presence of 1.5% chitosan in the coatings inhibited the growth of total coliforms and lactic acid bacteria throughout the storage period.

Hernandez-Munoz *et al.* (2006) evaluated the effectiveness of chitosan (CS) 1 and 1.5 percent or chitosan along with calcium gluconate to extend the storage of Strawberries. No sign of fungal decay was observed during the storage period for fruit coated with 1.5 percent CS (with or without the addition of CaGlu) or 1 percent CS + 0.5 percent CaGlu. By contrast, 12.5 percent of the strawberries coated with 1 percent CS lacking calcium salt were infected after five days of storage. The chitosan coating reduced respiration activity, thereby delaying ripening and senescence. Strawberries coated with 1.5 percent chitosan exhibited weight loss and reduced darkening than did those treated with 1 percent chitosan, independently of the presence or absence of CaGlu. However, the addition of calcium to the 1 percent chitosan solution increased the firmness of the fruit. Martýnez-

Romero *et al.* (2006) used a novel edible coating based on Aloe vera gel, as a postharvest treatment to maintain sweet cherry quality and safety. During cold temperature, uncoated fruit showed higher in respiration rate weight loss and color changes, softening and ripening, stem browning and microbial populations. On the contrary, sweet cherry treated with A. vera gel significantly delayed the above parameters related to postharvest quality losses, and storability could be extended. The sensory analyses revealed beneficial effects in terms of delaying stem browning and dehydration, maintenance of fruit visual aspect without any detrimental effect on taste, aroma or flavors.

Matuska *et al.* (2006) found that coating of whole strawberries with selected edible (polysaccharide) films before osmotic processing favor water removal and prevent solute uptake. Double coating with a 0.5% sodium alginate (SA) solution gave the best results in terms of a high water loss (WL) to solid gain (SG) ratio (WL/SG). Single or double sodium alginate coatinginhibited leakage losses upon freeze/thawing of osmotically treated strawberries.Vargas *et al.* (2006) used edible coatings based on high molecular weight chitosan combined with oleic acid to retain the quality of cold-stored strawberries. Coatings had no significant effects on acidity, pH and soluble solids contents of strawberries throughout storage. In contrast, coatings slowed down changes in the mechanical properties and slightly modified respiration rates of samples. Addition of oleic acid not only enhanced chitosan antimicrobial activity but also improved water vapor resistance of chitosan-coated samples. Sensory analysis showed that coating application led to a significant decrease in strawberry aroma and flavor, especially when the ratio oleicacid: chitosan was high in the film.Jayachandran *et al.* (2007) results showed that post-harvest application of antioxidants improved the shelf-life of the superior physical-nutritional status of guava fruit.Albanese *et al.* (2007) observed the effect of trehalose asan edible coating on minimally processed Annurca apple slices during cold storage. Decreases in weight loss and in the reduction of organic acids were observed in coated samples.Chien *et al.* (2007) observed the effect of treatment of sliced mango with aqueous solutions of 0%, 0.5%, 1% or 2% chitosan and then stored at 6°C. Changes in taste, color and water loss, were recorded. A chitosan coating decreased water loss and, increasing the soluble solids content, titratable acidity, and ascorbic acid content. It also inhibited the growth of microorganisms. Chlebowska-Smigiel *et al.* (2007) studied the influence of the pullulan and pullulan—protein edible coatings on the reduction of the apple mass loss during the storage. Pullulan edible coating significantly limited apple mass losses. Apples covered with coatings showed lower mass losses than the ones uncovered. The smallest mass losses were observed in apples covered with the coatings where the pullulan to protein ratios were: 6:4 and 5:5. It was observed that by adding protein to pullulan the coating stuck better to apple surface. During the storage process, the protein-containing layer was less susceptible to crumbling and to peel off.

Olivas *et al.* (2007) studied the effectiveness of alginate-based edible coatings to preserve the quality of mi processed apples. Apple wedges were immersed in a calcium chloride solution and subsequently coated with one of three different coating formulations: alginate, alginate-acetylated monoglyceride-linoleic acid, and alginate-butter-linoleic acid. It recorded thatcoatings prolonged the shelf-life of cut apples without causing anaerobic respiration. All coatings used minimized the weight loss during storage, and apples with coatings containing acetylated monoglyceride, in particular, remained the closest to the original weight. Higher production of hexanol and trans-2-hexenal was observed in coated apples containing butter and acetylated monoglyceride. Fisk *et al.* (2008) investigated the effect of calcium caseinate, chitosan, PrimaFresh® 50-V, and SemperfreshTM edible coatings for their potential to enhance the quality and extend the storage life of hardy kiwifruit cv Ananasnaya'. Coatings provided an attractive sheen to the fruit surface and did not impair ripening. The consumer test indicated that both coated and uncoated fruit was well-liked. Geraldine *et al.* (2008) evaluated the effects of agar-agar based (1 percent) coatings added with chitosan 0.2 percent acetic acid 0.2% on minimally processed garlic cloves. Moisture loss of treated garlic cloves was, three times lower when compared to the control. There was a marked increase in color difference values for control cloves compared to the other treatments. Filamentous fungus and aerobic mesophilic were noted when garlic cloves coated with acetic acid + chitosan incorporated antimicrobial compounds.Sothornvit and Rodsamran (2008) studied the effect of a mango edible film and storage conditions on quality and shelf-life of fresh mango determined by Sothornvit and Rodsamra. Tapia *et al.* (2008) used alginate- (2% w/v) or gellan-based (0.5% w/v) coating formulations on fresh-cut papaya pieces. Formulations containing 2% (w/v) glycerol+1% ascorbic acid or 1% glycerol+1% ascorbic acid exhibited slightly improved water barrier properties for both types of coatings, as compared to the uncoated samples. The incorporation of 0.025% (w/w) sunflower oil into the alginate or the gellan-based formulations resulted in a 16% and 66% increase in the WVR of the coated samples, respectively. In general, coatings improved the firmness of the fresh-cut product during the period studied. Furthermore, the incorporated of ascorbic acid as an antioxidant in the coatings aided to preserve the natural ascorbic acid content of the fresh-cut papaya, helping to maintain its nutritional quality throughout storage. The gas barrier properties of the formulated coatings were not modified to allow substantial changes on respiratory rate and ethylene production of the coated papayas.

Zhou *et al.* (2008) worked with pear cv. Huanghua. Coatings applied were shellac (14.3gm/100 ml water), Semperfresh TM (1.0gm/100 ml water) respectively, carboxy methyl chitosan (2.0 g/100mL water) during cold storage (4°C). The total soluble solids, titratableacidity and ascorbic acid levels in pears decreased significantly in all treatments after 60 days of storage. Compared with the control samples, the shellac coated pears had significantly higher total soluble solids, titratable acidity, and ascorbic acid levels. inhibited the respiratory ratesand retarded the overall metabolic activities of pears during storage. Zhou *et al.* (2008) reported that physiological loss in weight is important Soluble solid and organic acids of fruits are substrates that are consumed by respiration during storage. Ascorbic acid is primarily regulated by ascorbic acid oxidase and phenoloxidase, whose activities are influenced by the oxygen content in the storage condition. In this study, shellac coating was more effective in the retention of total soluble solids and the titratable acidity and ascorbic acid levels because of the lower gas permeability of shellac coating that indicator of the freshness of the fruit. Water loss can cause flesh softening, fruit ripening and senescence because of ethylene production and other metabolic reactions. Mahajan *et al.* (2009) reported that the 5% weight loss of guava fruits during storage is the maximum permissible limit above which the guava fruits show shriveling and become unmarketable. Mahajan *et al.* (2011) reported that citrashine coated pear fruits registered the lowest average physiological loss in weight (2.82%) followed by terpenoids oligomer (3.12%) and carnauba coated fruits (4.93%) from 3 to 24 days of storage as compared to the control lot (8.38%) store under ordinary market (30-32°C) and supermarket (20-22°C) conditions. This increase in physiological loss in weight might be due to the higher temperatures leading to increased respiration rate and moisture loss.

Hong *et al.* (2012) reported that 2.0% chitosan significantly reduced firmness, weight loss increases the anti-oxidant ability of guava by delaying the ripening process. Jiang and Li (2001) also reported that chitosan coating could extend post harvest life of longan fruit and maintain their quality.Velickova *et al.* (2013) reported that incorporation of the beeswax in the coating significantly reduced the respiration rate of the strawberries and hence resulted in better preservation. Krishna and Rao (2014) reported that post-harvest treatment of Allahabad Safeda guava fruits with 1% chitosan delayed the ripening process and prolonged shelf life up to 7 days at ambient condition and the fruits retained desirable texture and post-harvest quality till the end of their storage life. Gill (2014) reported that ascorbic acid (100 ppm) treated guava fruits registered the lowest mean PLW as compared to the control fruit. Petriccione and Scortichini (2015) carried out an experiment to study the effect of chitosan coating on loquat to judge its nutraceutical traits. They found that bio active compounds and activity of antioxidants was higher in treated fruits than the untreated fruits. It was also found that the rate of deterioration was higher in untreated fruits. Gardesh *et al.* (2016) conducted an experiment to study nano chitosan based coating on apple cv. GolabKohanz. They found that percentage of weight loss after harvesting was decreased comparatively and also the rate of respiration, ethylene production and peroxidase activity was significantly reduced.

Jawandha *et al.* (2017) studied the effect of aloe vera gel, chitosan and carboxymethyl cellulose on Punjab Beauty pear and they found out that the palatable quality of fruit was best till 67 days after harvesting but after 74 days the quality was poorly degraded. Adiletta *et al.* (2018) conducted an experiment by coating chitosan on loquat at 7°C for 21 days. They found the improved activity of enzyme catalase, superoxide, dismutase, ascorbate and peroxidase. Also fruit membrane integrity was maintained by chitosan. Romani and Martins (2018) the study on the effect of starch coating incorporated with pink pepper phenolic compounds on apple advocated that the coating was helpful in lowering enzymatic browning in apples by inhibiting the enzyme peroxidise.

CONCLUSION

Guava is highly perishable in nature and post-harvest loss is estimated to be at 3.4-15.1 percent. Under ambient conditions, fruit keeps well for only 2-3 days after harvest. Because of high moisture content and thin and soft skin, guava fruits are subjected to a higher rate of transpiration, respiration, ripening and other biological activities even after harvest which deteriorates the quality of the fruits in a short period and finally makes them unmarketable. Hence it is necessary to reduce rates of these physicochemical changes in order to enhance the shelf life of guava fruits.

REFERENCES

Agnihotri, B N and Ram H B A (1971) Comparative Study of Skin Coating and Smoking Treatment on Ripening and Storage Behaviour of Banana (Musacavendish cv. Basrai). *ProgHort* 24: 59-65.

Baldwidin A, Burns J Kand Kazokas W (1999) Effect of Two Edible Coatings with Permeability Characteristics Mango (Mangiferaindica L.) Ripening during Storage. *Postharvest Technol* 17: 215-226.

Bashir, H A and Abu-Goukh A A (2003) Compositional Changes during Guava Fruit Ripening. *Food Chem* 80: 557-563.

Bal, J S (2018) Fruit Science Culture and Technology vol. I Basic Aspect and Practices, New India Publishing Agency, New Delhi.

Banik D, Duha R S, Gosh S K and Sen S K (1988) Studies on Extension of Storage Life of Sapota (Achrassapota L.) *IndianJHort* 45: 241-248.

Banik D, Hore JK and Sen S K (1988) Studies on Storage of ber (Zizyphusmauritiana Lank). *Haryana J. HortSci* 17 (1-2): 49-55.

Chadha K L and Pareek O P (1993) Post-harvest Losses in Fruits. *Adv in Hort* 4; pp. 1795-1811.

Chauhan S K, Thakur K S and Kaushal B B L (2005). Effect of Post-harvest Coating Treatments on the Storage Behaviour of Starking Delicious Apple Fruits under Evaporative Cool Chamber. 696: 473-478.

Dalal V B, Eipeson W E and Singh M S (1971) Wax Emulsion for Fresh Fruits and Vegetables to Extend their Shelf Life. *Indian Fd Packer* 25 : 9-15.

Desai BB, Shukla AD and Chougule B A (1989) Biochemical Changes during Storage of Chemical Treated Banana Fruits. *J Maharashtra Agri Uni* 14 (1): 47-48.

Dhall R K (2012) Advances in Edible Coatings for Fresh Fruits and Vegetables: A Review. *Critical Reviews in Food Sci & Nutrition* 53: 435-450.

Section I:
Medicines in Nature

Pages: 99-111

Nutrition and Medicines in Nature
Edited by: Dr. Jairam Singh and Dr. Pawan Kumar 'Bharti'
ISBN: 978-93-88854-39-9
Edition: 2020
Published by: Discovery Publishing House Pvt. Ltd., New Delhi (India)

6

Rheum Emodi as Valuable Medicinal Plant and its Pharmacological Aspects

Showkat Ahmad Bhat[1], Gurjinder Singh[1], Sabhiya Majid[2]
Tehseen Hassan[2], Tariq Parvez Azad[3]

ABSTRACT

Medicinal plants, also called medicinal herbs, botanical drugs, or natural product drugs, have been discovered and used in traditional medicine practices since prehistoric times. India is one of the twelve mega-biodiversity countries of the world having rich vegetation with a wide variety of medicinal plants and a tradition of plant-based knowledge distributed amongst a vast number of ethnic groups. Rheum emodi (Polygonaceae), commonly known as revand-chini, is the Himalayan species of Indian rhubarb found wild at an altitude of 4000-12 000 feet in Kashmir, Nepal, Sikkim and Bhutan. It has been used in various traditional systems as laxative, tonic, diuretic and to treat fever, cough, indigestion, menstrual disorder since antiquity. This paper consists of literature of Rheum emodi regarding its ethnobotany, folkloric uses, chemical properties and pharmacological studies. The most common constituents of Rheum emodi are anthraquinone (rhein, chrysophanol, aloe-emodin, emodin, physcion, and their glycosides) and stilbene (picetannol, resveratrol and their glycosides). Studies have shown that Rheum emodi possess anticancer, antioxidant, anti-inflammatory, antimicrobial, antifungal, antidyslipidemic, antiplatelet, antidiabetic, antiulcer, hepatoprotective, immunoenhancing and nephroprotective activities. These studies raised the therapeutic efficacy of rhubarb

[1] **Department of Biochemistry, Govt. Medical College (GMC), Doda, Jammu & Kashmir, (India)**
[2] **Department of Biochemistry, Govt. Medical College (GMC), Srinagar, Jammu & Kashmir, (India)**
[3] **Principal Govt. Medical College (GMC), Doda, Jammu & Kashmir, (India)**

in diverse ailments. It is essential that this medicinal plant should study more extensively to confirm these therapeutic effects and to check the traditional claim that this plant have significant medicinal properties as is reported in the traditional knowledge of the indigenous people that the plant is used in the treatment of gastrointestinal infections, respiratory infections, liver and skin infections.

Keywords: *Rheum emodi; phytochemistry; antiulcer; antidyslipidemic; hepatoprotective; antioxidant.*

INTRODUCTION

Medicinal plants, also called medicinal herbs, botanical drugs, or natural product drugs, have been discovered and used in traditional medicine practices since prehistoric times. Plants synthesize hundreds of chemical compounds for botanical functions, including defence against insects, fungi, diseases, and herbivorous mammals. Numerous phytochemicals with potential or established biological activity have been identified. However, since a single plant contains widely diverse phytochemicals, the effects of using a whole plant as medicine are uncertain. Further, the phytochemical content and pharmacological actions, if any, of many plants having medicinal potential remain unassessed by rigorous scientific research to define efficacy and safety. In the United States over the period 1999 to 2012, despite several hundred applications for new drug status, only two botanical drug candidates had sufficient evidence of medicinal value to be approved by the Food and Drug Administration. The earliest historical records of herbs are found from the Sumerian civilisation, where hundreds of medicinal plants including opium are listed on clay tablets. The Ebers Papyrus from ancient Egypt describes over 850 plant medicines, while Dioscorides documented over 1000 recipes for medicines using over 600 medicinal plants in De materia medica, forming the basis of pharmacopoeias for some 1500 years. Drug research makes use of ethnobotany to search for pharmacologically active substances in nature, and has in this way discovered hundreds of useful compounds. These include the common drugs aspirin, digoxin, quinine, and opium. The compounds found in plants are of many kinds, but most are in four major biochemical classes: alkaloids, glycosides, polyphenols, and terpenes. Medicinal plants are widely used in non-industrialized societies, mainly because they are readily available and cheaper than modern medicines.

Rheum emodi (Polygonaceae), commonly known as revand-chini, is the Himalayan species of Indian rhubarb found wild at an altitude of 4000-12 000 feet in Kashmir, Nepal, Sikkim and Bhutan. Rhubarb has been successfully grown in certain parts of Assam. Roots of the Indian rhubarb is darker, inferior in aroma, is a well known stomachic, bitter and cathartic, and used all over the world. There have already been many reports about antibacterial and antifungal activities of the anthraquinones, the napthoquinones isolated from natural sources. In addition several other biological activities such as laxative, diuretic, and in vivo inhibitory effect towards P388 leukemia in mice are also reported. The present communication deals with naturally occurring antifungal principles from R. emodi rhizomes. A bioassay guided isolation, characterization and evaluation of their methanolic extracts exhibited antifungal activities which resulted in four anthraquinone derivatives as active components.

Rheum Emodi

Rheum emodi (Rhubarb) is a perineal stout herb belonging to family polygonaceae and has been cultivated over 5000 years for its medicinal properties. It is distributed in the temperate and subtropical regions of the world, especially in Asia and can be cultivated at an altitude above 1800m. The herb is reported to possess antioxidant, antimicrobial, antifungal, anticancer, wound healing and immune enhancing activity and is commonly used worldwide herb and often known as "the wondrous drug" because of its extensive medicinal uses. Rhubarb contains a variety of compounds like flavonoids, anthraquinone glycosides, tannins, volatile oils and saponins and has long been used as an ingredient of purgative, laxative and stomachic. Paradoxically, although larger doses were used as a laxative, small dose were used to treat dysentery and diarrhea. Rhubarb has also been used injams, jelly and sauce by its tart flavor. There are three main types of rhubarbs, viz. the Chinese Rhubarb, the Indian Rhubarb, and the Rhapontic Rhubarb. Chinese Rhubarb comprises of dried rhizomes of Rheum palmatum L., and Rheum officinale Baill. Rheum emodi, commonly known as Indian or Himalayan Rhubarb, is official in Indian Pharmacopeia [1-5].

HISTORIC OVERVIEW

The use of this drug has been traced in medicine from very early time. The Chinese appear to have been acquainted with the properties of Rhubarb from a period long anterior to Christian era around 2700BC. It was first documented in "The Shen Nong Ben Cao Jing", the earliest book on materia medica in the world. It was being imported in Greece and Rome for medicinal purposes in the 1st century. Dioscorides and Galen described the good medicinal properties of rhubarb in their manuscripts and Avicenna has quoted the use of rhubarb in almost all system of body. By the 10th century this root became a major export of Asia and gradually spreads to India, Russia, Europe and North America. In Europe it was much price drug even more than opium and in France (in 1542) it was sold for ten times the price of cinnamon and four times that of saffron [6-9].

ETYMOLOGY OF RHUBARB

The word rhubarb has been derived from Latin word "rha" (river) and "barb" (barbarian land). In ancient times, rhubarb roots were imported by Romans from barbarian lands which were beyond the Volga or Rha River. Imported from barbarians across the Rha, the plant became Rhabarbarum. According to Lindley's Treasury of Botany, some authorities derive the name from the Greek rheo ('to flow'), in allusion to the purgative properties of the root [8, 10].

PLANT DESCRIPTION

Different Names in different Languages

Rheum emodi or Himalayan rhubarb is known by various vernacular names in different geographical regions or system. Detail is mentioned in below table.

Language/System	Name
English	Indian Rhubarb or Himalayan Rhubarb [11]
Sanskrit	Gandhini, Revatchini Hindi Dolu, Pita [12]
Kashmiri	Pumbehakh [13]
Tamil	Nattu-ireval-chini, Nattu-manjal-chinni-kizhangu [12]
Telgu	Nattu-revalchini [11]
Arabic	Rewand [11]
Persian	Rewandchini [12]
Ayurvedic	Amlaparni, pitamuuli, Gandhini Revatikka [14]
Siddha	Revalchinikattai, Nattirevaichini [14]
Unani	Revandchini [13].
Synonym	Rheum austral D. Don [14]

Occurrence and Distribution

Rheum emodi is a stout herb, endemic to the Himalayan region distributed in the temperate and subtropical region from Kashmir to Sikkim at an elevation of 2800-3000m in India. It grows in the alpine zone on rocky soils, moraines and cervices.

Botanical Description

Rheum emodi Wall.exMeissn, is a leafy perennial herb, 1.5-3.0 m in height. Roots very stout. Radical leaves longpetioled, very large, often 60 cm in diameter, orbicular or broadly ovate obtuse, base cordate 5-7 nerved, papillose beneath, subscaberulous above; petiole 30-45 cm, very stout, scaberulous. Panicle is 0.6-0.9 m, papillosely puberulous, fastigiately branched and leafy with erect strict branches; flowers small 3 mm diameter, dark purple or pale red, in axillary panicles. Fruit ovoid-oblong, 13 mm long, purple, base cordate, apex notched, wings narrower than the disk. Roots and rhizomes are the main parts used as drug and are collected in October to November. Root of Indian Rhubarb is darker, inferior in aroma, coarser and untrimmed, is not decorticated. Fresh rhizome is 6 to 12 inches long, and the freshly fractured surface is dull orange to yellowish brown [15, 16].

PHARMACOLOGICAL ACTIONS AND TRADITIONAL USES

Many plant species belonging to different families have so far been reported to have a traditional medicinal use by different communities of India. However these days we have new and different medicines for these diseases, which unfortunately are accompanied by various side effects. Subsequently, there is a need to have the active principals of natural origin which can be used for the treatment and/or prevention of diseases/ infections with no side effects. Thus, there has been a growing interest in natural plant products as these are more compatible to the human body with little or no toxic side effects. Rheum emodi is considered as purgative, stomachic, and astringent tonic. It also possesses aperient, emmenagogue and diuretic properties. Root is regarded as expectorant and appetizer. Anti-inflammatory, anti-dysentery and alexentric actions have also been ascribed. Rhubarb is widely used in various traditional systems such as, Unani, Ayurveda, Chinese etc. The uses of Rhubarb by Unani scholars are described in Table 1. Indian rhubarb is used as a purgative and astringent tonic. Its primary action is of mild purgation; but it has also astringentproperty, so that it's secondary effect is to confine the bowels, hence it is well fitted for use in simple diarrhoea, but not in constipation or any affection in which a continuous aperient action is necessary. It is useful remedy in ailments of children. For the errors in diet of children and for the diarrhoea set up by undigested food, it is best given combined with sodium bicarbonate or magnesia. Rhubarb forms an important ingredient of a large variety of compound. Combined with ginger it may be given in the form of pills in cases where the bowels are sluggish. Root is regarded as panacea in local home remedies and is used in stomach problems, cuts, wound, and muscular swelling, tonsillitis and mumps. Some persons chew the root, and to them this is a very good way of taking it. Powdered roots are used for cleaning teeth and sprinkled over ulcers for quick healing. Ethno-medically leaf-stalk, leaves and flowers are consumed as vegetables after cooking. In Assam its leaves consumed as vegetables and cultivated for this purpose. Leaves are also dried and stored for consumption along with other foods, or made into a preserve. It is however stated that cook stalks act as a powerful purgative. Besides the medicinal uses, it is also used for coloration of textile and wooden material [11, 13, 15, 17].

PHYSICOCHEMICAL STUDY

Physicochemical study of Rheum emodi is carried out by Aslam *et al.* [2] The total-ash value of the plant is recorded as 4% whereas, acid insoluble and water insoluble is found to be 0.6% and 2.6% respectively.

PHYTOCHEMISTRY

Rheum emodi possess a number of phytoconstituents and these are: anthraquinones, anthrones, stilbenes, oxanthrone ethers and esters, flavonoids, lignans, phenols, carbohydrate and oxalic acid. The most common constituents of Rheum emodi are anthraquinone and stilbene. Anthraquinones include rhein, chrysophanol, aloe-emodin, emodin, physcion (emodin monomethyl ether), chrysophanein and emodin glycoside. Stilbene includes picetannol, resveratrol and their glycosides. Different derivatives of oxanthrone include oxanthrone ether (revandchinone-4), oxanthrone esters (revandchinone-1 and revandchinone-2), and revandchinone-3. Other complex compounds have also been reported, including torachrysone 8-O-b-D-glucoside, sulfated anthraquinone glycoside sulfemodin 8-O-b-D-glucoside b-asarone and rhein 11-O-b-D-glucoside. Tannins are also present in rhubarb which includes hydrolysable tannins, containing ester or glycosidic bonds composed of gallic acid, glucose and other monosaccharides and condensed tannins, derived primarily from the flavone derivatives catechin and leucocyanidin [17, 20-23].

PHARMACOLOGICAL ACTIVITIES OF R. EMODI

Recent studies have showed that Rheum emodi possess anticancer, antioxidant, antidiabetic, antifungal, antiulcer along with hepatoprotective and nephroprotective properties and theses action are due to a number of compounds isolated from it.

Table 6.1: Uses of Rhubarb

	Ailments	Approach
Gastrointestinal system	Jaundice Diarrhea Indigestion	Rhubarb taken with decoction of root of Foeniculum vulgare, Cichorium intybus, Capparis spinosa and Apium graveolens [18]. Taken with dried roses or pomegranate or gum of acacia [19]. Alone or taken with Aloe vera and Chebulic myrobalan. Taken with aniseeds or lukewarm water [18].
Urogenital system	Retention of urine Dysmenorrhoea with Oligomenorrhoea Menorrhagia	Rhubarb is taken along with seeds of Cucumis melo and Tribulus terrestris [8]. Powdered rhubarb admixed is taken 2 days beforemenstruation and continue three days during menstruation [8]. Taken with juice of Plantago major and Nardostachysjatamansi [18].
Respiratory system	Cough and asthma Haemoptysis	Rhubarb is crushed and make pill with resins of quince [8]. Crush root is chewed and kept in mouth for some time [18].
Nervous system	Headache, Migraine, Paralysis	Rhubarb is taken with Chebulic myrobalan and Polyporusofficinalis and Aloe vera [8, 18].
Musculoskeletal system	Bruises Muscular pain/body ache and Arthritis Swelling and Inflammation Abscess	Rhubarb together with tila (a preparation by grapes water) taken orally [19]. Externally rhubarb is recommended for hot swellings incombination with some liquid [18, 19]. Oil of rhubarb is applied on affected part [19].Its powder is also recommended for the management ofabscess [8]. Taken with decoction of asarum [18].
Skin	Freckle and other skin marks. Melasma	Root is crushed and grinded and makes paste with vinegarand applied externally on affected part [8, 18, 19]. Powder of root is applied with fresh milk [8].

Anticancer Activity

R. emodi has effective antiulcer activity probably by potentiating the defensive factors through the gastric cytoprotection. Some recent research studies found that the oral administration of an ethanolic extract of R. emodi to albino rats at a dose of 100 mg/kg body weight prevented the occurrence of pyloric ligation-induced ulcers. It also strongly inhibited gastric ulcers induced by ethanol and reserpine in albino rats. It was found from the study that there is reduction in ulcer index along with the reduction in volume and total acidity, and an increase in the pH of gastric fluid. Some researchers tested the methanolic and aqueous extracts of the Rheum emodi rhizome in human breast carcinoma (MDAMB- 435S) and liver carcinoma (Hep3B) cell lines for cytotoxicity. They found that the extracts exhibited extensive concentration-dependent cytotoxicity in tested cells [15, 24].

Antidiabetic Effect

Radhika *et al.* carried out a study to evaluate the antidiabetic effect of Rheum emodi rhizome extract and to study the activities of hexokinase, aldolase and phosphoglucoisomerase, and gluconeogenic enzymes such as glucose-6-phosphatase and fructose -1, 6-diphosphatase in liver and kidney of normal and alloxan induced diabetic rats. Oral administration of 75 % ethanolic extract (250 mg/kg body weight) for 30 days, resulted in decrease in the activities of glucose-6-phosphatase, fructose-1, 6-disphosphatase, aldolase and an increase in the activity of phosphoglucoisomerase and hexokinase in tissues. Radhika *et al.* also investigated therapeutic effects of Rheum emodi rhizome extract in another study on certain biochemical marker like asparate aminotransferase, alanine aminotransferase, alkaline phosphatase and LDH in the serum, liver and kidney tissue in alloxan – induced diabetes mellitus in rats. They have found that 250 mg/kg oral administration of Rheum emodi rhizome extract of 75% ethanolic extract to diabetic rat for 30 days restored all marker enzymes to near control level [25].

Antidyslipidemic Activity

Ethanolic extract of Rheum emodi shown antidyslipidemic effect in a study conducted by Mishra *et al.* Chrysophanol, emodin, chrysophanol 8-O-β-D-glucopyranoside and emodin 8-O-β-D glucopyranoside were active constituents and has significant effect in triton induced rats by reducing plasma lipids level. Emodin showed significant lipid lowering activity in high fed diet model [26].

Antifungal Activity

Rhein, physcion, aloe-emodin and chrysophanol isolated from Rheum emodi rhizomes exhibited antifungal activity against Candida albicans, Cryptococcus neoformans, Trichophyton mentagrophytes and Aspergillus fumigatus (MIC 25- 250μg/ml) responsible for skin diseases in India. In a different experiment, three compounds isolated from the Rheum emodi rhizome (revandchinone-1, 3 and 4) exhibited antifungal activity against Aspergillus niger and Rhizopus oryzae, with inhibition zone diameters of 8-9 and 9-11 mm for the 100 and 150 g/ml test concentrations, respectively [27, 21].

Anti-inflammatory Activity

Chauhan *et al.* studied the anti-inflammatory activity of the methanol extract of the rhizome (500 mg/kg). The anti-inflammatory activity was evaluated by using carrageenaninduced paw oedema. It was found that the degree of inhibition of oedema increased with time, reaching maximum inhibition after 5 h. This inhibitory activity was comparable to the control drug Ibuprofen (50 mg/kg body weight) [20].

Antimicrobial Activity

Antimicrobial activity compound of Rheum emodi was investigated by Babu *et al.* Compounds were tested against gram positive (Bacillus subtilis, Bacillus sphaericus and Staphylococcus aureus) and gram negative (Klebsiella aerogenes, Chromobacterium violaceum and Pseudomonas aeruginosa) bacteria. Revandchinone-1 and 3 had lower degrees of antibacterial activity (inhibition zone diameters of 7-9 mm for the 30 and 100 g/ml test concentrations) than didrevandchinone-4 (inhibition zone diameter of 12-14 mm at both the 30 and 100 g/ml test concentrations) [21].

Antioxidant Activity

The 2, 2-diphenyl-1-picrylhydrazyl (DPPH) and hydroxyl radical scavenging activities, inhibitory effects on lipid peroxidation (LPI) and Fe3+ reducing antioxidant properties of methanolic/aqueous extracts of the Rheum emodi rhizome were studied. Furthermore, the extracts proved to contain a high number of phenolic compounds, which were found to have strongly significant positive correlation with free radicals (DPPH and OH) scavenging efficacies, percentages of LPI and Fe3+ reductions [15].

Antiplatelet and Anticoagulant Activities

Seo EJ *et al.* investigated the effects of anthraquinone derivatives isolated from rhubarb on platelet activity. Of four anthraquinone derivatives isolated from rhubarb examined, chrysophanol-8-O-glucoside (CP- 8-O-glc) was found to have the most potent inhibitory effect on collagen- and thrombininduced platelet aggregation. CP-8-O-glc–treated mice showed significantly prolonged bleeding times. Furthermore, CP-8-Oglc was found to have a significant inhibitory effect on rat platelet aggregation ex vivo and on thromboxane A2 formation in vitro [28].

Antiulcer Activity

Antiulcer effect of ethanolic extract of rhizome of Rheum emodi was investigated on pyloric ligation-induced ulcers in rats by Amandeep *et al.* It was found that there is reduction in ulcer index along with the reduction in volume and total acidity, and an increase in the pH of gastric fluid [29].

Hepatoprotective Activity

The hepatoprotective activity of the ethanolic extracts of Rheum emodi rhizome against CCl4-induced liver damage in Wister rats has been evaluated by Ibrahim *et al.* Carbon tetrachloride administration caused a significant increase in the serum activities of AST, ALT and ALP and a similar increase in the total bilirubin. Oral administration of Rheum emodi at 3.0 g/kg significantly decreased the above elevated parameters, and the normal structure of the liver pattern was restored. Other similar study by Akhtar *et al.* has confirmed the hepatoprotective effect of aqueous extract of Rheum emodi against liver damage induced by paracetamol in albino rats [5, 30].

Immune-enhancing Effect

Konsar F *et al.* studied the immune-enhancing activity from ethyl acetate rhizome extract of Rheum emodi on the cell lines and it found to have an immune-enhancing effect through the release of various cytokines. There is a dose-dependent increase in the release of NO (Nitric Oxide) and cytokines TNF-α, IL-12, and a decrease in IL-10 by RAW 264.7 in macrophages cell line in the presence of extract alone [31].

Nephroprotective Effect

The renal effects of water-soluble (W-S) and water-insoluble (W-INS) portions of the alcoholic extract of Rheum emodi were investigated on cadmium chloride, mercuric chloride, potassium dichromate and gentamicin-induced nephrotoxicity in rats and normal rats by monitoring the levels of urea nitrogen and creatinine in serum. W-S fraction has nephroprotective effect on all the proximal tubule segments (S1, S2 and S3) possibly through antioxidant action of the tannins present in the fraction [32].

CONTRAINDICATIONS

Its use is prohibited for the patients suffering from gout, rheumatism, epilepsy and uric acid troubles, for people with a history of renal or gall bladder stones. The rhizome contains some oxalic acid, which, when consumed, can combine with calcium in the blood to form insoluble calcium oxalate crystals that may be deposited in the kidneys or gall bladder. It is not fitted for inflammatory or febrile cases although it seldom act as irritant. When given internally, the roots impart a deep tinge to urine.

CONCLUSION

Rheum emodi is an herb of enormous therapeutic effects and has been used in numerous ailments specially for constipation, indigestion, diarrhea, muscular pain, skin problems and menstrual disorder and. A number of compounds are isolated from it; antraquinones and stilbenes are the most common which are responsible for its extensive use. Further studies are required to isolate other biological active constituents responsible for its therapeutic use and also to validate the traditional knowledge of rhubarb.

REFERENCES

1. S. Bila, S.A. Bhat, I. Hussain, J.D. Parrah, S.P. Ahmad, M.R. Mir. The Use of a Rabbit Model to Evaluate the Influence of Age on Excision Wound Healing. Journal of Life Sciences Research 2015 2(3): 72-75.
2. Aslam M, Dayal R, Javed K, Fahamiya N, Mohd Mujeeb, Husain A. Pharmacognostical and Phytochemical Evaluation of Rheum emodi Wall. Current.
3. Qin Y, Wang J, Kong W, Zhao Y, Yang H, Dai C *et al*. The Diarrhoeogenic and Antidiarrhoeal bidirectional Effects of Rhubarb and its Potential Mechanism. Journal of Ethnopharmacology 2011; 133: 1096-1102.
4. Prior M. Rhubarbaria Recipes for Rhubarb. Prospect Books; 2009, 12.
5. Ibrahim M, Khaja NM, Aara A, Khan AA, Habeeb MA, Devi PY *et al*. Hepatoprotective Activity of Sapindus Mukorossi and Rheum emodi Extracts. World J Gastroenterol 2008; 14(16): 2566-2571.
6. Dymock W, Warden CJH, Hooper D. Pharmacographica Indica. A History of the Principal Drugs of Vegetable Origin. Vol. III. New Delhi: Shrishti Book Distributors; 2005, 153-157.
7. Fanga F, Wanga J, Zhaoa Y, Cheng Jin, Konga W, Zhaoc H, *et al*. A Comparative Study on the Tissue Distributions of Rhubarb Anthraquinones in Normal and CCl4-injured Rats Orally Administered Rhubarb Extract. Journal of Ethnopharmacology 2011; 137: 1492-1497.
8. Najmul Ghani, Khazianul Advia. Lucknow: Munshi Naval Kishore Press; YNM. 750-753.
9. Elaine L. Rhubarb: A Brief History of Rhubarb in Britain About.com Guide. http://britishfood.about.com/od/introtobritishfood/ss. [Access date: 03.07.2012]
10. The Rhubarb Compendium. http://www.rhubarbinfo.com/history [Access date: 27.06.2012].
11. Nadkarni KM. Indian Plants and Drugs. New Delhi: Srishti Book Distributors; 2009. p. 1056-58.
12. Anonymous. The Unani Pharmacopoeia of India. Part I. Vol. II. New Delhi: Govt. of India Ministry of Health & Family Welfare Dept. of AYUSH; 2007. p. 91-92.
13. Medicinal Plants in Folklores of Kashmir Himalayas. 1st ed. New Delhi: CCRUM; 2001, 184.
14. Khare CP. Indian Medicinal Plants: An Illustrated Dictionary. New Delhi: Springer India (P) Ltd; 2007: 543-44.
15. Rajkumar V, Guha G, Kumar RA. Antioxidant and Anti-Cancer Potentials of Rheum emodi Rhizome Extract. Evidenced-Based Complementary and Alternative Medicine 2011 June; 1-9.

16. Kirtikar KR, Basu BD. Indian Medicinal Plants with Illustrations. 2nd ed. Vol. IX. Uttaranchal: 2003: 2907-Nadkarni KM. Indian Plants and Drugs. New Delhi: Srishti Book Distributors; 2009: 1056-58.
17. Parvaiz A. Wani, Irshad A. Nawchoo and B.A. Wafai. The Role of Phenotypic Plasticity, Phenology, Breeding Behaviour and Pollination Systems in Conservation of Rheum emodi Wall. exMeisn. (Polygonaceae) — A Threatened Medicinal Herb of North West Himalaya. The International Journal of Plant Reproductive Biology 2009; 1(2): 179-189.
18. Ibn Baitar. Jami al Mufradat al Advia wa al Aghzia (Urdu Translation). Vol. II. New Delhi: CCRUM; 2000, 275-282.
19. Ibn Sina. Al Qanoon Fil Tib (Urdu trans. by Kantoori GH). New Delhi: Ejaz Publication house; 2010, 447-48.
20. Malik S, Sharma N, Sharma UK, Singh NP, Bhushan S, Sharma M *et al*. Qualitative and Quantitative Analysis of Anthraquinone Derivatives in Rhizomes of Tissue Culture-raised Rheum emodi Wall. Plants Journal of Plant Physiology 2010; 167(9):749-756.
21. Babu KS, Srinivas PV, Praveen B, Kishore KH, Murty US, Rao JM. Antimicrobial Constituents from the Rhizomes of Rheum emodi. Phytochemistry 2003; 62: 203-207.
22. Singh SS, Pandey SS, Singh R, Aggarwal S. 1, Dihydroxyanthraquinone Derivates from the Rhizome of Rheum emodi Wall. Indian Journal of Chemistry 2005; 42B: 1494-1496.
23. Krenn L, Pradhan R, Presser A, Reznicek G, Kopp B. Anthrone C-Glucosides from Rheum emodi. Chem Pharm Bull 2004; 52(4): 391-393.
24. Rajkumar V, Guha G, Kumar RA. Apoptosis Induction in MDA-MB-435S, Hep3B and PC-3 Cell Lines by Rheum emodi Rhizome Extracts. Asian Pacific Journal of Cancer Prevention 2011; 12: 1197-1200.
25. Radhika R, Ragavan B, Pawar SD, Sudarsanam D. Action of Marker Enzymes of Rheum emodi in Alloxane induced Diabetic Rats. Asian J ExpBiol Sci 2012; 3(2): 420-423.
26. Mishra SK, Tiwari S, Shrivastava A, Srivastava S, Boudh GK, Chourasia SK. Antidyslipidemic Effect and Antioxidant Activity of Anthraquinone Derivatives from Rheum emodi Rhizomes in Dyslipidemic rats. J Nat Med 2013; Dec. 17.
27. Agarwal SK, Sudhir SS, Sushma V, Kumar S. Antifungal Activity of Anthraquinone Derivatives from Rheum emodi. Journal of Ethnopharmacology 2000; 72(1-2): 43-46.
28. Seo EJ, Ngoc TM, Lee SM, Kim YS, Jung YS. Chrysophanol-8-O-glucoside, an Anthraquinone Derivative in Rhubarb, Has Antiplatelet and Anticoagulant Activities. J Pharmacol Sci 2012; 118: 245-254.
29. Kaur A, Kumar S, Sharma R. Assessment of Anti-Ulcer Activity of Rheum emodi Rhizomes Extract. Indo Global Journal of Pharmaceutical Sciences 2012; 2(3): 333-341.
30. Akhtar MS, Amin M, Ahmad M, Alamgeer. Hepatoprotective Effect of Rheum emodi Roots (Revandchini) and Akseer-e-Jigar Against Paracetamol-induced Hepatotoxicity in Rats. Ethnobotanical Leaflets 2009; 13: 310-315.

31. Kausar F, Rather MA, Ghani BA, Zargar MA. Immune-enhancing Effects of the Herbal Extract from Himalayan Rhubarb Rheum emodi Wall. Ex Meissn Food Chemistry 2011 June; 126(3): 967-71.
32. Alam MMA, Javed K, Jafri MA. Effect of Rheum emodi (Revand Hindi) on Renal Functions in Rats. Journal of Ethnopharmacology 2005; 96: 121-125.

Pages: 112-144

Nutrition and Medicines in Nature
Edited by: Dr. Jairam Singh and Dr. Pawan Kumar 'Bharti'
ISBN: 978-93-88854-39-9
Edition: 2020
Published by: Discovery Publishing House Pvt. Ltd., New Delhi (India)

7

Scenario of Diabetes and Medicinal Plants as a Source of its Treatment

Showkat Ahmad Bhat[1], Gurjinder Singh[1], Sabhiya Majid[2]
Tehseen Hassan[2], Tariq Parvez Azad[3]

SUMMARY

Diabetes mellitus (DM), both insulin-dependent DM (IDDM) and non-insulin dependent DM (NIDDM) is a common and serious metabolic disorder throughout the world with the characteristic feature of hyperglycemia i.e increased glucose levels. It usually occurs due to the disturbances in carbohydrate metabolism. Glucose is an important aldohexose sugar whose level gets raised during diabetes. Normally in the body glucose is acted upon by the hormone Insulin which is secreted by the beta islet cells of the pancreas. However during diabetes either the level of insulin decreases or the cells become insensitive to the action of insulin. Diabetes mellitus is associated with a number of complications affecting eyes, kidney, heart, nerves etc. A lot of research is done or is still is going on, but diabetes mellitus still is the leading cause of death worldwide. The number of diabetic cases in developing countries is increasing day by day and no huge effort has been put into action to stop this sweet but deadly disease. Traditional plant treatments have been used throughout the world for the therapy of diabetes mellitus. Among many medications and other alternative medicines, several herbs have been known to cure and control diabetes; additionally they have no side effects. The present paper is an attempt to list of the plants with

[1] **Department of Biochemistry, Govt. Medical College (GMC), Doda, Jammu & Kashmir, (India)**
[2] **Department of Biochemistry, Govt. Medical College (GMC), Srinagar, Jammu & Kashmir, (India)**
[2] **Principal Govt. Medical College (GMC), Doda, Jammu & Kashmir, (India)**

anti-diabetic and related beneficial effects originating from different parts of world. History showed that medicinal plants have been used in traditional healing around the world for a long time to treat diabetes; this is because such herbal plants have hypoglycemic properties and other beneficial properties, as reported in scientific literature. There are 136 such plants described in this review which clearly shows the importance of herbal plants in the treatment of diabetes mellitus. The effects of these plants may delay the development of diabetic complications and provide a rich source for antioxidants that are known to prevent/delay different diseased states.

Keywords: *Diabetes mellitus, Medicinal plants, Hypoglycemic, Antioxidant.*

INTRODUCTION

The term Diabetes Mellitus describes a metabolic disorder of multiple etiologies characterized by chronic hyperglycemia with disturbances of carbohydrate, fat, and protein metabolism resulting from defects in insulin secretion and/or insulin action. Diabetes, for the whole world is not an epidemic anymore but has turned into pandemic. The worldwide survey reported that diabetes is affecting nearly 10% of the population. According to the World Health Organization (WHO) projections, the prevalence of diabetes is likely to increase by 35% by the year 2025. India has high prevalence of diabetes and the numbers are increasing at an alarming rate. In India alone, diabetes is expected to increase from 40.6 million in 2006 to 79.4 million by 2030.

History

Diabetes was one of the first diseases described, with an Egyptian manuscript from 1500 BC mentioning "too great emptying of the urine". The first described cases are believed to be of type 1 diabetes Indian physicians around the same time identified the disease and classified it as *madhumeha* or "honey urine", noting the urine would attract ants. The term "diabetes" or "to pass through" was first used in 230 BCE by the Greek Appollonius of Memphis. The disease was considered rare during the time of the Roman empire, with Galen commenting he had only seen two cases during his career. This is possibly due the diet and life-style of the ancient people, or because the clinical symptoms were observed during the advanced stage of the disease. Galen named the disease "diarrhea of the urine" (diarrhea urinosa). The earliest surviving work with a detailed reference to diabetes is that of Aretaeus of Cappadocia (2nd or early 3rd century CE). He described the symptoms and the course of the disease, which he attributed to the moisture and coldness, reflecting the beliefs of the "Pneumatic School". He hypothesized a correlation of diabetes with other diseases and he discussed differential diagnosis from the snakebite which also provokes excessive thirst. His work remained unknown in the West until the middle of the 16th century when, in 1552, the first Latin edition was published in Venice.

Type 1 and type 2 diabetes were identified as separate conditions for the first time by the Indian physicians Sushruta and Charaka in 400-500 CE with type 1 associated with youth and type 2 with being overweight. The term "mellitus" or "from honey" was added by the Briton John Rolle in the late 1700s to separate the condition from diabetes insipidus, which is also associated with frequent urination.

Types of Diabetes

The global rise in diabetes is due to population growth, ageing, increasing trends towards an unhealthy diet, obesity and sedentary lifestyles. According to World Health Organization, diabetes can be classified into two major classes:

Type 1 Diabetes

Type 1 insulin-dependent diabetes is present in 5-10 percent of all diabetics, but is increasing in adolescent minority groups. The prevalence of type 1 diabetes increases with age and the overall incidence of the disease may be increasing. T1DM is the classical form of diabetes and these subjects cannot survive without insulin treatment.

Etiology

Genetic predisposition, autoimmunity and viral infection are the main etiological factors implicated in the pathogenesis of type 1 diabetes mellitus. Type 1 diabetes, which may develop at any age is a chronic autoimmune disease, characterized by irreversible autoimmune destruction of the insulin secreting β-cells of the islets in the pancreas. There is hepatic overproduction of glucose by glycogenolysis and gluconeogenesis and decreased cellular uptake of glucose from the circulation. Type 1 diabetes requires lifelong treatment with exogenous insulin for survival. Genetic screening seems to be essential in the identification of individuals at increased risk for T1DM.

Type 2 Diabetes

Type 2 diabetes is the most common form of the disease, accounting for about 90 to 95% of all diagnosed cases of diabetes. In type 2 diabetes, the body does not produce enough insulin or the cells ignore the insulin. The incidence of type 2 diabetes is increasing among all age groups, including adolescents, among whom type 2 diabetes was formerly very rare T2DM is a group of genetically determined diseases which may be controlled by diet and/or hypoglycemic agents and/or exogenous insulin. T2DM is mainly characterized by insulin resistance, but impairment in insulin secretion also occurs in type 2 diabetes. Subjects with T2DM cannot compensate for insulin resistance at hyperglycemic levels by increasing insulin secretion.

Etiology

Type 2 diabetes occurs usually in individuals over 40 years of age and dramatically increases as a result of changes in human behavior and increased body mass index. The increasing proportion of the aging population, consumption of calorie rich diet, obesity and sedentary ifestyle have led to a tremendous increase in the number of diabetics worldwide. This form of diabetes, previously referred to as non–insulin dependent diabetes, type 2 diabetes, or adult-onset diabetes, encompasses individuals who have insulin resistance and usually have relative (rather than absolute) insulin deficiency. At least initially and often throughout their lifetime, these individuals do not need insulin treatment to survive. Most patients with this form of diabetes are obese and obesity itself causes some degree of insulin resistance. This form of diabetes frequently goes undiagnosed for many years. Impaired intrauterine growth/nutrition results in the programming of systems that regulate insulin sensitivity, insulin secretion and energy storage and utilization throughout the lifetime of the individual. The familial predisposition to type 2 diabetes is mediated by both genetic and intrauterine environmental factors (*Seshiah et al., 2008*). The effect of insulin resistance on the endothelial cells is shown as:

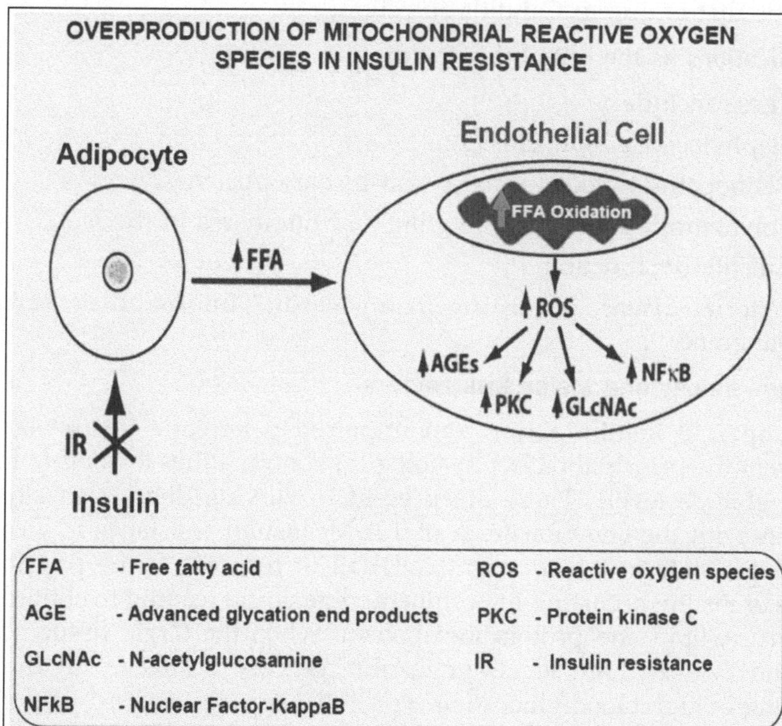

Fig. 7.1: Over production of mitochondrial ROS in Insulin resistance

Clinical Presentation of Diabetes

Presentation may be acute, subacute or asymptomatic.

Acute Presentation

Young people often present with a 2- to 6-week history and report the classic triad of symptoms:

- Polyuria – due to the osmotic diuresis that results when blood glucose levels exceed the renal threshold
- Thirst – due to the resulting loss of fluid and electrolytes
- Weight loss – due to fluid depletion and the accelerated breakdown of fat and muscle secondary to insulin deficiency.

Ketonuria is often present in young people and may progress to ketoacidosis if these early symptoms are not recognized and treated.

Subacute Presentation

The clinical onset may be over several months or years, particularly in older patients. Thirst, polyuria and weight loss are typically present but patients may complain of such symptoms as lack of energy, visual blurring (owing to glucose-induced changes in refraction), or pruritus vulvae or balanitis that is due to Candida infection.

Complications as the presenting feature

These include:

- Staphylococcal skin infections
- Retinopathy noted during a visit to the optician.
- Polyneuropathy causing tingling and numbness in the feet.
- Erectile dysfunction.
- Arterial disease, resulting in myocardial infarction or peripheral gangrene.

Pathophysiology and Major Risk Factors

Impaired insulin action and impaired pancreatic insulin secretion represent the principal pathophysiological abnormalities leading to increase blood glucose levels. These are present to varying degrees in almost all patients with the common form of T2DM. Insulin resistance is a common pathologic state in which target cells fail to respond to the physiological effects of insulin occurring in peripheral organs and leading to abnormalities in glucose, lipid and protein metabolism. When the target tissue does not respond to even high levels of insulin, glucose builds up in the blood resulting in high blood glucose or type 2 diabetes. In fact, insulin resistance is present in the majority of patients with impaired glucose tolerance or T2DM, and it is also found in up to 25 % of the general, apparently healthy population. Insulin secretion from pancreatic β-cells in the islets of Langerhans is in two phases and is mainly regulated by glucose entry via its transporters. In nondiabetic subjects after glucose administration, the insulin secretion is abundant and rapid, lasting approximately 10 minutes, to compensate for an acute postprandial glucose peak and this state is defined as the first-phase response. The second-phase insulin secretion is the subsequent sustained increase in insulin secretion which is slower and lasts longer. InT2DM, the first-phase secretion of insulin as a response to glucose is missing or considerably weakened. A secretory defect in the second phase is also characteristic of T2DM, and the ability of glucose to potentiate the effects of other stimulants of insulin secretion is diminished. In response to elevated blood glucose concentration due to insulin resistance, β-cells need to increase the insulin secretion to maintain homeostasis in glucose levels. Finally, β-cells become unresponsive to glucose due to pancreatic β-cells dysfunction and eventually type 2 diabetes develops. Although the etiology of the β-cell dysfunction of diabetes is incompletely understood, it is thought to result from both genetic and environmental factors. Many researchers have postulated that, among individuals with type 2 diabetes, roughly half of their disease risk can be attributed to environmental exposure and half to genetics. Family history, diet, and lack of physical activity are all major risk factors for developing T2DM. Dyslipidemia and high blood pressure are other risk factors that often appear before the clinical disease is evident. Elevated levels of free fatty acids are also strong predictor of diabetes and correlate with hepatic glucose output, a major cause of diabetic hyperglycemia and obesity.

Complications of Diabetes

Severe long term abnormalities can result such as eye complications, heart disease, kidney and foot problems if blood sugar levels are poorly controlled. These complications are of two types microvascular complications that include retinopathy, nephropathy, neuropathy and peripheral vascular disorders and macrovascular complications that include cardiovascular and cerebrovascular disorders. The complications of diabetes can involve multiple systems throughout the body that are susceptible to the detrimental effects of oxidative stress and apoptotic cell injury. Innovative strategies are necessary for the implementation of new treatments for diabetes that are generated by further understanding the cellular pathways that govern the pathological consequences of diabetes. Furthermore, significant portion of the population has undiagnosed diabetes, illustrating the need for improved early diagnosis. Diabetes also leads to long-term complications throughout the body involving cardiovascular, renal and nervous disorders. Plasma C-peptide concentrations provide an indirect measure of the insulin secretory reserve. Low serum level of C-peptide is a possible factor of the progression of diabetic angiopathies. Accumulated clinical experience indicates that there is an inverse association between beta-cell function and chronic complications of autoimmune diabetes- higher the C-peptide levels (an indirect measure of viable beta-cell function), lower the incidence of microvascular complications of autoimmune diabetes. The chronic hyperglycemia of diabetes is associated with long-term damage, dysfunction and failure of various organs especially the eyes, kidneys, nerves, heart and blood vessels. The importance of protecting the body from hyperglycemia cannot be overstated; the direct and indirect effects on the human vascular tree are the major source of morbidity and mortality in both type 1 and type 2 diabetes. Generally, the injurious effects of hyperglycemia are separated into macrovascular complications (coronary artery disease, peripheral arterial disease and stroke) and microvascular complications (diabetic nephropathy, neuropathy, and retinopathy).

Type 2 Diabetes and Microvascular Complications

Diabetic Retinopathy

Diabetes results in characteristic lesions in the retinal blood vessels. Diabetic Retinopathy is still the most common cause of acquired blindness in the Western world. Its prevalence increases most steeply between 5 to 15 years of diabetes duration, being about 60% after 20 years in the European population. This can result in formation of microaneurysms (minimal retinopathy), haemorrhages and increased leakage, causing retinal edema and lipid exudates (background retinopathy). These changes do not threaten visual acuity unless they are located in the macular region, where they can cause macular edema. When pathological development of new vessels in the retina or abnormal blood vessels and fibrous tissue (i.e. neovascularisation), occurs, the retinopathy is classified as proliferative retinopathy. Microaneurysm may be reversible even if a higher count is predictive of higher rates of proliferative retinopathy and macular oedema in the coming years. The formation of fibrous tissue may eventually cause retinal detachment and severe visual impairment. Also, an excess of glucose activates the polyol pathway, which causes accumulation of sorbitol in the lens and is accompanied by cataracts. The etiology of retinopathy includes yperglycemia-associated biochemical, anatomical and functional changes.

Diabetic Nephropathy

Diabetic nephropathy is estimated to develop in one third of both main types of diabetes. Nephropathy is characterised by glomerular basement membrane thickening and arteriosclerosis of small arterioles. The mechanisms proposed to induce glomerulosclerosis include hyperglycemia, a hyperfiltration-related increase of glomerular pressure, and increased blood viscosity. The hallmark of renal damage in diabetes is increased excretion of albumin in the urine. The natural history of diabetic nephropathy has been viewed as a descending path from normoalbuminuria to microalbuminuria, clinically overt diabetic nephropathy; i.e macroalbuminuria, and eventually to end-stage renal disease. The term microalbumiuria; i.e. incipient diabetic nephropathy, has been defined as urine albumin excretion rate 20-200 µg/min in a timed overnight or 30-300mg/24h urine collection as determined by sensitive laboratory measurements. Urine albumin excretion rate exceeding these values is called macroalbuminuria and considered a sign of manifest diabetic nephropathy. It has been estimated that approximately half the patients with microalbuminuria will progress to overt nephropathy. The rate of the development of diabetic nephropathy varies in individual patients and improvement in glycemic control may result in the disappearance of microalbuminuria. Along with macroalbuminuria the glomerular filtration rate falls consistently. Nephropathy may culminate in uremia and, in fact, most of the hemodialysis patients and the patients receiving renal transplants have diabetes.

Diabetic Neuropathy

The term diabetic neuropathy includes either a clinical or subclinical disorder without any additional causes of peripheral neuropathy other than diabetes. In fact, damage to the microvasculature in peripheral nerves is now becoming recognized as a major pathogenic factor in diabetic neuropathy. It may affect both sensory and autonomic nerves, but distal symmetric polyneuropathy is probably the most common consequence which, together with peripheral vascular disease, is an important etiologic factor for foot ulcerations and lower limb amputations.

Autonomic dysfunction is common in people with diabetes, but is only clinically apparent in a small percentage. Diabetic neuropathy is encountered in about half of all people with diabetes either as a polyneuropathy or mononeuropathy especially in patients over 60 years age with T2DM. Although exact prevalence depends on the diagnostic criteria used to identify neuropathy, most studies suggest that 50% of patients with a 20-years history of either type 1 or type 2 diabetes have neuropathy. Around 10% of these cases of neuropathy are associated with abnormal sensations and pain. The incidence of neuropathy increases with duration of diabetes and is accelerated bypoor control. Additionally, the death rate is as high as 50% at three years after diagnosis of overt autonomic neuropathy.

Type 2 Diabetes and Macrovascular Complications

Macrovascular complications of DM are due to accelerated atherosclerosis and have an important role in the increased morbidity and mortality suffered by these individuals. People with diabetes are at a high risk of suffering from cerebrovascular disease, peripheral vascular disease and cardiovascular complications such as myocardial infarction, coronary heart failure, and stroke and these chronic illnesses take 10-20 years to manifest. Observations from the United Kingdom Prospective Diabetes Study demonstrated that the 10-year risk for macrovascular complications is more than four fold higher than the risk for microvascular complications. However, patients with T2DM are more at risk to develop macrovascular disease, both at an earlier age and in a higher frequency as compared to the general non-diabetic population.

The presence of diabetes, in addition to any or all the other risk factors (such as smoking, hypertension, dyslipidemia, and genetic factors), approximately doubles the probability of developing macrovascular diseases and the available evidence suggests that strict diabetic control does not prevent or delay these complications. Coronary heart disease, cerebrovascular accidents and peripheral vascular disease are the most important complications in T2DM. They are responsible for at least 50-60% of all deaths in subjects with type 2 diabetes.

Cardiovascular disease accounts for about 70% of all deaths in patients with diabetes. Epidemiological studies show that the risk of cardiovascular mortality is two to three times higher in men and three to five times higher in women with diabetes than in non-diabetic subjects. Cardiovascular complications are often present already at the time of diagnosis of T2DM. Subjects with impaired glucose tolerance (IGT) have an approximately two-fold increase in the risk of macrovascular diseases.

Causes of Diabetic Complications

The complications of diabetes are the result of multiple factors in particular, cellular pathways that lead to diabetes. The complications of diabetes have been tied to oxidant stress. Studies with diabetic animals have shown that oxidative stress leads to DNA damage in renal cortical cells. Although early effects of elevated glucose may increase the presence of potentially protective pathways, more prolonged exposure of elevated glucose with the rise in insulin levels can lead to reactive oxygen species (ROS) and can be detrimental even if glucose levels are controlled.

Major Risk Factors

Hypertension: The standard definition of hypertension is a blood pressure e"140/90 mmHg. Hypertension is a major conventional risk factor for CHD and successful treatment with antihypertensive drugs reduces the incidence of CHD. Up to 70% of adults with type 2 diabetes have raised blood pressure. Together, hypertension and overt diabetes double the risk of cardiovascular disease. Raised blood pressure is more common in people with T2DM than in the general population. For example, an epidemiological analysis of the UKPDS Group data demonstrated that, with each 10 mm Hg increase in systolic blood pressure, the risk of a person with type 2 diabetes sustaining a myocardial infarction was increased by 11%. In addition to assessing the effect of improving bloodglucose control in people with T2DM, the UKPDS also compared the effects of tight blood pressure control to poor blood pressure control.

Smoking: Smoking is a major conventional risk factor for CHD. Smoking increases the risk of coronary heart disease and stroke in people with diabetes and also increases their overall mortality. People with diabetes who stop smoking can substantially reduce their risk of developing complications. Indeed, stopping smoking is one of the most effective ways of reducing the risk of developing the long-term complications of diabetes, particularly cardiovascular disease.

Low Density Lipoprotein: The Major Player

In type 2 diabetes lipid abnormalities are almost the rule. LDL cholesterol is a well-known risk factor for coronary heart disease and is now recognized as the primary target of lipid lowering therapy (Adult Treatment Panel III, 2001). Elevated LDL cholesterol has been associated with CHD in follow-up studies. Increased LDL cholesterol predicts CHD in patients without macroangiopathy at baseline indicating that elevated LDL cholesterol becomes important after exclusion of high-risk patients with CHD at baseline. More than 70% of people with type 2 diabetes have raised LDL cholesterol levels. The risk of a cardiovascular event increases as the level LDL cholesterol level increases. In the UKPDS, the risk of either angina or a myocardial infarction in people with type 2 diabetes increased 1.57 fold for every 1 mmol/l increase in LDL cholesterol. Those withan LDL cholesterol > 3.89 mmol/l were 2.3 times more likely to develop angina or a myocardial infarction than people with an LDL cholesterol < 3 mmol/l. People with diabetes also tend to have a combination of raised triglyceride levels and decreased high density lipoprotein (HDL) cholesterol levels, both of which are also risk factors for cardiovascular disease.

DIABETIES MEDICINAL PLANTS WITH ANTIDIABETIC AND RELATED BENEFICIAL PROPERTIES

Diabetes mellitus is a common and very prevalent disease affecting the citizens of both developed and developing countries. It is estimated that 25% of the world population is affected by this disease. Diabetes mellitus is caused by the abnormality of carbohydrate metabolism which is linked to low blood insulin level or insensitivity of target organs to insulin. Despite considerable progress in the treatment of diabetes by oral hypoglycemic agents, search for newer drugs continues because the existing synthetic drugs have several limitations. The herbal drugs with antidiabetic activity are yet to be commercially formulated as modern medicines, even though they have been acclaimed for their therapeutic properties in the traditional systems of medicine. The plants provide a potential source of hypoglycemic drugs because many plants and plant derived compounds have been used in the treatment of diabetes. Many Indian plants have been investigated for their beneficial use in different types of diabetes and reports occur in numerous scientific journals. Ayurveda and other traditional medicinal system for the treatment of diabetes describe a number of plants used as herbal drugs. Hence, they play an important role as alternative medicine due to less side effects and low cost. The active principles present in medicinal plants have been reported to possess pancreatic beta cells re-generating, insulin releasing and fighting the problem of insulin resistance. Hyperglycemia is involved in the etiology of development of diabetic complications. Hypoglycemic herbs increase insulin secretion, enhance glucose uptake by adipose or muscle tissues and inhibit glucose absorption from intestine and glucose production from liver. Insulin and oral hypoglycemic agents like sulphonylureas and biguanides are still the major players in the management but there is quest for the development of more effective anti-diabetic agents [1-4].

Abelmoschus moschatus **Medik (Malvaceae):** It is an aromatic medicinal plant, which is native to India. Abelmoschus moschatus is a delightful, soft, herbaceous trailing plant, 0.5- 2.5 meters high with soft hairy stems and a long slender tap root. It has an underground tuber and dies back to this tuber in the dry season, emerging again with the first substantial rains of the wet season. Myricelin, an active principle of *A. moschatus*, improves insulin sensitivity through increased post-receptor insulin signaling mediated by enhancements in IRS-1-associated PI3-kinase and GLUT 4 activity in muscles of obese Zucker rats. Myricetin might be used as a model substance for the development of antidiabetic compounds [5].

Acacia arabica **(Lam) Wild. (Mimosaceae):** It is found all over India. The plant extract acts as an antidiabetic agent by acting as secretagouge to release insulin. It induces hypoglycemia in control rats but not in alloxanized animals. Powdered seeds of *A. arabica* when administered (2, 3 and 4 g/kg body weight) to normal rabbits, induces hypoglycemic effect by initiating release of insulin from pancreatic beta cells [6].

Achyranthes aspera **L (Amaranthaceae):** It is distributed throughout the tropical world. Oral administration of *A. aspera* powder produces a significant dose-related hypoglycemic effect in normal as well as in diabetic rabbits. The water and methanol extracts also decreases blood glucose levels in normal and alloxan diabetic rabbits. The acute toxicity study in rabbits does not reveal any adverse or side effects of this folk medicine at dosages up to 8 g/kg orally. The plant could act by providing certain necessary elements like calcium, zinc, magnesium, manganese and copper to the beta-cells [7].

***Achyrocline satureioides* (Less) DC (Asteraceae):** It is a medicinal plant symbol of Rio Grande do Sul state in Brazil. A new prenylated dibenzofuran, achyrofuran, a compound derived from *A. satureioides* significantly lowered blood glucose levels when administered orally at 20 mg/kg q.d. The aqueous extract of the aerial parts of *A. satureioides* administered before bromobenzene (BB), at the dose of 300mg/kg, inhibited the increase of liver ALT and AST, whereas, the BB-induced liver shows increase of thiobarbituric acid reacting substances (TBARS) content. Also it significantly increases the depleted levels of liver glutathione and bile flow in rats. In addition, at the same dose, a significant increase in the bile flow of rats was found. The results obtained with the aqueous extract of *A. satureioides* support its use in popular medicine as a hepatoprotective and digestive agent, and the effects might be mediated through the antioxidant and choleretic activities [8, 9].

***Acosmium panamense* Schott. (Leguminosae):** Oral application of water extracts at doses of 20 and 200 mg/kg and of butanol extracts at doses of 20 and 100 mg/kg significantly lowers the plasma glucose levels in diabetic rats within 3 h in streptozotocin (STZ)-induced diabetic rats [10].

***Aegle marmelose* (L) Corr. (Rutaceae):** A species of tree native to India, it is present throughout Southeast Asia as a naturalized species. A significant decrease in liver glycogen of diabetic rats is reversed to almost the normal level by the leaf extract and it also decreases the blood urea and serum cholesterol. A similar effect is seen with insulin treatment and the results indicate that the active principle in *A. marmelos* leaf extract has similar hypoglycemic activity to insulin treatment [11].

***Agrimony eupatoria L. (agrimony)* (Rosaceae):** Agrimony, when incorporated into the diet (62.5 g/kg) and drinking water (2.5 g/L) counters the weight loss, polydipsia, hyperphagia and hyperglycemia of STZ-diabetic mice. Aqueous extract (1mg/mL) stimulates insulin secretion from the BRIN-BDII pancreatic B-cell line, 2-deoxy-glucose transport, glucose oxidation and incorporation of glucose into glycogen in mouse abdominal muscle comparable with 0.1μM-insulin. These results demonstrate the presence of antihyperglycemic, insulin-releasing and insulin-like activity in *A. eupatoria* [12].

***Ajuga iva* L. Schreberr (Medit) (Lamiaceae):** A species native to Europe, Asia and Africa. Single and repeated oral administration of the water extract of *A. iva* L (AT) at a dose of 10 mg/kg produces a slight and significant decrease in plasma glucose levels in normal rats 6 h after administration and after 3 weeks of treatment. It continuously decreases thereafter and shows rapid normalization, which concludes *A.iva* possess a strong hypoglycemic effect in diabetic rats, and supports its traditional use in diabetes mellitus control [13].

Allium cepa **L. (onion): (Liliaceae):** *Allium cepa* is known only in cultivation but related wild species occur in Central Asia. Various ether soluble fractions as well as insoluble fractions of dried onion powder show anti-hyperglycemic activity in diabetic rabbits. *A. cepa* also known to have antioxidant and hypolipidemic activity. Administration of a sulfur containing amino acid, S-methyl cysteine sulphoxide (SMCS) (200 mg/kg for 45 days) to alloxan induced diabetic rats significantly controlled blood glucose as well as lipids in serum and tissues. It normalizes the activities of liver hexokinase, glucose 6-phosphatase and HMG Co A reductase When diabetic patients were given single oral dose of 50 g of onion juice, it significantly controlled post-prandial glucose levels [14-16].

Allium sativum **L. (garlic): (Liliaceae):** It is a perennial herb cultivated throughout India. Oral administration of the garlic extract significantly decreases serum glucose, total cholesterol, triglycerides, urea, uric acid, creatinine, AST and ALT levels, while increases serum insulin in diabetic rats but not in normal rats when compared with antidiabetic drug glibenclamide. The antidiabetic effect of the extract was more effective than glibenclamide. It is concluded that the plant must be considered as excellent candidate for future studies on diabetes mellitus [17].

Aloe barbadensis **Mill.(Liliaceae):** The species has been widely cultivated throughout the world. Treatment of chronic but no single dose of exudates of *Aloe barbadensis* leaves shows hypoglycemic effect in alloxanized diabetic rats. Single as well as chronic doses of bitter principle of the same plant also show hypoglycemic effect in diabetic rats. This action is through stimulation of synthesis and/or release of insulin from pancreatic beta cells [18].

Aloe vera **(L) Burm.(Asphodelaceae):** It grows in arid climates and is widely distributed in Africa, India and other arid areas. *Aloe vera* gel at 200 mg/kg 1 possesses significant antidiabetic, cardioprotective activity, reduces the increased TBARS, maintains the Superoxide dismutase and Catalase activity up to the normal level and increases reduced glutathione by four times in diabetic rats. The leaf pulp extract showed hypoglycemic activity on IDDM and NIDDM rats, the effectiveness being enhanced for type II diabetes in comparison with glibenclamide [19, 20].

Andrographis paniculata **Burm. (Acanthaceae):** It is a herbaceous plant native to India, Sri Lanka and widely cultivated in southern Asia. Oral administration of andrographis significantly increases the activity of SOD and Catalase. Also decreases blood glucose levels due to its antioxidant properties. The ethanolic extract of *A. paniculata* possesses antidiabetic property and may be attributed at least in part to increase glucose metabolism. Its hypotriglyceridemic effect is also beneficial in the diabetic state [21, 22].

Annona squamosa **L (Annonaceae):** It is a small well-branched tree or shrub, grows at lower altitudes. Administration of 15 mg/kg/day of isolated juercetin-3-O-glucoside from *Annona squamosa* leaves for 10 consecutive days to the hyperglycemic animals reverse these effects and simultaneously inhibits the activity of hepatic Glucose-6-phosphatase. It further decreases the hepatic and renal lipid peroxidation with a concomitant increase in the activities of antioxidative enzymes, such as Catalase and Superoxide dismutase as well as glutathione content, indicating its safe and antiperoxidative effects [23].

Artemisia herba-alba **Asso (Med). (Asteraceae):** It is a perennial shrub that grows commonly on the steppes of Northern Africa, Arabian Peninsula, Western Asia and Southwestern Europe. Oral administration of 0.39 g/kg body weight of the aqueous extract of the leaves or barks produces a significant reduction in blood glucose level, while the aqueous extract of roots and methanolic extract of the aerial parts of the plant produce almost no reduction in blood glucose level. The extract of the aerial parts of the plant seem to have minimal adverse effect and high LD50 value [24].

Artemisia dracunculus L. **(Asteraceae):** Commonly known as "dragon herb". It is native to a wide area of the Northern Hemisphere from easternmost Europe across central and eastern Asia to India, western North America, and south to northern Mexico. At doses of 50-500 rag/kg/day, the hypoglycemic activity of the extract enhances 3-5-fold with the bio-enhancer Labrasol, making it comparable to the activity of the anti-diabetic drug metformin. Tarralin, an ethanolic extract lowers elevated blood glucose levels by 24% relative to control animals. The extract also increases the binding of glucagon-like peptide to its receptor in vitro. These results indicate that tarralin has antihyperglycemic activity and plays a potential role in the management of diabetic status [25, 26].

Astragalus membranaceus **Bunge (Fisch.): (Leguminosae):** It is used in traditional Chinese medicine. The protective mechanism of AGS-IV, a new glycoside of cycloartane-type triterpene isolated from the root of *A. membranaceus* (Fisch.) decreases the blood glucose concentration and HbAlC levels, and increases plasma insulin levels. AGS-IV increases the activity of glutathione peroxidase in nerves, depress the activation of aldose reductase in erythrocytes, and decreases the accumulation of advanced glycation end products in both nerves and erythrocytes. Moreover, elevates Na+, K+-ATPase activity in both the nerves and erythrocytes of diabetic rats. These results indicate that AGS-IV exerts protective effects against the progression of peripheral neuropathy in STZ-induced diabetes in rats through several interrelated mechanisms [27].

Averrhoa bilimbi **L (Oxalidaceae):** The plant is mainly found in Asia and in some other parts of the world. At a dose of 125-mg/kg-body weight, the aqueous fraction (AF), butanol-soluble fraction (BuF) and the reference drug metformin (500 mg/kg body weight), produces significant blood glucose-lowering effect in the diabetic rats when compared to the vehicle (distilled water). Also Hepatic glucose-6-phosphatase activity in AF- and metformin-treated groups is lower, but not in BuF-treated groups, compared to that in vehicle-treated group. These results indicate that AF is more potent than BuF in the amelioration of hyperglycemia in STZ-diabeiic rats and is a potential source for the isolation of new orally active agent(s) for anti-diabetic therapy [28].

***Azadirachta-indica* A. Juss. (Meliaceae):** Commonly known as Neem. It is a tree native to India, Burma, Bangladesh, Sri Lanka, Malaysia and Pakistan, growing in tropical and semi-tropical regions. A low (0.5g tid) and high (2g tid) doses of powdered part, aqueous extract and alcoholic extract of *A. indica* shows significant hypoglycemic activity in high dose and can be successfully combined with oral hypoglycemic agents in type-2 diabetic patients whose diabetes is not controlled by these agents [29].

***Bauhinia candicans* Benth (Leguminosae):** A medicinal plant indigenous to sub-tropical regions of Argentina and southern Brazil. The effect of different fractions of methanolic extract of *B. candicans* leaves (8 mg/kg) shows hypoglycemic activity along with a reduced urinary glucose excretion. Among the fractions, the butanolic fraction (fraction III) exhibits highest activity. Moreover, fraction III reduces plasma glucose level in normal, as well as, glucose loaded rabbits. These results suggest that *B. candicans* increases the peripheral metabolism of glucose [30].

***Bauhinia forficate* Link. (Caesalpinaceae):** Commonly known as Pata de Vaca, native to Brazil and Peru. Oral administration of kaempferilrin, a major flavonoid compound of the n-butanol fraction from *B. forficata* leaves leads to a significant hypoglycemic effect in normal and in alloxan-induced diabetic rats. In normal rats, kaempferitrin lowers blood glucose only with the higher dose of (200 mg/kg) at 1 h after treatment and also shows antioxidant properties. Administraton of aqueous, ethanolic and hexanic extracts daily for 7 days at doses of 200 and 400 mg/kg, p.o., to the alloxan-diabetic rats shows significant reductions in plasma glucose, triglycerides, total cholesterol and HDL-cholesterol after treatment with the extracts and glibenclamide (standard drug) as compared to the diabetic controls [31, 32].

***Bidens pilosa* L (Asteraceae):** It is known as Spanish Needle. The butanol fraction *of B. pilosa* inhibits the differentiation of naive helper T (ThO) cells into Thl cells but enhances their transition into type II helper T (Th2) cells, thus can prevent diabetes pausibly via suppressing the differentiation of ThO cells into Thl cells and promoting that of ThO cells into Th2 cells, thus preventing autoimmune diabetes in non-obese diabetic mice [33].

Biophytum sensitivum **(L) DC. (Oxalidaceae):** The annual perennial herbaceous plant is a traditional medicine in Nepal. Initial dose-response studies shows a dose of 200 mg/kg body weight is optimum for hypoglycemia. In 16-h fasted non-diabetic rabbits, a single administration brings about a 16.1% fall in fasting plasma glucose at the end of 1 and 2 h, and the hypoglycemic effect persists at the end of 6 h (13.8% fall). Serum insulin levels shows a significant rise in the treated animals, which suggests a pancreatic mode of action (i.e. insulinotropic effect), suggesting that the hypoglycemic response of *B. sensitivum* may be mediated through stimulating the synthesis/release of insulin from the beta cells of Langerhans [34].

Bixa orellana **L. (Bixaceae):** It is a shrub or small tree from the tropical region of the Americas. This annatto extract decreases blood glucose levels in fasting normoglycaemic and streptozotocin-induced diabetic dogs. In normal dogs, it suppresses the postprandial rise in blood glucose after an oral glucose load and also causes an increase in insulin-to-glucose ratio in normal dogs. Increased insulin levels were not due to increased insulin synthesis as after 1h residence time and half-hour postprandial, decreases C-peptide levels. It is concluded that *B. orellana* (annatto) lowers blood glucose by stimulating peripheral utilization of glucose, and it is possible that this glucose-lowering extract might be of pharmacological importance [35].

Brassica nigra **(L) Koch (Brassicaceae):** It is an annual weedy plant cultivated for its seeds and is native to the southern Mediterranean region of Europe. Administration of 200 mg/kg body weight of aqueous extract to diabetic animals daily once for one month brings down fasting serum glucose (FSG) levels while in the untreated group FSG remains at a higher value. In the treated animals the increase in glycosylated hemoglobin (HbAlc) and serum lipids is much less when compared with the levels in untreated diabetic controls [36].

Bryonia alba **L. (Cucurbitaceae):** It is a flowering plant native to western Eurasia and adjacent regions, such as North Africa, the Canary Islands and South Asia. Administration of trihydroxyoctadecadienoic acids obtained from the roots of the native Armenian plant *B. alba* L. (0.05 mg/kg/day for 15 days. Lin.) restores the disordered lipid metabolism of alloxan-diabetic rats. Metabolic changes induced in diabetes significantly restores towards their normal values with the exception of diminished triglyceride content of muscle which does not restores. Thus, they can influence the profile of the formation of stable prostaglandins by actions downstream of prostaglandin endoperoxides [37].

Bumelia sartorum **Mart. *(Sapotaceae):*** It has been mentioned in Brazilian folklore for its reputed use in the treatment of diabetes mellitus and inflammatory disorders. Bassic acid, an unsaturated triterpene acid isolated from ethanol extract *of B. sartorum* root bark, elicits significant hypoglycemic activity and increases plasma insulin levels significantly in alloxan-diabetic rats and alters the pattern of glucose tolerance in these animals. Besides hypoglycemic activity, the extract also elicits significant anti inflammatory activity, but shows no significant effects on blood pressure, respiration or on the various isolated tissue preparations [38, 39].

***Caesalpinia bonducella* (L) Roxb. (Caesalpinaceae):** The oral administration of the extracts (300 mg/kg) produces significant antihyperglycemic action as well as lowers the BUN levels significantly. The action of the extracts on diabetes induced hyperlipidemia significantly lowers the elevated cholesterol as well as LDL level. The antihyperglycemic action of the extracts may be due to the blocking of glucose absorption. The drug has the potential to act as antidiabetic as well as antihyperlipidemic [40].

***Cajanus cajan* (L) Millsp. (Papilionaceae):** Single doses of unroasted seeds (60% and 80%) on administration to normal as well as alloxanized mice shows significant reduction in the serum glucose levels after 1-2 hr and a significant rise at 3 hr. In case of roasted seeds, on other hand serum glucose levels increases during 3 hr experimental period. It is therefore concluded that roasting of seeds at high temperature for half an hour period results in the total loss of hypoglycemic principle but not the hyperglycemic principle present in the seeds [41].

Carum carvi* L.(CC) (Apiaceae)/*Capparis spinosa* L. (CS) (Capparidaceae)*: (CC) is a biennial plant native to western Asia, Europe and Northern Africa and (CS) is native in Israel and eastern part of Mediterranean. After a single dose or 14 daily doses, oral administration of the aqueous CC and CS extracts (20 mg/kg) produces a significant decrease on blood glucose levels in STZ diabetic rats, and brings down to nearly normal after 2 weeks. There is no high significant change on blood glucose levels or basal plasma insulin concentrations in normal rats after both acute and chronic treatments with CS and CC [42].

***Casearia esculenta* Roxb. (Flacourtiaceae):** *Casearia esculenta* root (Roxb.) is widely used in traditional system of medicine to treat diabetes in India. Oral administration of aqueous extract of root (300 mg/kg body weight) for 45 days results in a significant reduction in blood glucose and in the activities of glucose-6-phosphatase and fructose-1,6-bisphosphatase and an increase in the activity of liver hexokinase. However, in the case of 200 mg/kg body weight of extract, it shows less activity. The study clearly shows that the root extract of *C. esculenta* possesses potent antihyperglycemic activity but weaker than that of glibenclamide [43].

***Cassia auriculata* L.(Caesalpinaceae):** It occurs in the dry regions of India and Sri Lanka. Oral administration of CLEt- to mildly diabetic (MD) and severely diabetic (SD) rats at a dose of 400 mg/kg once a day for 15 days shows significant reduction in fasting blood glucose, also enhances the activity of hepatic hexokinase, phosphofructokinase, suppresses glucose-6-phosphatase and fructose-l,6-bisphosphatase in both MD and SD rats. Histopathological examination of pancreatic sections reveals increased number of islets and beta-cells in CLEt-treated MD as well as SD rats [44].

***Catharanthus roseus* (L)G.Don.(Apocynaceae):** Oral administration at dose-dependent of 0.5, 0.75 and 1.0 mL/kg body weight reduced the blood glucose of both normal and diabetic rabbits comparable with that of the standard drug, glibenclamide. The results indicate a prolonged action in reduction of blood glucose by *C. roseus* and the mode of action of the active compound(s) is probably mediated through enhance secretion of insulin from the betacells of Langerhans or through extra pancreatic mechanism [45].

***Chamaemelum nobile* (L) All. (Asteraceae):** It is a low perennial plant found in dry fields and around gardens in Europe, North America, and Argentina. Single oral administration at a dose of 20mg/kg body weight of *C. nobile* aqueous extract reduces blood glucose levels after 6h in normal rats and in STZ diabetic rats. After 15 days of treatment, Basal plasma insulin concentrations remain unchanged [46].

***Cichorium intybus* L.(Asteraceae):** A bushy perennial herbaceous plant, which lives as a wild plant on roadsides in its native Europe, and in North America and Australia. A dose of 125 mg of plant extract/kg body weight exhibits the most potent hypoglycemic effect. Moreover, daily administration of *Cichorium intybus* (C1E) (125 mg/kg) for 14 days to diabetic rats attenuates serum glucose by 20%, triglycerides by 91% and total cholesterol by 16%. In addition, hepatic glucose-6-phosphatase activity (Glc-6-Pase) markedly reduces by CIE [47].

***Clausena anisata* (Willd) Benth. (Rutaceae):** At a dose of 800 mg/kg p.o., *Clausena anisata* (Wild) Hook (CAME) reduces the mean basal blood glucose concentrations of fasted normal and fasted diabetic rats by 57.52 and 51.30%, respectively [48].

***Coccinia indica* Wt & Arn. (Cucurbitaceae):** An indigenous plant used in Ayurvedic medicine in India. Dried extracts of *C. indica* (500 mg/kg body weight) administered to diabetic patients for 6 weeks restores the activities of enzyme lipoprotein lipase (LPL), glucose-6-phosphatase and lactate dehydrogenase, which rises in untreated diabetics [49].

***Coriandrum sativum* L (Apiaceae):** An annual herb native to southern Europe and North Africa to southwestern Asia. Coriander seed extract (200 mg/kg) significantly increases the activity of the beta cells in comparison with the diabetic control rats and decreases serum glucose in streptozotocin-induced diabetic rats and releases insulin from the beta cells of the pancreas. The extract shows antihyperglycemic, insulin-releasing and insulin-like activity [50, 51].

***Cuminum cyminum* L (Apiaceae):** A flowering plant native from the East Mediterranean to East India. The seeds extract of *C. cyminum* (CC) causes a reduction in blood glucose, glycosylated hemoglobin, creatinine, blood urea nitrogen and improved serum insulin and glycogen (liver and skeletal muscle) content. It shows significant reduction in renal oxidative stress and AGE when compared to diabetic control and glibenclamide. CC and glibenclamide improved antioxidant status in kidney and pancreas of diabetic rats [52].

***Cuminum nigrum* L (Apiaceae):** It grows mainly in Central Asia and India. Oral administration of the flavonoid contents of the plant causes hypoglycemic effect at a dose range of 0.5 to 1.5 g/kg, both in normal and alloxan-diabetic rabbits. Curcumin promotes AMPK activation and glucose uptake with increased insulin sensitivity in muscle cells as a potential anti-diabetic therapeutic agent [53, 54].

***Cyamopsis tetragonoloba* (L) Taubert. (Papilionaceae):** The species are distributed across Africa, Asia and the Pacific. The aqueous extract of beans at 250 mg/kg body wt. significantly lowers blood glucose levels in alloxan-induced diabetic rats within 3 h of administration. Continuation for 10 days produces statistically significant reduction in the blood glucose levels while shows marginal activity is in normal and glucose-loaded rats [55].

***Dioscorea dumetorum* (Kunth) Pax. (Dioscoreaceae):** It is mainly found in West and Central Africa. At a dose of 20 mg/kg, the fasting blood sugar in normoglycemic rabbits reduces from 112 mg/100 mL to 55 mg/100 mL after 4h. In alloxan diabetic rabbits, the blood sugar lowers from 520 mg/100 mL to 286 mg/100 mL at the same time interval. The aqueous fraction of the methanol extract produces comparable effects at 100 mg/kg. Whereas, chloroform fraction rises the fasting blood sugar of normal rabbits to 196 mg/100 mL after 6h. The hypoglycemic effects are compared to those of tolbutamide [56].

***Eclipta alba* (L) Hassk. (Asteraceae):** It is widely distributed throughout India, China, Thailand, and Brazil. Oral administration of leaf suspension of *E. alba* (2 and 4 g/kg body weight) for 60 days results in significant reduction in blood glucose, glycosylated hemoglobin HbA(l)c. The extract decreases the activities of glucose-6-phosphatase and fructose-1,6-bisphosphatase, and increase the activity of liver hexokinase. Thus, oral administration of *E. alba* possess potent antihyperglycemic activity [57].

***Emblica officinalis* Gaertn. (Euphorbiaceae):** Different solvent extracts of *E. officinalis* acts as α-amylase and α-glucosidase inhibitor. Significant antiglycation activity also confirms the therapeutic potential of these extracts against diabetes. Methanol extracts significantly inhibits the oxidation of LDL under in vitro conditions [58].

***Enicostema littorale blume* (Gentianaceae):** Dried plant equivalent extract of 1.5 g/100 g body weight causes significant decrease in glycosylated haemoglobin, liver glucose-6-phosphatase activity and increase in serum insulin levels of the diabetic rats. There is no toxicity parameter of extract treated diabetic rats as compared to diabetic control rats. The above results suggest that *E. littorale* is a potent antidiabetic agent without any toxic effect [59].

***Ficus bengalensis* L. (Moraceae):** A reputed plant commonly known as "banyan tree" in Ayurvedic literature. At a dose of 100 mg/kg for one month, there is significant decrease in blood and urine sugar, certain lipid components in serum, tissues and glucose-6- phosphatase activity in liver, but increase in body weight, the activities of hexokinase and HMG-COA reductase in tissues as compared to diabetic control. The mechanism of action of the principle may be related to its protective/inhibitory action against the insulin degradative processes [60].

***Fraxinus excelsior* L (Oleaceae):** The aqueous extract at a dose of 10 mg/kg/h produces a significant decrease in blood glucose levels in normal rats and even more in diabetic rats. A potent increase of glycosuria concludes inhibition of renal glucose reabsorption. This renal effect might be at least one mechanism explaining the hypoglycemic activity of this plant in normal and diabetic rats [61].

***Garcinia kola* Heckel (W & C Afr) (Clusiaceae):** It is found in Africa mainly in subtropical or tropical moist lowland forests. The extract decreases the activity of microsomal glucose-6-phosphatase and lipid peroxidation (LPO) products. At a dose of 100 mg/kg, the fasting blood sugar in normoglycemic rabbits reduces from 115 mg/100 mL to 65 mg/100 mL after 4 h. In alloxan diabetic rabbits, the blood sugar lowers from 506 mg/100 mL to 285 mg/100 mL at 12 h. Kolaviron, a mixture of C-3/C-8 linked biflavonoids obtained from Garcinia kola produces significant hypoglycemic effects [62, 63].

***Gongronema latifolium* Endl. (Asclepiadaceae):** The origin of the plant is traced to Nigeria in West Africa. The aqueous extract of *G. latifolium* is able to significantly increase the activities of hepatic hexokinase and decrease the activities of glucokinase, but does not produce any change in the hepatic glycogen and both hepatic and blood glucose content of diabetic rats. The effects of oral administration of aqueous and ethanolic leaf extracts increase the activity of superoxide dismutase and the level of reduced glutathione. The aqueous extract further increases the activity of glutathione reductase while the ethanolic extract causes a significant increase in the activity of glutathione peroxidases and glucose-6-phosphate dehydrogenase and a significant decrease in lipid peroxidation. These results suggest that the extracts from *G. latifolium* leaves could exert their antidiabetic activities through their antioxidant properties [64, 65].

Helicteres isora **L., As.(Sterculiaceae):** Distributed widely in forests throughout India. The hot water extract of fruit of *H. isora* exhibits significant antioxidant activity and moderate antidiabetic activity, at 200 mg/mL dose it shows glucose uptake activity and found to be active comparable with insulin and metformin. The ethanolic extract has insulin-sensitizing and hypolipidemic activity and has the potential for use in the treatment of type- 2 diabetes [66-68].

Hypoxis hemerocallidea conn **Corm (African potato) (Hypoxidaceae):** At a dose of 800 mg/kg, the plant extract causes 30.20% and 48.54% reductions in the blood glucose concentrations of fasted normal and STZ-treated diabetic rats respectively. Thus, possesses hypoglycemic activity [69].

Inula racemosa **Hook.f.(Asteraceae):** It grows in the temperate and alpine western Himalayas. The petroleum ether extract of roots lowers plasma insulin and glucose levels within 75 min of oral administration to albino rats and it significantly counteracts adrenaline-induced hyperglycemia in rats. The extract further shows negative inotropic and negative chronotropic effects on frog heart. All these findings indicate that one of the constituents of *I. racemosa* may have adrenergic beta-blocking activity [70].

Lagerstroemia speciosa **(L) Pers. (Lythraceae):** *L. speciosa* standardized to 1% corosolic acid (Glucosol) at daily dosages of 32 and 48mg for 2 weeks shows significant reduction in the blood glucose levels. Glucosol in a soft gel capsule formulation shows a 30% decrease in blood glucose levels compared to 20% drop with dry-powder filled hard gelatin capsule formulation, suggesting that the soft gel formulation has a better bioavailability than a dry-powder formulation [71].

Lepidium sativum **L. (Brassicaceae):** It is a fast-growing, edible herb. The aqueous LS extract at a dose of 10 mg/kg/h causes a potent inhibition of renal glucose reabsorption which in turn reduces blood sugar. This renal effect is at least one mechanism explaining the hypoglycemic activity of this plant in normal and diabetic rats [72].

Mangifera indica **L.(Anacardiaceae):** The aqueous extract produces reduction of blood glucose level in normoglycemic and glucose induced hyperglycemia, but does not have any effect on streptozotocin-induced diabetic mice under the same conditions when compared with that of an oral dose of chlorpropamide. The result indicates that the aqueous extract of the leaves of *M. indica* possess hypoglycemic activity [73].

Momordica charantia **L. (Cucurbitaceae):** *M. charantia* (bitter melon) is commonly known as vegetable insulin. An oral sucrose tolerance test reveals that administration of aqueous extract (AE), methanol fraction (MF) or methanol insoluble fraction (MIF) each significantly suppresses plasma glucose levels at 30 min as compared with control. In addition, the plasma insulin level at 30 min also lowers after MF administration than the control in the oral sucrose tolerance test, these results demonstrates that bitter melon suppresses postprandial hyperglycemia by inhibition of α-glucosidase activity [74].

Morinda lucida **Benth.(Rubiaceae):** The extract demonstrates a significant and dose dependent hypoglycemic activity within 4 h after oral administration in normal rats. In hyperglycemic rats, the extract produces a significant anti-diabetic effect from day 3 after oral administration, with 400 mg/kg extract-treated animals. These results suggest that the leaves of *M. lucida* have a strong glucose lowering property when administered to streptozotocin-treated rats [75].

Myrcia uniflora **Barb., Rods.(Myricaceae):** A plant is widely used in northern Brazil for treatment of diabetes. The aqueous extracts of Myrcia has a beneficial effect on the diabetic state, mainly by improving metabolic parameters of glucose homeostasis which reduces hyperglycemia, polyphagia, polydipsia, urine volume and the urinary excretion of glucose and urea. Also, Myrcia administration for 3 weeks has no effect on the weight of epididymal and retroperitoneal adipose tissue, or on the concentrations of pancreatic and serum insulin [76].

Nigella sativa **L (Ranunculaceae):** Oral administration of ethanol extract of *N. sativa* seeds (300 mg/kg body weight/day) to streptozotocin induced diabetic rats for 30 days significantly reduces the elevated levels of blood glucose, lipids, plasma insulin and improved altered levels of lipid peroxidation products (TBARS and hydroperoxides) and antioxidant enzymes like catalase, superoxide dismutase, reduced glutathione and glutathione peroxidase in liver and kidney. The results confirm the antidiabetic activity of *N. sativa* seeds extract [77].

Ocimum sanctum **L. (Lamiaceae):** It is commonly known as Tulsi. Since ancient times, this plant is known for its medicinal properties. The aqueous extract of leaves shows significant reduction in blood sugar level in both normal and alloxan induced diabetic rats. Significant reduction in fasting blood glucose, uronic acid, total amino acid, total cholesterol, triglyceride and total lipid indicate the hypoglycemic and hypolipidemic effects of tulsi in diabetic rats. Oral administration of plant extract (200 mg/kg) for 30 days leads to decrease in the plasma glucose level. Renal glycogen content increases 10 fold while skeletal muscle and hepatic glycogen levels decreases by 68 and 75% respectively in diabetic rats as compared to control. This plant also shows antioxidant, antibacterial, antifungal, antiviral, antiasthemitic, antistress, antitumor, gastric antiulcer activity, antimutagenic and immunostimulant activities [78-80].

***Origanum vulgare* L. (Lamiaceae):** It is native to warm-temperate western and southwestern Eurasia and the Mediterranean region. Oral administration of the aqueous extract (20 mg/kg) produces significant decrease on blood glucose levels in STZ diabetic rats. However, the blood glucose levels gets normalised from the fourth day after daily repeated oral administration of aqueous OV extract (20 mg/kg). This concludes that an aqueous extract of *O. Vulgare* exhibits anti-hyperglycemic activity in STZ rats without affecting basal plasma insulin concentrations [81].

***Otholobium pubescens* L. (Papilionaceae):** The known compound bakuchiol, isolated from an extract of *O. pubescens* reduces blood glucose levels in a dosedependent fashion in db/db mice and displays no hypoglycemic effect in lean mice at 250 mg/kg q.d. An oral dose of bakuchiol at 150 mg/kg q.d. in the fat-fed, streptozotocin (STZ)-treated rat, a new rodent model for type 2 diabetes, significantly lowers plasma glucose and triglyceride levels [82].

***Paeonia lactiflora* Pall.(Paeoniaceae):** Paeoniflorin and 8-debenzoylpaeoniflorin isolated from the dried root of *P. lactiflora* pall produces a significant blood sugar lowering effect in streptozotocin-treated rats and has a maximum effect at 25 min after treatment and this hypoglycemic action is also observed in normoglycemic rats only at 1 mg/kg. Plasma insulin does not change in paeoniflorin-treated normoglycemic rats indicating an insulin-independent action [83].

***Panax ginseng* C. Meyer. (Araliaceae):** The roots are taken orally in the treatment of type II diabetes. Extracts of ginseng species shows antihyperglycemic activity associated with increased peroxisome proliferator-activated receptor gamma expression and adenosine monophosphate-activated protein kinase phosphorylation in liver and muscle. Oral administration of *P. ginseng* root improves insulin sensitivity and may be used as an adjuvant therapy for treating diabetic patients with insulin resistance [84, 85].

***Phyllanthus amarus* Schum & Thonn. (Euphorbiaceae):** A traditional Ayurveda herb used in southern India. Methanolic extract of P. *amarus* has potential anti-oxidant activity as it could inhibit lipid peroxidation, and scavenge hydroxyl and superoxide radicals in vitro. This extract also reduces the blood sugar in alloxanized diabetic rats [86].

***Psidium guajava* L. (Myrtaceae):** An indigenous medicinal plant used to control diabetes in Indian System of Medicine. Ethanol stem bark extract exhibits statistically significant hypoglycemic activity in alloxan-induced hyperglycemic rats but devoid of hypoglycemic effect in normal and glucose loaded rats (OGTT). Aqueous extract shows hypolipidaemic activity in addition to its hypoglycemic and antidiabetic activity [87, 88].

Pterocarpus marsupium **Roxb. (Papilionaceae):** It is widely used in 'Ayurveda' as 'Rasayana' for management of various metabolic disorders. An aqueous extract of *P. marsupium* wood, at an oral dose of 250 mg/kg, shows statistically significant hypoglycemic activity. Marsupin, pterosupin and liquiritigenin obtained from this plant show antihyperlipidemic activity. (-) Epicatechin, its active principle, has been found to be insulinogenic, enhancing insulin release and conversion of proinsulin to insulin in vitro. Like insulin, (-)epicatechin stimulates oxygen uptake in fat cells and tissue slices of various organs, increases glycogen content of rat diaphragm in a dosedependent manner [89-91].

Retama raetam (RR) **(Forssk) Webb. (Papilionaceae):** The aqueous extract of RR at a dose of 20mg/kg significantly reduces the blood glucose in normal rats 6h after a single oral administration and two weeks after repeated oral administration. This hypoglycemic effect is more pronounced in streptozotocin (STZ) diabetic rats. The aqueous extract of RR has no effect on basal plasma insulin levels. Also causes a potent inhibition of renal glucose reabsorption. These findings suggest that the aqueous extract of RR possess significant hypoglycemic effect in both normal and STZ diabetic rats [92, 93].

Salacia reticulate **W. (Celastraceae):** Supplementation of 0.01 % solution of the extract as drinking water prevents the elevation of the plasma glucose level and intestinal α-glucosidase activities in type 1 diabetic mice. This treatment also prevents the elevation of the plasma, pancreatic, and kidney lipid peroxide levels, lowering of the plasma insulin level, and elevation of the kidney aldose reductase activities in diabetic mice. These results suggest that the water extract of the leaves of *S. reticulata* could be a beneficial food material for the prevention of diabetes and obesity because of its multiple effects [94].

Spergularia purpurea **(SP) (Pers) G, Donf.(Caryophyllaceae):** The aqueous extract at a dose of 10 mg/kg produces a significant decrease in blood glucose levels in normal rats, and even more in diabetic rats. This hypoglycemic effect might be due to an extra-pancreatic action of the aqueous extract of SP, since the basal plasma insulin concentrations unchange after SP treatment. This concludes that aqueous extract perfusion of SP inhibits endogenous glucose production in mice [95].

Suaeda fruticosa (SF) **Euras (Chenopodiaceae):** The aqueous extract at a dose of 192 mg/kg produces a significant decrease in blood glucose levels in normal rats, and even more in diabetic rats. This hypoglycemic effect might be due to an extra-pancreatic action of the aqueous extract of SF, since that the levels of plasma insulin unchanged between the values before and after treatment. The effect of the aqueous extract on the plasma cholesterol is significant in both normal and diabetic rats but, there is no significant effect of SF on plasma triglycerides in both groups [96].

***Syzigium cumini* (L) Skeels. (Myrtaceae):** Commonly known as 'Jamun', is widely used in Indian folk medicine for the treatment of diabetes mellitus. Oral administration of 2.5 and 5.0 g/kg body weight of the aqueous extract of the seed for 6 weeks results in significant reduction in blood glucose and an increase in total haemoglobin, but in the case of 7.5 g/kg body weight the effect is not significant. The aqueous extract also decreases free radical formation which clearly shows the antioxidant property. Thus the study shows that Jamun seed extract (JSEt) has hypoglycemic action [97].

***Tamarindus indica* L. (Caesalpinaceae):** Aqueous extract of seed of *T. indica* when given to mild diabetic (MD) and severe diabetic (SD) rats at the dose of 80 mg and 120 mg/0.5 mL distilled water/100 g body weight/d respectively for 14 days, the extract shows attenuation of hyperglycemia and hyperlipidemia in streptozotocin-induced diabetic rats [98].

***Telfaria occidentalis* Hook. (Cucurbitaceae):** It is a tropical vine grown in West Africa as a leaf vegetable and for its edible seeds. The aqueous extract given orally in 1 g/kg to the mice 60 minutes before glucose administration reduces the blood glucose level from day two when compared with that of chlorpropamide (200 mg/kg) under the same conditions. The results of this study indicates that the aqueous extract of the leaves of *T. occidentalis* possess hypoglycemic activity [99].

***Tinospora cordifolia* Miers. (Menispermaceae):** Commonly known as Guduchi, an herbaceous vine indigenous to the tropical areas of India, Myanmar and Sri Lanka. Oral administration of an aqueous *T. cordifolia* root extract to alloxan diabetic rats causes a significant reduction in blood glucose and brain lipids. Though the aqueous extract at a dose of 400 mg/kg could elicit significant antihyperglycemic effect in different animal models, its effect is equivalent to only one unit/kg of insulin [100].

***Trigonella foenum* graecum L. (fenugreek) (Papilionaceae):** Used both as an herb (the leaves) and as a spice (the seed) and cultivated worldwide as a semi-arid crop. Oral administration of 2 and 8 g/kg of plant extract produces dose dependent decrease in the blood glucose levels in both normal as well as diabetic rats. Administration of fenugreek seeds improves glucose metabolism and normalizes creatinine kinase activity in heart, skeletal muscle and liver of diabetic rats. It also reduces hepatic and renal glucose-6-phosphalase and fructose -1, 6-biphosphatase activity [101, 102].

SYNTHETIC DRUGS AND HERBAL MEDICINE

Oral hypoglycemic drugs are used only in the treatment of type 2 diabetes which is a disorder involving resistance to secreted insulin. Type 1 diabetes involves lack of insulin and requires insulin for treatment. There are now four classes of hypoglycemic drugs: These drugs are approved for use only in patients with type 2 diabetes and are used in patients who have not responded to diet, weight reduction, and exercise. They are not approved for the treatment of women who are pregnant with diabetes. Sulfonylureas are the most widely used drugs for the treatment of type 2 diabetes and appear to function by stimulating insulin secretion. The net effect is increased responsiveness of ß-cells (insulin secreting cells located in the pancreas) to both glucose and non-glucose secretagogues, resulting in more insulin being released at all blood glucose concentrations. Sulfonylureas may also have extra-pancreatic effects, one of which is to increase tissue sensitivity to insulin, but the clinical importance of these effects is minimal. Metformin is an oral antidiabetic drug in the biguanide class. It is the first-line drug of choice for the treatment of type 2 diabetes, in particular, in overweight and obese people and those with normal kidney function. It is effective only in the presence of insulin. But, in contrast to sulfonylureas, it does not directly stimulate insulin secretion. Its major effect is to increase insulin action. One important effect appears to be suppression of glucose output from the liver. Thiazolidinediones or TZDs act by binding to PPARs (peroxisome proliferator-activated receptors), a group of receptor molecules inside the cell nucleus, specifically *PPARã* (gamma). The ligands for these receptors are free fatty acids (FFAs) and eicosanoids. When activated, the receptor migrates to the DNA, activating transcription of a number of specific genes. TZDs reverse insulin resistance by acting on muscle, fat and to a lesser extent liver to increase glucose utilization and diminish glucose production and are also effective when given in combination with metformin. Alpha-glucosidase inhibitors inhibit the upper gastrointestinal enzymes that convert dietary starch and other complex carbohydrates into simple sugars which can be absorbed. The result is to slow the absorption of glucose after meals. Alpha-glucosidase inhibitors are used to establish greater glycemic control over hyperglycemia in diabetes mellitus type 2, particularly with regard to postprandial hyperglycemia. They may be used as monotherapy in conjunction with an appropriate diabetic diet and exercise or with other anti-diabetic drugs. Herbs have been used for healing purposes and to promote wellness since from the ancient times and are not categorized as medicines but treated as food since they are natural products. Nowadays, herbal medicines, health and dietary supplements are flooding the markets. The use in the right way provides effective and safe treatment for many ailments and the effectiveness is mostly subjective to the patient. The potency varies based on the genetic variation, growing conditions, timing and method of harvesting, exposure to air, light, moisture, and type of preservation of the herbs. Herbal medicines can be used for healing purposes and to promote wellness and are not addictive or habit forming, but are powerful nutritional agents that support the body naturally. They promote health and serve as excellent healing agents without side effects. Chinese herbs are taken as tonics to enhance physical and mental well-being and can nourish the body's deepest and most basic elements. They are also safe and effective for health, healing, weight loss/gain/maintenance. Herbal medicines are great body balancers that help regulate body functions, can be used to support balance process of our body and offer the nutrients that the body fails to receive due to poor diet or environmental deficiencies in the soil and air. They can be used to treat many diseases such as diabetes, asthma, eczema, premenstrual syndrome, rheumatoid arthritis, migraine, menopausal symptoms, chronic fatigue, and irritable bowel syndrome, etc., and can be used for maintaining general health. Herbal preparations are best when taken under the guidance of a trained professional. When used correctly, herbal medicines are considered safer than conventional medications. People are greatly concerned about the efficacy and side effects of many synthetic drugs, and hence choose herbal medicines for providing a safe and natural alternative treatment for many health problems. The use is widespread and growing, In fact, herbs are always the alternative medicine and primary source.

The advantages of using herbal medicines are numerous. They tend to be more effective for long-standing health complaints that don't respond well to traditional medicine. Herbs typically have fewer side effects, and may be safer to use over time.

CONCLUSION

Diabetes mellitus (DM), both insulin-dependent DM (IDDM) and non-insulin dependent DM (NIDDM) is a common and serious metabolic disorder throughout the world with the characteristic feature of hyperglycemia i.e increased glucose levels. It usually occurs due to the disturbances in carbohydrate metabolism. Differences in social structure, psychic stress, obesity, hormonal imbalance and heredity are optimizing the growth of pandemic. At present, the treatment of diabetes mainly involves a sustained reduction in hyperglycemia by the use of biguanides, thiazolidinediones, sulphonylureas, D-phenylalanine derivatives, meglitinides and α-glucosidase inhibitors in addition to insulin. However, due to unwanted side effects the efficacies of these compounds are debatable and there is a demand for new compounds for the treatment of diabetes. Hence, plants have been suggested as a rich, as yet unexplored source of potentially useful antidiabetic drugs. However, only a few have been subjected to detailed scientific investigation due to a lack of mechanism-based available in vitro assays. These efforts may provide treatment for all and justify the role of novel traditional medicinal plants having anti-diabetic potentials.

REFERENCES

1. Maiti R, Jana D, Das UK, Ghosh D. Antidiabelic Effect of Aqueous Extract of Seed of Tamarindus Indica in Streptozotocin induced Diabetic Rats. J Ethnopharmacol 2004, 92, 85-91.
2. Wadkar KA, Magdum CS, Patil SS, Naikwade NS. Antidiabetic Potential and Indian Medicinal Plants. J Herbal Med and Toxicol 2008, 2, 45-50.
3. Welihinda J, Arvidson G, Gylfe E, Hellman B, Karlsson E.Ada Biol MetLGer 1982, 41, 1229.
4. Hongxiang Hui, George Tang, and Vay Liang W Go. VLW. Hypoglycemic Herbs and their Action Mechanisms. Chin Med 2009, 4, 11-14.
5. Liu IM, Tzeng TF, Liou SS, Lan TW. Improvement of Insulin Sensitivity in Obese Zucker Rats by Myricetin Extracted from Abelmoschus moschatus. Planta Med 2007, 73, 1054-1060.
6. Wadood A, Wadood N, Shah SA. Effects of Acacia arabica and Caralluma edulis on Blood Glucose Levels on Normal and Alloxan Diabetic Rabbits. J Pakistan Med 1989, 39, 208-212.
7. Akhtar MS, Iqbal J. Evaluation of the Hypoglycaemic Effect of Achyranthes aspera in Normal and Alloxan-diabetic Rabbits. J Ethnopharmacol 1991, 31, 49-57.
8. Ruffa MJ, Ferraro G, Wagner ML, Calcagno ML, Campos RH, Cavallaro L. Cytotoxic Effect of Argentine Medicinal Plant Extracts on Human Hepatocellular Carcinoma Cell Line. J Ethnopharmacol 2002, 79, 335-339.
9. Kadarian C, Broussalis AM, Miño J, Lopez P, Gorzalczany S, Ferraro G, Acevedo C.Hepatoprotcctive Activity of Achyrocline Satureioides (Lam) D. C. Pharmacol Res 2002, 45, 57-61.
10. Andrade-Cetto A, Wiedenfeld H. Hypoglycemic Effect of Acosmium panamense Bark on Streptozotocin Diabetic Rats. J Ethnopharmacol 2004, 90, 217-220.
11. Ponnachan PT, Paulose CS, Panikkar KR. Effect of Leaf Extract of Aegle Mannelose in Diabetic Rats. Indian J Exp Biol 1993, 31, 345-347.
12. Gray AM, Flatt PR.Actions of the Traditional Anti-diabetic Plant, Agrimony Eupatoria (agrimony): Effects Onhyperglycaemia, Cellular Glucose Metabolism and Insulin Secretion. Br J Nutr 1998, 80, 109-114.
13. El Hilaly J, Lyoussi B. Hypoglycaemic Effect of the Lyophilised Aqueous Extract of Ajuga ivain Normal and streptozotocin Diabetic Rats. J Ethnopharmacol 2002, 80, 109-113.
14. Roman-Ramos R, Flores-Saenz JL, Alarcon-Aguilar FJ. Antihyperglycemic Effect of some Edible Plants. J Ethnopharmacol 1995, 48, 25-32.
15. Kumari K, Mathew BC, Augusti KT. Antidiabetic and HypoHpidaemic Effects of S-methyl Cysteinesulfoxide, Isolated from Allium cepa Linn. Ind J Biochem Biophys 1995, 32, 49-54.
16. Mathew PT, Augusti KT. Hypoglycemic Effects of Onion, Allium cepa Linn, on Diabetes Mellitus- apreliminary Report. Ind J Physiol Pharmacol 1975, 19, 213-217.
17. Eidi A, Eidi M, Esmaeili E. Antidiabetic Effect of Garlic (Allium sativum L.) in Normal and Streptozotocin-induced Diabetic Rats. Phytomedicine 2005, 13, 624-629.
18. Ajabnoor MA. Effect of Aloes on Blood Glucose Levels Innormal and Alloxan Diabetic Mice. J Ethnopharmacol 1990, 28, 215-220.

19. Jain N, Vijayaraghavan R, Pant SC, Lomash V, Ali M. Aloe vera gel Alleviates Cardiotoxicity in Streptozocin-induced Diabetes in Rats. J Pharm Pharmacol 2010, 62, 115-123.
20. Okyar A, Can A, Akev N, Baktir G, Sütlüpinar N. Effect of Aloe vera Leaves on Blood Glucose Level in Type I and type II Diabetic Rat Models. Phytother Res 2001, 15, 157-161.
21. Dandu AM, Inamdar NM. Evaluation of Beneficial Effects of Antioxidant Properties of Aqueous Leaf Extract of Andrographis Paniculata in STZ induced Diabetes. Pak J Pharm Sci 2009, 22, 49-52.
22. Zhang XF, Tan BK. Anti-diabetic Property of Erhanolic Extract of Andrographis Paniculata in Streptozotocin-diabetic Rats, Acta Pharmacol Sin 2000, 21, 157-164.
23. Panda S, Kar A. Antidiabetic and Antioxidative Effects of Annona squamosa Leaves are Possibly Mediated through quercetin-3-O-glucoside. Biofactors 2007, 31, 201-210.
24. Khazraji SM, Shamaony LA, Twaij HA. Hypoglycaemic Effect of Artemisia Herba alba. Effect of Different Parts and Influence of the Solvent on Hypoglycemic Activity. J Ethnopharmacol 1993, 40, 163-166.
25. Ribnicky DM, Kuhn P, Poulev A, Logendra S, Zuberi A, Cefalu WT, Raskin I. Improved Absorption and Bioactivity of Active Compounds from an Anti-diabetic Extract of Artemisia dracunculus L. Int J Pharm 2009, 370, 87-92.
26. Ribnicky DM, Poulev A, Watford M, Cefalu WT, Raskin I. Poulev A, Watford M, Cefalu WT, Raskin I. Antihyperglycemic Activity of Tarralin, an Ethanolic Extract of *Artemisia dracunculus* L. Phytomedicine 2006, 13, 550-557.
27. Yu J, Zhang Y, Sun S, Shen J, Qiu J, Yin X, Yin H, Jiang S. Inhibitory Effects of Astragaloside IV on Diabetic Peripheral Neuropathy in Rats. Can J Physiol Pharmacol 2006, 84, 579-587.
28. Pushparaj PN, Tan BK, Tan CH. The Mechanism of Hypoglycemic Action of the Semi-purified Fractions of Averrhoabilimbi in Streptozotocin-diabetic Rats. Life Sci 2001, 70, 535-547.
29. Waheed A, Miana GA, Ahmad SI. Clinical Investigation of Hypoglycemic Effect of Seeds of *Azadirachta-inidca* in type-2 (NIDDM) Diabetes Mellitus. Pak J Pharm Sci 2006, 19, 322-325.
30. Fuentes O, Arancibia-Avila P, Alarcón J.Hypoglycemic Activity of *Bauhinia candicans* in Diabetic induced Rabbits. Fitoterapia 2004, 75, 527-532.
31. de Sousa E, Zanatta L, Seifriz I, Creczynski-Pasa TB, Pizzolatti MG, Szpoganicz B, Silva FR. Hypoglycemic Effect and Antioxidant Potential of kaempferoI-3,7-O-(alpha)-dirhamnoside from *Bauhinia foificata* Leaves. J Nat Prod 2004, 67, 829-832.
32. Lino Cde S, Diógenes JP, Pereira BA, Faria RA, Andrade Neto M, Alves RS, de Queiroz MG, de Sousa FC, Viana GS. Antidiabetic Activity of *Bauhinia forficata* Extracts in Alloxan-diabetic Rats. Biol PharmBull 2004, 27, 125-127.
33. Chang SL, Chang CL, Chiang YM, Hsieh RH, Tzeng CR, Wu TK, Sytwu HK, Shyur LF, Yang WC. Polyacetylenic Compounds and Butanol Fraction from Bidens pilosa can Modulate the differentiation of helper T Cells and Prevent Autoimmune Diabetes in Non-obese Diabetic mice. Planta Med 2004, 70, 1045-1051.
34. Puri D. The Insulinotropic Activity of a Nepaiese Medicinal Plant Biophytum Sensitivum: Preliminary Experimental Study. J Ethnopharmacol 2001, 78, 89-93.

35. Russell KR, Omoruyi FO, Pascoe KO, Morrison EY. Hypoglycaemic Activity of *Bixa orellana* Extract in the Dog. Methods Find Exp Clin Pharmacol 2008, 30, 301-305.
36. Anand P, Murali KY, Tandon V, Chandra R, Murthy PS. Preliminary Studies on Antihyperglycemic Effect of Aqueous Extract of *Brassica nigra* (L.)Koch in Streptozotocin induced Diabetic Rats. Indian J Exp Bioi 2007, 45, 696-701.
37. Karageuzyan KG, Vartanyan GS, Agadjanov MI, Panossian AG, Hoult JR. Restoration of the Disordered Glucose-fatty Acid Cycle in Alloxandiabetic Rats bytrihydroxyoctadecadienoic Acids from *Bryonia alba*, a Native Armenian Medicinal Plant. Planta Med 1998, 64, 417-422.
38. Naik SR, Barbosa Filho JM, Dhuley JN, Deshmukh V. Probable Mechanism of Hypoglycemic Activity of Bassic Acid, a Natural Product isolated from *Bumelia sartorum*. J Ethnopharmacol 1991, 33, 37-44.
39. Almeida RN, Filho J, Naik SR. Chemistry and Pharmacology of an Ethanol Extract of *Bumelia sartorum*. J Ethnopharmacol 1985, 14, 173-185.
40. Kannur DM, Hukkeri VI, Akki KS. Antidiabetic Activity of *Caesalpinia bonducella* Seed Extracts in Rats. Filoterapia 2006, 77, 546-549.
41. Amalraj T, Ignacimuthu S. Hypoglycemic Activity of *Cajanus cajan* (seeds) in Mice. Indian J Exp Biol 1998, 36, 1032-1033.
42. Eddouks M, Lemhadri A, Michel JB.Caraway and Caper: Potential Anti-hyperglycaemic Plants in Diabetic Rats. J Ethnopharmacol 2004, 94, 143-148.
43. Prakasam A, Sethupathy S, Pugalendi KV. Antihyperglycaemic Effect of *Casearia esculenta* Root Extracts in Streptozotocin-induced diabetic Rats. Pharmazie 2002, 57, 758-760.
44. Gupta S, Sharma SB, Singh UR, Bansal SK, Prabhu KM. Elucidation of Mechanism of Action of *Cassia auriculata* Leaf Extract for its antidiabetic Activity in strep to zotocin-induced Diabetic Rats. J Med Food 2010, 13, 528-534.
45. Nammi S, Boini MK, Lodagala SD, Behara RB. The Juice of Fresh Leaves of *Catharanthus roseus* Linn, reduces Blood Glucose in Normal and Alloxan Diabetic Rabbits. BMC Complement Altern Med 2003, 2, 3- 4.
46. Eddouks M, Lemhadri A, Zeggwagh NA, Michel JB. Potent Hypoglycaemic Activity of the Aqueous Extract of *Chamaemelum nobite* in Normal and Streptozotocin-induced Diabetic Rats. Diabetes Res Clin Pract 2005, 67, 189-195.
47. Pushparaj PN, Low HK, Manikandan J, Tan BK, Tan CH. Anti-diabetic Effects of *Cichorium intybus* in Streptozotocin-induced Diabetic Rats. J Elhnopharmacol 2007,111, 430-434.
48. Ojewole JA. Hypoglycaemic Effect of *Clausena anisata* (Willd) Hook Methanolic Root Extract in Rats. J Ethnopharmacol 2002, 81, 231-237.
49. Kamble SM, Kamlakar PL, Vaidya S, Bambole VD. Influence of *Coccinia indica* on Certain Enzymes in Glycolytic and Lipolytic Pathway in Human Diabetes. Indian J 1998, 52, 143-146.
50. Eidi M, Eidi A, Saeidi A, Molanaei S, Sadeghipour A, Bahar M, Bahar K. Effect of Coriander Seed (*Coriandrum sativum* L.) Ethanol Extract on Insulin Release from Pancreatic beta Cells in streptozotocin-induccd Diabetic Rats. Phytother Res 2009, 23, 404-406.
51. Gray AM, Flatt PR. Insulin-releasing and Insulin-like Activity of the Traditional Anti-diabetic Plant *Coriandrum sativum* (coriander). Br J Nutr 1999, 81, 203-209.

52. Jagtap AG, Patil PB. Antihyperglycemic Activity and Inhibition of Advanced Glycation end Product Formation by *Cuminum cyminum* in Streptozolocin Induced Diabetic Rats. Food Chem Toxicol 2010, 48, 2030-2036.
53. Ahmad M, Akhtar MS, Malik T, Gilani AH. Hypoglycaemic Action of the Flavonoid Fraction of *Cuminum nigrum* Seeds. Phytother Res 2000, 14, 103-106.
54. Kang C, Kim E. Synergistic Effect of Curcumin and Insulin on Muscle Cell Glucose Metabolism. Food ChemToxicol 2010, 48, 2366-2373.
55. Mukhtar HM, Ansari SH, Ali M, Bhat ZA, Naved T. Effect of Aqueous Extract of *Cyamopsis tetragonoloba* Linn, Beans on Blood Glucose Level in Normal and Alloxan-induced Diabetic Rats. Indian J Exp Biol 2004, 42, 1212-1215.
56. Iwu MM, Okunji CO, Ohiaeri GO, Akah P, Corley D, Tempesta MS. Hypoglycaemic Activity of Dioscoretine from Tubers of *Dioscorea dumetorum* in Normal and Alloxan Diabetic Rabbits. Planta Med 1990, 56, 264-267.
57. Ananthi J, Prakasam A, Pugalendi KV. Antihyperglycemic Activity of *Eclipta alba* Leaf on Alloxan-induced Diabetic Rats. Yale J Biol Med 2003, 76, 97-102.
58. Nampoothiri SV, Prathapan A, Cherian OL, Raghu KG, Venugopalan VV, Sundaresan A. In vitro Antioxidant and Inhibitory Potential of *Tetminalia bellerica* and *Emblica officinalis* Fruits against LDL Oxidation and Key Enzymes Linked to type 2 Diabetes. Food Chem Toxicol 2010.
59. Maroo J, Vasu VT, Gupta S. Dose Dependent Hypoglycemic Effect of Aqueous Extract of *Enkostemma litturale* Blume Inalloxan Induced Diabetic Rats. Phytomedicine 2003, 10, 196-199.
60. Kumar RV, Augusti KT. Antidiabetic Effect of a Leucocyanidin Derivative Isolated from the Bark of *Ficus bengalensis* Linn. Indian J Biochem Biophys 1989, 26, 400-404.
61. Eddouks M, Maghrani M. Phlorizin-like Effect of *Fraxinus excelsior* in Normal and Diabetic Rats. J Ethnopharmacol 2004, 94, 149-154.
62. Adaramoye OA, Adeyemi EO. Hypoglycaemic and Hypolipidaemic Effects of Fractions from Kolaviron, Abiflavonoid Complex from *Garcinia Kola* in Streptozotocin-induced Diabetes Mellitus Rats. J Pharm Pharmacol 2006, 58, 121-128.
63. Iwu MM, Igboko OA, Okunji CO, Tempesta MS. Antidiabetic and aldose Reductase Activities of Biflavanones of Garcinia kola. J Pharm Pharmacol 1990, 42, 290-292.
64. Ugochukwu NH, Babady NE. Antihyperglycemic Effect of Aqueous and Ethanolic Extracts of Gongronemalatifolium Leaves on Glucose and Glycogen Metabolism in Livers of Normal and Streptozotocin-induced Diabetic Rats. Life Sci 2003, 29, 73, 1925-1938.
65. Ugochukwu NH, Babady NE. Antioxidant Effects of *Gongronema latifolium* in Hepatocytes of Rat Models of Non-insulin Dependent Diabetes Mellitus, Fitoterapia 2002, 73, 612-618.
66. Suthar M, Rathore GS, Pareek A. Antioxidant and Antidiabetic Activity of *Helicteres isora* (L.) Fruits. Indian J Pharm Sci 2009, 71, 695-699.
67. Gupta RN, Pareek A, Suthar M, Rathore GS, Basniwal PK, Jain D. Study of Glucose uptake Activity of *Helicteres isora* Linn, Fruits in L-6 cell Lines. Int J Diabetes Dev Ctries 2009, 29, 170-173.
68. Chakrabarti R, Vikramadithyan RK, Mullangi R, Sharma VM, Jagadheshan H, Rao YN, Sairam P, Rajagopalan R. Antidiabetic and Hypolipidemic Activity of *Helicteres isora* in Animal Models. J Ethnopharmacol 2002, 81, 343-349.

69. Mahomed IM, Ojewole JA. Hypoglycemic Effect of *Hypoxis hemerocallidea* conn (African Potato) Aqueous Extract in Rats. Methods Find Exp Clin Pharmacol 2003, 25, 617-623.

70. Tripathi YB, Tripathi P, Upadhyay BN. Assessment of the Adrenergic Beta-blocking Activity of Inula racemosa. J Ethnopbarmacol 1988, 23, 3-9.

71. Judy WV, Hari SP, Stogsdill WW, Judy JS, Naguib YM, Passwater R. Antidiabetic Activity of a Standardized Extract (Glucosol) from *Lagerstmemia speciosa* Leaves in Type II Diabetics. A Dose-dependence Study. J Elhnopharmacol 2003, 87, 115-117.

72. Eddouks M, Maghrani M. Effect of *Lepidium sativum* L. on Renal Glucose Reabsorption and Urinary TGF-beta 1levels in Diabetic Rats. Phytother Res 2008, 22, 1-5.

73. Aderibigbe AO, Emudianughe TS, Lawal BA. Evaluation of the Antidiabetic Action of *Mangifera indica* in Mice. Phytother Res 2001, 15, 456-458.

74. Uebanso T, Arai H, Taketani Y, Fukaya M, Yamamoto H, Mizuno A, Uryu K, Hada T, Takeda E. Extracts of *Momordica charantia* Suppress Postprandial Hyperglycemia in Rats. Nutr Sci Vitaminol (Tokyo) 2007, 53, 482-488.

75. Olajide OA, Awe SO, Makinde JM, Morebise O. Evaluation of the Antidiabetic Property of *Morinda lucida* Leaves in Streptozotocin-diabetic Rats. J Pharm Pharmacol 1999, 51, 1321 -1324.

76. Pepato MT, Oliveira JR, Kettelhut IC, Migliorini RH. Assessment of the Antidiabetic Activity of *Myrcia uniflora* Extracts in Streptozotocin Diabetic Rats. Diabetes Res 1993, 22, 49-57.

77. Kaleem M, Kirmani D, Asif M, Ahmed Q, Bano B. Biochemical Effects of *Nigella saliva* L Seeds in Diabetic Rats. Indian J Exp Biol 2006, 44, 745-748.

78. Vats V, Grover JK, Rathi SS. Evaluation of Antihyperglycemic and Hypogiycemic Effect of *Trigonella foenumgraecum* Linn, *Ocimum sanctum* Linn and *Pterocarpus marsupium* Linn in Normal and Alloxanized Diabetic Rats. J Ethnopharmacol 2002, 79, 95-100.

79. Rai V, Iyer U, Mani UV. Effect of Tulasi (*Ocimum sanctum*) Leaf Powder Supplementation on Blood Sugar Levels, Serum Lipids and Tissue Lipid in Diabetic Rats. Plant Food for Human Nutrition 1997, 50, 9-16.

80. Vats V, Yadav SP, Grover JK. Ethanolic Extract of *Ocimum sanctum* Leaves Partially Attenuates Streptozotocin induced Alteration in Glycogen Content and Carbohydrate Metabolism in Rats. J Etnnopharmacol 2004, 90, 155-160.

81. Lemhadri A, Zeggwagh NA, Maghrani M, Jouad H, Eddouks M. Antihyperglycemic Activity of the Aqueous Extract of *Origanum vulgare* Growing Wildin Tafilalet Region. J Ethnopharmacol 2004, 92, 251-256.

82. Krenisky JM, Luo J, Reed MJ, Carney JR. Isolation and Antihyperglycemic Activity of Bakuchiol from *Otholobium pubescens* (Fabaceae), a Peruvian Medicinal Plant used for the Treatment of Diabetes. Biol Pharm Bull 1999, 22, 1137-1140.

83. Hsu FL, Lai CW, Cheng JT. Antihyperglycemic Effects of Paeoniflorin and 8-debenzoylpaeoniflorin, Glucosides from the Root of *Paeonia lactiflora*. Planta Med 1997, 63, 323-325.

84. Lim S, Yoon JW, Choi SH, Cho BJ, Kim JT, Chang HS, Park HS, Park KS, Lee HK, Kim YB, Jang HC. Effect of Ginsam, a Vinegar Extract from *Panax ginseng*, on Body Weight and Glucosehomeostasis in an Obese Insulin-resistant Rat Model. Metabolism 2009, 58, 8-15.

85. Liu TP, Liu IM, Cheng JT. Improvement of Insulin Resistance by *panax ginseng* in Fructose-rich chow-fed Rats. Horm Metab Res 2005, 37, 146-151.

86. Raphael KR, Sabu MC, Kuttan R. Hypoglyccmic Effect of Methanol Extract of *Phyllanthus amarus* Schum & *Thonn onalloxan* Induced Diabetes mcllitus in Rats and its Relation with Antioxidant Potential. Indian J Exp Biol 2002, 40, 905-909.

87. Mukhtar HM, Ansari SH, Bhat ZA, Naved T, Singh P. Antidiabctic Activity of an Ethanol Extract Obtained from the Stem Bark of *Psidium guajava* (Myrtaceae). Pharmazie 2006, 61, 725-727.

88. Rai PK, Mehta S, Watal G. Hypolipidaemic & Hepatoprotective Effects of *Psidium guajava* Raw Fruit Peel Inexperimental Diabetes. Indian J Med Res 2010, 131, 820-824.

89. Mukhtar HM, Ansari SH, Ali M, Bhat ZA, Naved T. Effect of Aqueous Extract of *Pterocarpus marsupium* Wood on Alloxan-induced Diabetic Rats. Pharmazie 2005, 60, 478-479.

90. Jahromi MA, Ray AB. Antihyperlipidemic Effect of Flavonoids from *Pterocarpus marsupium*. J Nat Prod 1993, 56, 989-994.

91. Ahmad F, Khalid P, Khan MM, Rastogi AK, Kidwai JR. Insulin like Activity in (-) epicatechin. Acta. Diabetol 1989, 26, 291-300.

92. Maghrani M, Lemhadri A, Jouad H, Michel JB, Eddouks M. Effect of the Desert Plant Retama raetam on glycaemia in Normal and Streptozotocin-induced Diabetic Rats. J Ethnopharmacol 2003, 87, 21-25.

93. Maghrani M, Michel JB, Eddouks M.Hypoglycaemic Activity of Retama Raetam in Rats. Phytother Res 2005, 19, 125-128.

94. Yoshino K, Miyauchi Y, Kanetaka T, Takagi Y, Koga K. Anti-diabetic Activity of a Leaf Extract Prepared from Salacia reticulata in Mice, Biochem 2009, 73, 1096-1104.

95. Eddouks M, Jouad H, Maghrani M, Lemhadri A, Burcelin Rl. Inhibition of Endogenous Glucose Production Accounts for Hypogiycemic Effect of *Spergularia purpurea* in Streptozotocin Mice. Phytomedicine 2003, 10, 594-599.

96. Benwahhoud M, Jouad H, Eddouks M, Lyoussi B.Hypogiycemic Effect of *Suaeda fruticosa* in Streptozotocin-induced Diabetic Rats. J Ethnopharmacol 2001, 76, 35-38.

97. Prince PS, Menon VP, Pari L.Hypoglycaemic Activity of *Syzigium cumini* Seeds: Effect on Lipid Peroxidation in Alloxandiabetic Rats. J Ethnopharmacol 1998, 61, l-7.

98. Maiti R, Das UK, Ghosh D. Attenuation of Hyperglycemia and Hyperlipidemia in Streptozolocin-induced Diabetic Rats by Aqueous Extract of Seed of *Tamarindus indica*. Biol Pharm Bull 2005, 28, 1172-1176.

99. Aderibigbe AO, Lawal BA, Oluwagbemi JO. The antihyperglycamic Effect of *Telfaria occidentals* Mice. Afr J Med Med Sci 1999, 28, 171-175.

100. Dhaliwal, K.S. Method and Composition for Treatment of Diabetes 1999, US Patent 5886029.

101. Khosla P, Gupta DD, Nagpal RK.Effect of Trigonella foenum graecum (fenugreek) on Blood Glucose in Normal and Diabetic Rats. Indian J. Physiol. Pharmacol 1995, 39, 173-174.

102. Gupta D, Raju J, Baquer NZ. Modulation of some Gluconeogenic Enzyme Activities in Diabetic Rat Liver and Kidney: Effect of Antidiabetic Compounds. Indian J Expt Biol 1999, 37, 196-199.

Pages: 145-160

Nutrition and Medicines in Nature
Edited by: Dr. Jairam Singh and Dr. Pawan Kumar 'Bharti'
ISBN: 978-93-88854-39-9
Edition: 2020
Published by: Discovery Publishing House Pvt. Ltd., New Delhi (India)

8

Recent Advances in Antimicrobial Therapy for Combating Multi-Drug Resistance by Plant Molecular Medicine - A Review

Dhananjay Pandey[1,2] and A.K. Gupta[1]

ABSTRACT

Plant molecular medicine as therapeutics is often effective for patients with serious infections caused by multi-drug resistant microorganisms. The increased drug resistance among microbes due to the profuse use of commercially available antibiotics has drawn the attention of the researchers globally to look for the alternative therapy of healing infections. One of the best strategy to overcome these resistant mechanisms is the use of combination of drugs. The search for such novel plant derived molecular compounds which can be combined with antibiotics in the treatment of MDR strains may be an alternative to overcome the problem of antibiotic resistance. Synergism is a positive interaction created when two agents combined and exert an inhibitory effect that is greater than the sum of their individual effects. Thus, in current scenario the efforts to standardize and look into the use of bioactive plant products as molecular medicine in combination with standard antibiotics and its implications in antimicrobial therapy deserves attention. However, the assessment of pharmacological activity through bio-efficacy testing and characterization of the plant molecular medicine as antimicrobial compound by several analytical instruments viz., HPLC, HPTLC, UV-Visible, FT-IR, NMR (^{1}H & ^{13}C), GC-MS and ESI-MS is the need of the hour.

Keywords: *Bio-efficacy; Bioactive; Multi-drug resistant; Synergism; Antagonism.*

[1] School of Studies in Life Science, Pt. Ravishankar Shukla University, Raipur - 492 010, Chhattisgarh (India)

[2] School of Studies in Biotechnology, Bastar Vishwavidyalaya, Dharampura, Jagdalpur - 494 001, Chhattisgarh (India)

INTRODUCTION

The integration of traditional and modern medicine is gaining increased recognition globally (WHO, 2000). Drug synergism between known antimicrobial agents and bioactive plant extracts has been recently reported (Rakholiya and Chanda, 2012; Syed *et al.*, 2015). Combination therapy could be an alternative to monotherapy for patients with invasive infections caused by multi-drug resistant pathogens (Kamatou *et al.*, 2006; Dawis *et al.*, 2003). Antimicrobial compounds used in combination might promote the effectiveness of each agent, with higher efficacy being achieved using a lower dose of each drug (Williamson, 2001). This therapy can be used to expand the antimicrobial spectrum to prevent the emergence of resistant mutants, to minimize toxicity and to obtain synergistic antimicrobial activity (Ranjan *et al.*, 2012). Although, several studies have been carried out to extract various medicinal plants for screening antimicrobial activity but attention has not been focused intensively on studying the combinations of these products for their antimicrobial efficacy (Abu-Shanab *et al.*, 2004). There is, therefore, an urgent need of novel antimicrobials and to develop new approaches for alternative antimicrobial agents for the amelioration of dreadful infectious diseases.

Antibiotics are the most powerful weapons in combating microbial infections. Over the past few decades these health benefits are under threat as many commonly used antibiotics have become quite less effective against certain illnesses not only because many of them produce toxic reactions but also due to the emergence of multi-drug resistant bacteria (Wong *et al.*, 2010). The increasing failures of chemo therapeutics and antibiotic resistance exhibited by pathogenic microbial infectious agents have led to the screening of several medicinal plants for their potential antimicrobial activity (Pavithra *et al.*, 2009).

According to the World Health Organization (WHO, 2001) a medicinal plant is any plant which contains substances useful for the therapeutic purposes and are the precursors for the synthesis of useful drugs. Medicinal plants are considered as clinically effective and safer alternatives to the synthetic antibiotics (Modi *et al.*, 2012). There are several reports on the antimicrobial activity of herbal extracts in different parts of the world (Sainkhediya and Ray, 2012; Joselin *et al.*, 2013; Florence *et al.*, 2014 and Sumathi and Uthayakumari, 2014; Lee and Choi, 2015; Deshpande and Naik, 2016). The common view in the society and the medical community is that green medicines are healthier, safer, harmless and more reliable than synthetic ones (Yadav *et al.*, 2015). Therefore, there is an urgent need of extensive research in the area of medicinal plants with the aim of exploring their ethno-medicinal efficacy and subsequently the isolation, purification and characterization of bioactive compounds by HPLC, HPTLC, UV-Visible spectrophotometer, FT-IR, NMR (^1H & ^{13}C), GC-MS and ESI-MS which will contribute for the better, safer and cost effective novel drug development in future.

ADVANCES IN ANTIMICROBIAL THERAPY

Synergistic effects resulting from the combination of antibiotics with various plant extracts has been studied and experimented by a number of researchers (Chatterjee *et al.*, 2009; Rubaka *et al.*, 2014; Abidi *et al.*, 2015; Manosalva *et al.*, 2016). The increased resistance to antibiotics has led to the emergence of infectious diseases. One strategy employed to overcome these resistance mechanisms is the use of combination of drugs, such as β-lactams together with β-lactamase inhibitors. Recently several plant extracts have been reported to show synergistic activity against microorganisms. The synergy between natural products including flavonoids, essential oils and synthetic drugs was found to be effective in combating bacterial, fungal and mycobacterial infections. The mode of action of combination differs significantly from that of the same drugs acting individually (Hemaiswarya *et al.*, 2008). Thus to combat increased antimicrobial resistance against pathogenic microorganisms the use of bioactive plant products in combination with standard antibiotics is widely implicated in antimicrobial chemotherapy. Adwan and Mhanna (2008) evaluated the synergistic activity of water extracts of *Laurus nobilis, Majorana syriaca, Ocimum basilucum, Psidium guajava, Rosa damascene, Rosmarinus officinalis, Salvia fruticosa,* and *Syzygium aromaticum* with known antimicrobials of different mode of action *viz.*, oxytetracycline, gentamicin, penicillin G, cephalexin, sulfadimethoxine and enrofloxacin against five *S. aureus* isolates. These plants exhibited *in-vitro* synergistic interactions with antimicrobial agents with a significant reduction in the MICs of the test antibiotics.

Adwan *et al.* (2009) assessed the synergistic activity of ethanol leaf extracts of *Lawsonia inermis, Psidium guajava, Rhus coriaria* and seed of *Sacropoterium spinosum* with antibiotics such as oxytetracyclin, enrofloxacin, gentamicin and sulphadimethoxin against four clinical isolates of methicillin-resistant *S. aureus*. The results revealed that the combination of plant crude extracts with antibiotics enhanced the antimicrobial activity as compared from the compounds and antibiotic used alone except in case of enrofloxacin. Aiyegoro and Okoh (2009) emphasized that multi-drug resistance in the microorganisms is the major threat to the public health in global perspectives. However, the plant antimicrobials have been documented to be synergistic enhancers. The combination of plant extract and antibiotic showing synergism are the new choice for curing infectious diseases. Moreover, the synergistic effect will also reduce the problem of overdose and toxicity. They advocated exploration of bioactive principles of plant origin for their synergistic effect. Kumar *et al.* (2009) evaluated the synergistic activity of methanol extract of *Thespesia populnea* with oxytetracycline against 12 different Gram-positive and Gram-negative bacteria and reported low MIC of combination as compared from individual compound (Fig. 8.1-8.2). The maximum synergism rate was recorded against *Shigella boydii* (ATCC8700). Moghaddam *et al.* (2009) evaluated the synergistic antibacterial activity of curcumin with different antibiotics against *S. aureus*. The antibacterial activity of cefixime, cephotaxime, vancomycin and tetracycline increased in the presence of sub-inhibitory concentration of curcumin (500 µg/disc). The highest increase in inhibition area was recorded for cefixime against *S. aureus* followed by cephotaxime, vancomycin and tetracycline. However, with nalidixic acid, curcumin showed an antagonistic effect on the antibacterial activity.

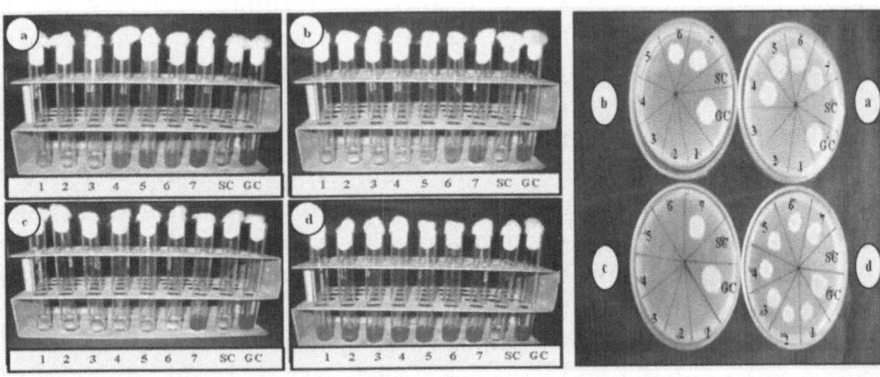

Fig. 8.1: MIC and MBC of the crude methanol root extract and purified pooled fraction of *C. caesia* for *B. cereus* (a) crude extract (b) purified fraction (c) positive control (d) negative control (SC- Sterility control and GC- Growth control)

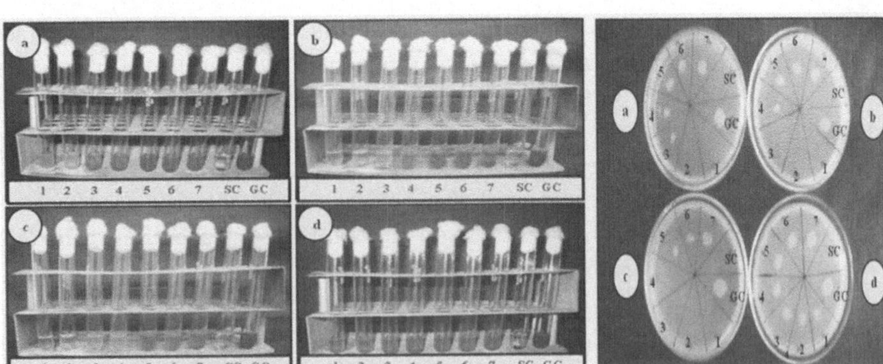

Fig. 8.2: MIC and MBC of the crude methanol root extract and purified pooled fraction of *C. caesia* for *K. pneumoniae* (a) crude extract (b) purified fraction (c) positive control (d) negative control (SC- Sterility control and GC- Growth control)

Ahmed *et al.* (2010) evaluated the synergistic activity of two antibiotics *viz.*, penicillin and tetracycline with ethanol extracts of stem and leaf of *Salvadora persica* against *S. aureus* separately and in combination. The results revealed that the maximum inhibition was recorded with tetracycline plus *S. persica* stem extract followed by tetracycline plus *S. persica* leaf extract. The combination of stem and leaf extract with tetracycline was found to be more effective as compared from the same extract with penicillin. Majid *et al.* (2010) evaluated the synergistic and antimicrobial activity of *Echinophora platyloba* ethanol extract against Gram-positive bacteria and *C. albicans*. The synergistic effect of 5% ethanol extract of *E. platyloba* and Amphotericin B against *C. albicans* was determined by MIC and MLC values. The results revealed that the Gram-positive bacteria were resistant to the extract whereas, *Trichophyton schenlaini* and *T. verucosum* were sensitive to concentrations $\geq$ 35 mg/ml. MIC value of 5% ethanol extract against *C. albicans* was 2 mg/ml. However, there was a reduction of 50% in MIC and a 75% in MLC by the combinations against *C. albicans*. Purushotham *et al.* (2010) evaluated the synergistic activity of methanol extract of *Tectona grandis* with tetracycline against nine different Gram-positive and Gram-negative bacteria exhibiting the MIC ranging from 62.5-2000 µg/ml. The highest synergistic activity was recorded against *Salmonella typhimurium* (MTCC 98) and *K. pneumoniae* (MTCC 432) and lowest activity against *Pichia pastoris* (MTCC 34), *E. coli,* (MTCC 729) and *P. aeruginosa* (MTCC1688). However, no synergistic activity was recorded in case of *Citrobacter freondii* (MTCC 1658).

Elmanama *et al.* (2011) assessed independent and synergistic effect of extracts of *Hibiscus sabdariffa*, *Lawsonia inermis* and *Punica granatum* with antibiotics on pathogenic organisms. The results revealed that highest antibacterial activity was shown by methanol extract of *P. granatum* against *S. aureus* while *K. pneumoniae and E. coli* showed least sensitivity to the extract. The combinations of *P. granatum* methanol extract with ciprofloxacin and erythromycin increased antibacterial potentiality with *P. aeruginosa* and *S. aureus* respectively. The activity of ketoconazole and fluconazole drugs in combination with the aqueous extract of *H. sabdariffa* increased antifungal activity many folds. The synergistic effect against fungi was higher as compared from the bacteria.

Rakholiya and Chanda (2012) documented *in-vitro* interaction between leaf methanol extracts of *Terminalia catappa* and *Carica papaya* with known antibacterials, such as amikacin, amoxyclav, ampicillin, cephalothin, chloramphenicol, gentamicin, nilidixic acid, ofloxacin, penicillin, polymyxin and rifampicin against five Gram-positive and five Gram-negative bacteria. The results revealed that synergism between methanol extract of *C. papaya* and antibiotics enhanced antimicrobial activity though methanol extract of *C. papaya* alone did not show any antibacterial activity. The study illustrates that the combination of plant extract and antibiotics could be novel and better alternative for combating drug-resistant pathogens. Ranjan *et al.* (2012) analyzed the synergetic effect of leaf extracts of *Adhatoda vasica* and *Tinospora cardifolia* with nalidixic acid and rifampicin against *B. cereus* and *K. pneumoniae*. The results revealed that several combinations were highly effective and showed almost double effect. However, some of the combinations showed antagonistic activity as well. The synergistic combinations of antibiotics with plant extracts against resistant bacteria and fungi could be helpful in amelioration of infectious diseases.

Stefanovic and Comic (2012) reported the synergistic antimicrobial activity between aqueous, ethanol and ethyl acetate extracts of *Melissa officinalis* with five commonly used antibiotics *viz.*, amoxicillin, chloramphenicol, rifamycine, streptomycin and tetracycline against susceptible and resistant human-pathogenic bacteria. The extract and antibiotic combinations exhibited higher zone of inhibition as compared with control against antibiotic resistant bacteria. Further, ethanol and ethyl acetate extracts showed better synergy than aqueous extract. However, the least susceptible bacteria to the combinations were *E. coli, P. aeruginosa* and *P. mirabilis*.

Cabral *et al.* (2013) reported the antifungal synergism between statins, *viz.*, atorvastatin, lovastatin, pravastatin, rosuvastatin and simvastatin and azoles, *viz.*, clotrimazole, fluconazole, itraconazole, ketoconazole or miconazole with *Saccharomyces cerevisiae* ATCC 32051 and *Candida utilis*. Inhibition was significantly enhanced when clotrimazole, fluconazole, itraconazole, ketoconazole and miconazole were combined with atorvastatin, lovastatin, rosuvastatin and simvastatin. Highest growth inhibition was observed in *S. cerevisiae* followed by *C. utilis*. However, the highest interaction ratios between antifungal corresponded to simvastatin–miconazole combinations and were indicative of synergism. The synergistic activity was confirmed by the increased reduction in cellular ergosterol levels in *S. cerevisiae* and *C. utilis*. Jain *et al.* (2013) assessed antibacterial activity of crude extracts of *Pterocarpus santalinus* against *E. coli, P. aeruginosa, S. aureus, Streptococcus mutans, C. albicans, C. glabrata, C. parapsilosis* and *C. tropicalis* compared with standard antibiotic ciprofloxacin and fluconazole. The ethanol and methanol extracts showed inhibitory activity while chloroform, petroleum ether and butanol were ineffective. MIC for ethanol extract ranged from 4-8 mg/ml while that of methanol extract ranged from 6-10 mg/ml. The synergistic combination of plant extract with known antibiotics resulted in significant reduction in the MIC of the test antibiotics.

Alshami and Alharbi (2014) investigated the antimicrobial activity of *H. sabdariffa* extract in combination with fluconazole and voriconazole against six strains of fluconazole resistant *C. albicans* isolated from the patients with recurrent candiduria. The interaction effect of *H. sabdariffa* with voriconazole showed good synergy whereas, the extract showed indifferent effect with fluconazole. However, no antagonistic effect was recorded. Atteia and Hussein (2014) assessed the antimicrobial and synergistic activity in aqueous and ethanol extracts of *Allium sativum, Commiphora molmol* and *Syzygium aromaticum* with antibiotics against *S. aureus* and *K. pneumoniae*. The results revealed that the aqueous extract of *S. aromaticum* exhibited higher inhibitory effect on *S. aureus* as compared from *A. sativum* extract whereas, the aqueous extract of *C. molmol* showed no antibacterial activity. The ethanol extracts of all the three plants exhibited inhibitory effect against *K. pneumoniae*. The synergistic activity assessment revealed that the ethanol extracts of *A. sativum, C. molmol* and *S. aromaticum* alone and in combination with antibiotics exhibited significantly higher antimicrobial activity.

Bansal *et al.* (2014) tested the synergistic antifungal activity of crude DMSO and petroleum ether leaves extract of *Cassia fistula* with fluconazole against *Candida* sp. isolated from Candidasis patients. The antifungal activity of *C. fistula* leaves extract in combination with fluconazole increased three-fold antimicrobial activity. Similarly, Kim *et al.* (2014) investigated the efficacy of an antifungal agent from *Eisenia bicyclis*. The methanol extract of *E. bicyclis* showed potential antifungal activity against *Candida* sp. Among five solvent extracts tested, the ethyl acetate extract from *E. bicyclis* demonstrated the stron-gest antifungal activity with a MIC ranging from 4-8 mg/ml. The MIC values decreased significantly in combination of ethyl acetate extract and fluconazole from 64-4 µg/ml against *Candida* sp. Sharma and Kaur (2014) assessed the synergetic effect in leaves of different medicinal plants, *i.e., Adhatoda vasica, Calotropis gigantean* and *Ficus carica* from Kangra valley with tetracycline, gentamicin, streptomycin and ampicillin. Antimicrobial activity of these extracts were tested alone and in combination with antibiotics against *B. subtilis, E. coli, P. aeruginosa, S. aureus, S. mutans, A. brasiliensis* and *C. albicans*. The methanol extract of *A. vasica* and ampicillin showed increased synergistic effect against *S. aureus* whereas methanol extract of *Ficus carica* showed synergistic effect with gentamycin and tetracyclin against *E. coli* and *S. aureus*. However, some combinations showed antagonistic effect as well.

Teow and Ali (2015) reported the antibacterial activity of curcumin with eight different antibiotic groups against one clinical, two reference, and ten environmental strains of *S. aureus*. The results revealed that curcumin (25 µg/ml) exhibited synergistic antibacterial activity in combination with a majority of tested antibiotics against *S. aureus*. However, checkerboard micro dilution assay showed only synergism with fractional inhibitory concentration index (FICI) < 0.5 in three antibiotics *viz.*, gentamicin, amikacin, and ciprofloxacin whereas, other antibiotics showed indifferent interactions but no antagonism was recorded. The time-kill curve showed appreciable reduction of bacterial cells in combination therapy compared to monotherapy. The antibiotics with higher synergistic interaction with curcumin were amikacin followed by gentamicin and ciprofloxacin.

STRUCTURAL ELUCIDATION OF PLANT BIOACTIVE MOLECULES

One of the most challenging objectives of medicinal plant research is to purify and identify the bioactive compounds present in the extracts. The crude extracts of medicinal plant are complex mixture of diverse group of chemical components. Thus, the separation of active components of plant from the other components has always been a difficult task for researchers. However, this can be achieved by applying various chromatographic techniques. The structural information of isolated and purified compounds can be drawn by using different sophisticated analytical techniques *viz.*, Ultraviolet-Visible (UV-VIS), Fourier Transmission Infrared Spectroscopy (FT-IR), Nuclear Magnetic Resonance (NMR) and Mass Spectroscopy (MS) etc (Fig. 8.3).

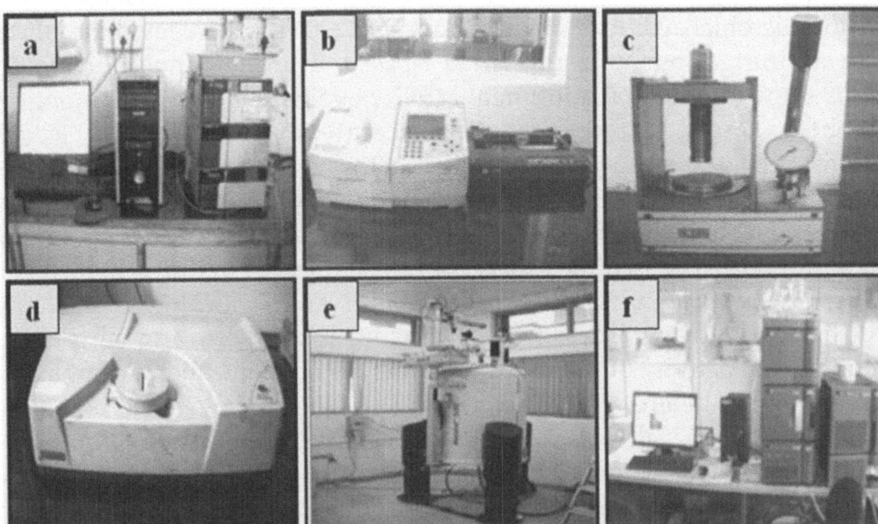

Fig. 8.3: Sophisticated instruments for spectral analysis of the plant bioactive molecules (a) High performance liquid chromatography (b) UV-Visible spectrophotometer (c) Kbr press for FT-IR (d) FT-IR spectroscopy (e) Nuclear magnetic resonance spectroscopy (f) Electron spray ionization mass spectrometry

Madan *et al.* (2008) studied the antimicrobial activity in butanol, dichloromethane and methanol root extracts of *Flemingia strobilifera* against some bacteria and fungi. The isolation and characterization of compounds by column chromatography, UV, FT-IR, NMR and MS revealed the presence of Flemingiaflavanone (8, 3'-diprenyl-5, 7, 4'-trihydroxy flavanone), Genistin

(5, 4′- dihydroxy isoflavone 7-O-glucoside) and β-sitosterol-D glucoside. Flemingiaflavanone showed significant antimicrobial activity against Gram-positive (*S. aureus, S. epidermidis,* MRSA), Gram-negative bacteria (*P. aeruginosa, E. coli*) and fungi (*C. albicans*). However, Genistin exhibited moderate activity against Gram-positive, Gram-negative bacteria and fungi.

Muhit *et al.* (2010) focused on the purification of crude leaf methanol extract of *Dillenia indica* L. by column chromatography using different solvent system of increasing polarity (n-hexane, carbon tetrachloride and chloroform). The purified compound characterized by ^{1}HNMR revealed the presence of four compound viz., dillenetin, betulinic acid, β-sitosterol and stigmasterol all being rich source of triterpenoids and flavonoids.

Revathy *et al.* (2011) isolated and purified curcuminoids from *Curcuma longa* by column chromatography followed by purity analysis by HPLC. Several mobile phase combinations were pre-tested in TLC for separation of curcuminoids but chloroform: methanol at (95:5) was found to show better resolution with three bands of Curcumin, Demethoxycurcumin and Bisdemethoxycurcumin respectively. The crude extract was subjected to silica gel column chromatography with chloroform: methanol at increasing polarity. Different fractions were collected and checked for its bioefficacy and finally analyzed by UV spectrophotometry. The purified crude extracts from column chromatography showed single peak on HPLC. Senthilkumar and Reetha (2011) screened the antibacterial activity of *Aegle marmelos, Cassia auriculata, Chloris Virgata, Clausena anisata* and *Feronia limonia* against human pathogenic bacteria such as *E. coli, K. pneumoniae, P. mirabilis* and *S. typhi* at different concentrations. The results revealed that the leaf extract of the *C. auriculata* exhibited highest antibacterial activity. Further, the compound showing highest bioefficacy was isolated and identified by FT-IR spectrum, ^{1}H NMR, ^{13}C NMR and Mass spectrum, as oleanolic acid with a molecular formula of $C_{30}H_{48}O_3$. Sukanya *et al.* (2011) studied the methanol, ethanol, ethyl acetate, hexane and chloroform extracts of *Chromolaena odorata* against clinical isolates of bacteria *viz., E. coli* and *S. aureus* and phytopathogenic bacteria *viz., R. solanacearum* and *X. vesicatoria*. The results revealed that methanol extracts of *C. odorata* exhibited inhibition against all the organisms. The purified antimicrobial compound by TLC and column chromatography recorded MIC value between 0.35-4.0 mg/ml and 0.25-4.0 mg/ml respectively for clinical and phytopathogenic bacteria. The structural elucidation of the HPLC purified antimicrobial compound by FT-IR, 2D NMR and LC-MS was found to be phenolic groups with molecular weight of 437.4129.

Bama *et al.* (2012) studied the antibacterial activity from the leaf extract of *Tridax procumbens* against *E. coli, P. mirabilis, S. aureus,* and *V. cholarae*. The result revealed that the terpenoid extract exhibited significantly higher antimicrobial activity against the pathogenic microorganisms. The bioactive terpenoid exhibiting antibacterial activity was further characterized by FT-IR, NMR and mass spectroscopy. Patra *et al.* (2012) characterized crude leaf methanol extract of *Excoecaria agallocha,* from Bhitarkanika, Odisha having potential against *S. aureus* (MTCC-1141) and *P. aeruginosa* (MTCC 1034). TLC and HPLC of the crude methanol plant extract produced seven peaks for the leaf and two peaks for the stem/bark. The spectral analysis by ^{1}H NMR revealed the presence of á- mono substituted aliphatic and acyclic aliphatic group of compounds in the sample.

Sahaya *et al.* (2012) analyzed antimicrobial constituents present in different leaf extracts of *Vitex altissima* L. using UV-Visible spectroscopy, FT-IR and GC-MS. The UV-Visible spectroscopy showed different peaks ranging from 400-700 nm and the FT-IR spectrum of crude extracts confirmed the presence of alcohols, phenols, alkanes, alkynes, alkyl halides, aldehydes, carboxylic acids, aromatics, nitro compounds and amines in different extracts. Further, GC-MS analysis ascertained the presence of 21 phytocompounds in the extract with major phytoconstituents such as 9, 12-Octadecadienoic acid (23.41%), n-Hexadecanoic acid (23.74%) and Squalene (14.74%). Saxena and Saxena (2012) reported bioactive compounds in the methanol leaf extracts of *Acorus calamus* through UV-Visible spectroscopy and FT-IR. The results revealed the presence of two peaks at 304.00nm and 237.00nm which were characteristic for flavonoid groups. The FT-IR spectra showed the characteristic peak at 3363.97 cm^{-1} corresponding to the presence of hydroxyl group in the extract. Sen *et al.* (2012) purified crude extract of the leaves of *M. charantia* by silica gel column chromatography and reported a single spot with Rf value of 0.55 with TLC. The purified compound was further characterized by FT-IR and NMR spectral analysis and was found to be β-sitosterol. The purified compound exhibited effective antimicrobial activity against *E. coli, K. pneumoniae P. aeruginosa* and *S. aureus* with reference to gentamicin.

Sharma and Paliwal (2013) isolated the saponin from successive benzene extract of *Moringa oleifera* pods and separated them through TLC using chloroform: methanol: water (7:3:1) as mobile phase. A single spot with Rf value of 0.90 revealed the purity of the compound. The characterization of the isolated saponin was done using HPLC, FT-IR and ^{1}H NMR. The FT-IR spectrum of isolated compound showed the presence for hydroxyl group (-OH), carboxylic acids (-COOH), alkynes, esters (–C=O), ethers (>C-O) and aromatic structures. ^{1} H NMR spectrum of isolated compound revealed the presence of protons in the compound.

Bhubaneswari and Gobalakrishnan (2014) studied the antimicrobial potential and characterization of the bioactive compound from flower extract of *Cassia javanica* L. against human pathogens. The result revealed that ethyl acetate and ethanol crude extracts exhibited effective antimicrobial activity against all the human pathogens tested and showed the presence of bioactive constituents such as alkaloids, flavonoids, saponins, phenolic compounds, cardiac glycosides, glycosides, phlobatannins, tannins, triterpenoides and volatile oils. The GC-MS analysis revealed the presence of fourteen bioactive compounds in different solvent extracts of *C. javanica* flower. Emmanuel *et al.* (2014) studied the ethyl acetate rhizome extract of *Zingiber officinale* against *B. cereus* CIP 6624, *B. substilis* ATCC 6636, *Enterococcus faecalis* CIP 76117, *E. coli* CIP 548, *Listeria monocytogenes* CIP 82110, *Pseudomonas fluorescents* CIP 6913, *S. aureus* CIP 7625, *Candida lusitaniae* ATCC 200950, *Candida tropicalis* ATCC 750, *Cryptococcus neoformans* CIP 95026, *Aspergillus flavus*, and *Aspergillus parasiticus*. The extract was further purified by column chromatography and preparative TLC using a gradient system of hexane, ethyl acetate and methanol. The structural elucidation of the purified compounds by 1D and 2D NMR, mass spectroscopy and chemical reactions revealed the presence of two compounds *viz.*, nonyl-3-phenylpropanoate (1) and 8-hepthyl-12- propyldecanol (2). Both the compounds exhibited antibacterial and antifungal activity and the minimal inhibitory concentration against test fungi varied from (3.34-5.08 mM) for compound 1 and (3.81-5.08 mM) for compound 2.

Karpagasundari and Kulothungan (2014) reported the bioactive compound of *Physalis minima* leaves using GC-MS, HPLC, UV-Visible spectroscopy and FT-IR. The HPLC profiles of *P. minima* revealed four phenolic compounds *viz.*, Catechol (3.59 min), Catechin (7.41 min), Ellagic acid (4.13 min) and Gallic acid (4.12 min). The UV-Visible spectra showed the three peaks at 315.09 nm, 408.09 nm and 676.50 nm. FT-IR analysis confirmed the presence of alkanes, aldehyde, amino acid, aromatic amines, phenol, secondary alcohol and halogen compound. The GC-MS analysis of extract of *P. minima* leaves revealed the presence of Heneicosanoic acid (25.22), Bicyclo [4.1.0] Hepta-2, 4-dien (27.41) Octadecanoic acid (CAS), Stearic acid (31.19) and Octadeca-9, 12-dienoic acid (32.02). Pillai and Nair (2014) studied the methanol extracts of two species of *Cleome* such as *C. burmanni* and *C. viscosa* using FT-IR spectrum profile. The results revealed similar absorption peaks by the two species at different transmission percentages. Also, most of the functional groups recorded were similar in the two species with a difference in their wave numbers. Aromatic amines and alkynes were observed in *C. viscosa* while *C. burmanni* contained phenols which could distinguish both the species.

Edilu *et al.* (2015) assessed the antibacterial activity of the crude methanol root extract of *Caylusea absyssinica* (fresen) against clinical bacterial strains, *E. coli* (ATCC25722), *P. aeruginosa* (DSMZ1117), *Salmonella thyphimurium* (ATCC13311) and *S. aureus* (ATCC25903). The active crude showing higher efficacy was further purified and identified by spectral analysis *viz.*, ^{1}H NMR, ^{13}C NMR and FT-IR as β-sitosterol and stigmasterol. The antimicrobial activity of the purified compound showed zone of inhibition ranging from 12-15 mm for β-sitosterol and 11-18 mm for stigmasterol against different test strains. Kumar *et al.* (2015) studied the purification and characterization of bioactive compound from methanol leaf extract of *Millingtonia hortensis* using silica gel column chromatography. The sixth fraction obtained from column chromatography was identified to have potent antimicrobial, antioxidant and antiproliferative activity. TLC of the active fraction showed the Rf value of 0.41 using ethyl acetate: methanol (9:1) as mobile phase. The structural elucidation was done using HPLC, FT-IR, ^{1}H and ^{13}C NMR spectroscopy and mass spectrometry. FT-IR spectroscopy revealed the presence of hydroxyl, phenolic, methoxy and aromatic functional groups. The molecular weight of the isolated compound was 301 daltons. The purified compound was identified as 5, 7-dihydroxy-2-(4-hydroxyphenyl)-6-methoxy-4H-chromen-4-one).

Mickymaray *et al.* (2016) evaluated antibacterial activity of five Indian medicinal plants *viz.*, *Acalypha indica*, *Aerva lanata*, *Clerodendrum inerme*, *Pergularia daemia* and *Solanum surattense* against pathogens isolated from HIV infected patients such as *E. coli*, *P. aeruginosa*, *Salmonella typhi*, *Serratia marcescens* and *S. aureus*. *A. indica* showed potential antibacterial activity against *S. aureus* and *E. coli* whereas, *A. lanata* exhibited antibacterial activity against *E. coli*, *S. typhi* and *P. aeruginosa*. The results revealed the presence of total 19 phytoconstituents in the ethanol extract of *A. indica* and *A. lanata* by GC-MS analysis.

CONCLUSION

Medicinal plant as therapeutics would be one of the key source for obtaining a variety of newer drugs as phytochemicals are more specific, biodegradable and are supposed to have fewer side effects, clinically effective and safer alternatives to the synthetic antibiotics. They also offer a vital and unique platform for biological functionality and structural diversity which is indispensable for novel drug discovery. In future multi-dimension research aimed at correlating phytochemicals and botanical properties to specific pharmacological activity is also expected. Further, the plant based antimicrobials have enormous potentials and would open an avenue for the formulation of antimicrobial agents in combating several dreadful microbial diseases. However, not only testing these plant extracts on clinical microbial culture but also their toxicological evaluation *in-vivo* and looking towards the development of combination therapy against MDR strains with the view to formulate novel chemotherapeutic agents and scientific validation of the same will lay the foundation for alternative antimicrobial therapy against multi-drug resistant microorganisms.

REFERENCES

Abidi SH, Ahmed K, Sherwani SK and Kazmi SU (2015): Synergy between Antibiotics and Natural Agents Results in Increased Antimicrobial Activity against *Staphylococcus epidermidis*. *The Journal of Infection in Developing Countries*, 9, 925-929.

Abraham Z (1981): *Glimpses of Indian Ethnobotany*. Oxford & Publishing Co., New Delhi, P. 308-320.

Abu-Shanab B, Adwan G and Abu-Safiya D (2004): Antibacterial Activities of some Plant Extracts Utilized in Popular Medicine in Palestine. *Turkish Journal of Biology*, 28, 99-102.

Adwan G and Mhanna M (2008): Synergistic Effects of Plant Extracts and Antibiotics on *Staphylococcus aureus* Strains Isolated from Clinical Specimens. *Middle East Journal of Scientific Research*, 3, 134-139.

Ahmed Z, Khan SS, Khan M, Tanveer A and Lone ZA (2010): Synergistic Effect of *Salvadora persica* Extracts, Tetracycline and Penicillin against *Staphylococcus aureus*. *African Journal of Basic and Applied Sciences*, 2, 25-29.

Aiyegoro OA and Okoh AI (2009): Use of Bioactive Plant Products in Combination with Standard Antibiotics: Implications in Antimicrobial Chemotherapy. *Journal of Medicinal Plants Research*, 3, 1147-1152.

Alshami I and Alharbi AE (2014): Antibacterial Effect of *Hibiscus sabdariffa* (Roselle) Extract in Synergism with Voriconazole and Fluconazole against Fluconazole-resistant *Candida albicans* isolates: An *in-vitro* Study. *Biomedical Research*, 25, 401-404.

Astal ZY, Ashour A. and Kerrit AAM (2005): Antimicrobial Activity of some Medicinal Plant Extracts in Palestine. *Pakistan Journal of Medical Sciences*, 21, 187-193.

Atteia HG and Hussein EAM (2014): *In-vitro* Antibacterial and Synergistic Effects of some Plant Extracts against *Staphylococcus aureus* and *Klebsiella pneumoniae*. *Journal of Antimicrobials*, 129, 338-346.

Bama SS, Kingsley JS, Sankaranarayanan S and Bama P (2012): Antibacterial Activity of different Phytochemical Extracts from the Leaves of *T. procumbens* L.: Identification and Mode of Action of the Terpenoid Compound as Antibacterial. *International Journal of Pharmacy and Pharmaceutical Sciences*, 4, 557-564.

Bansal Y, Charulata and Negi DS (2014): *In-vitro* Synergistic Effect of *Cassia fistula* Leaves Extract with Fluconazole against Clinical Isolates of *Candida albicans*. *International Journal of Pharmaceutical and Clinical Research*, 6, 201-205.

Bhuvaneswari R and Gobalakrishnan R (2014): Antimicrobial Potential and Structural Elucidation of Bioactive Compounds from Flower Extract of *Cassia javanica* L. *Indian Journal of Natural Products and Resources*, 5, 34-39.

Boyd M, Hallock Y, Cardellina J, Manfredi K, Blunt J, McMahon J, Buckheit R, Bringmann G, Schaffer M, Cragg G, Thomas D and Jato J (1994): Anti-HIV michellamines from *Ancistrocladus korupensis*. *Medicinal Chemistry*, 37, 1740-1745.

Cabral ME, Figueroa LIC and Farina JI (2013): Synergistic Antifungal Activity of Statin-azole Associations as witnessed by *Saccharomyces cerevisiae* and *Candida utilis* Bioassays and Ergosterol Quantification. *Revista Iberoamericana de Micologia*, 30, 31-38.

Chatterjee SK, Bhattacharjee I and Chandra G (2009): *In-vitro* Synergistic Effect of Doxycycline and Ofloxacin in Combination with Ethanolic Leaf Extract of *Vangueria spinosa* against Four Pathogenic Bacteria. *Indian Journal of Medicinal Research*, 130, 475-478.

Dawis MA, Isenberg HD, France KA and Jenkins SG (2003): *In-vitro* activity of Gatifloxacin Alone and Incombination with Cefepime, Meropenem, Piperacillin and Gentamicin against Multidrug-resistant Organisms. *Journal of Antimicrobial Chemotherapy*, 51, 1203-1211.

Deshpande SR and Naik SB (2016): Evaluation of *in-vitro* Antimicrobial Activity of Extracts from *Cassia obtusifolia* L. and *Senna sophera* (L.) Roxb. against Pathogenic Organisms. *Journal of Applied Pharmaceutical Science*, 6, 83-85.

Edilu A, Adane L and Woyessa D (2015): *In-vitro* Antibacterial Activities of Compounds Isolated from Roots of *Caylusea abyssinica*. *Annals of Clinical Microbiology and Antimicrobials*, 14, 1-8.

Elmanama AA, Alyazji AA and Abu GNA (2011): Antibacterial, Antifungal and Synergistic Effect of *Lawsonia inermis, Punica granatum* and *Hibiscus sabdariffa*. *Annals of Alquds Medicine*, 7, 33-41.

Emmanuel T, Aristide B, Leopold TN, Benoît NM, Duplex WJ, Gbaveng Y, Bernard D, Alain M, Joseph MT and Roch A (2014): Antimicrobial Activity of Phenylpropanoyle from the Rhizome of *Zingiber officinale* Roscoe (Zingiberaceae). *European Journal of Medicinal Plants*, 4, 126-134.

Florence AR, Joselin J, Brintha TSS, Sukumaran S and Jeeva S, (2014): Preliminary Phytochemical Studies of Select Members of the Family Annonaceae for Bioactive Constituents. *Bioscience discovery*, 5, 85-96.

Hemaiswarya S, Kruthiventi AK and Doble M (2008): Synergism between Natural Products and Antibiotics against Infectious Diseases. *Phytomedicine*, 15, 639-652.

Jain P, Agrawal V and Singh A (2013): *In-vitro* Evaluation of Antimicrobial Properties of Extracts of *Pterocarpus santalinus* against Oral Pathogens and its Synergistic Effect with Ciprofloxacin and Fluconazole. *International Journal of Pharmaceutical Sciences Review and Research*, 19, 31-35.

Joselin J, Brintha TSS, Florence AR and Jeeva S, (2013): Phytochemical Evaluation of Bignonaceae Flowers. *Journal of Chemical and Pharmaceutical Research*, 5, 106-111.

Kamatou GPP, Vanzyl RL, Vuuren SF and Viljoen AM (2006): Chemical Composition, Leaf Trichome Types and Biological Activities of the Essential Oils of Four Related Salvia species Indigenous to Southern Africa. *Journal of Essential Oil Research*, 18, 72-79.

Karpagasundari C and Kulothungan S (2014): Analysis of Bioactive Compounds in *Physalis minima* Leaves using GC-MS, HPLC, UV-VIS and FT-IR Techniques. *Journal of Pharmacognosy and Phytochemistry*, 3, 196-201.

Kim KH, Eom SH, Kim HJ, Lee DS, Nshimiyumukiza O, Kim D, Kim YM and Lee MS (2014): Antifungal and Synergistic Effects of an Ethyl Acetate Extract of the Edible Brown Seaweed *Eisenia bicyclis* against *Candida* species. *Fisheries and Aquatic Sciences*, 17, 209-214.

Kumar M, Agrawal RC, Dey S, Rai VK and Johnson B (2009): Antimicrobial Activity of Aqueos Extrat of *Terminalia chebula* on Gram-positive and Gram-negative Microorganisms. *International Journal of Current Pharmaceutical Research*, 1, 235.

Kumar MMVS, Prasad TVSSL and Rajagopal SV (2015): Purification and Characterization of Bioactive Compound from the Methanolic Leaf Extract of *millingtonia hortensis* L. *International Journal of Pharma and Bio Sciences*, 6, 348-358.

Lee JH and Choi HJ (2015): Antiviral and Antimicrobial Activity of Medicinal Plant Extracts. *Microbial and Biochemical Technology*, 7, 286-288.

Madan S, Singh GN, Kumar Y, Kohli K, Singh RM, Mir SR and Ahmad S (2008): A New Flavanone from *Flemingia strobilifera* (Linn) R. Br. and its Antimicrobial Activity. *Tropical Journal of Pharmaceutical Research*, 7, 921-927.

Majid A, Mohaddesse M, Mahdi D, Mahdi S, Sanaz S and Kassaiyan N (2010): Overview on *Echinophora platyloba*, a Synergistic Antifungal Agent Candidate. *Journal of Yeast and Fungal Research*, 1: 88-94.

Manosalva L, Mutis A, Urzúa A, Fajardo V and Quiroz A (2016): Antibacterial Activity of Alkaloid Fractions from *Berberis microphylla* G. Forst and Study of Synergism with Ampicillin and Cephalothin. *Molecules*, 21, 1-10.

Melendez PA and Capriles VA (2006): Antibacterial Properties of Tropical Plants from Puerto Rico. *Phytomedicine*, 13, 272-276.

Mickymaray S, Al Aboody MS, Rath PK, Annamalai P and Nooruddin T (2016): Screening and Antibacterial Efficacy of Selected Indian Medicinal Plants. *Asian Pacific Journal of Tropical Biomedicine*, 6, 185-191.

Modi C, Mody S, Patel H, Dudhatra G, Kumar A, and Awale M. (2012): Herbal Antibacterials, a Review. *Journal of Ethnopharmacology*, 1, 52-61.

Moghaddam KM, Iranshahi M, Yazdi MC and Shahverdi AR (2009): The Combination Effect of Curcumin with Different Antibiotics against *Staphylococcus aureus*. *International Journal of Green Pharmacy*, 3, 141-143.

Muhit MA, Tareq SM, Apu AS, Basak D and Islam MS (2010): Isolation and Identification of Compounds from the Leaf Extract of *Dillenia indica* Linn. *Bangladesh Pharmaceutical Journal*, 13, 49-53.

Patra JK, Gouda S, Sahoo SK and Thatoi HN (2012): Chromatography Separation, ^{1}H NMR Analysis and Bioautography Screening of Methanol Extract of *Excoecaria agallocha* L. from Bhitarkanika, Orissa, India. *Asian Pacific Journal of Tropical Biomedicine*, 2, S50-S56.

Pavithra PS, Sreevidya N and Verma RS (2009): Antibacterial Activity and Chemical Composition of Essential Oil of *Pamburus missionis*. *Journal of Ethnopharmacology*, 124, 151-153.

Purushotham KG, Arjun P, Jayarani J Johnsy, Vasnthakumari R, Sankar L and Reddy BR (2010): Synergistic *in-vitro* Antibacterial Activity of *Tectona grandis* Leaves with Tetracycline. *International Journal of Pharm Tech Research*, 2, 519-523.

Rakholiya K and Chanda S (2012): *In-vitro* Interaction of Certain Antimicrobial Agents in Combination with Plant Extracts against some Pathogenic Bacterial Strains. *Asian Pacific Journal of Tropical Biomedicine*, 2, S876-S880.

Rakholiya K and Chanda S. (2012): *In-vitro* Interaction of Certain Antimicrobial Agents in Combination with Plant Extracts against some Pathogenic Bacterial Strains. *Asian Pacific Journal of Tropical Biomedicine*, 2, S876-S880.

Ranjan S, Bhavya K, Muntaj SK, Basumata G and Matcha R (2012): Synergistic Effect of some Medicinal Plants and Antibiotics against Few Pathogenic Bacteria. *International Journal of Biological and Pharmaceutical Research*, 3, 1000-1004.

Ranjan S, Bhavya K, Muntaj SK, Basumata G and Matcha R (2012): Synergistic Effect of some Medicinal Plants and Antibiotics against Few Pathogenic Bacteria. *International Journal of Biological and Pharmaceutical Research*, 3, 1000-1004.

Revathy S, Elumalai S, Benny M and Antony B (2011): Isolation, Purification and Identification of Curcuminoids from Turmeric *Curcuma longa* L. by Column Chromatography. *Journal of experimental Sciences*, 2, 21-25.

Rojas A, Hernandez L, Pereda-Miranda R and Mata R (1992): Screening for Antimicrobial Activity of Crude Drug Extracts and Pure Natural Products from Mexican Medicinal Plants. *Journal of Ethnopharmacology*, 35, 275-283.

Rubaka C, Ndakidemi P, Malebo HM and Shahada F (2014): Individual and Combined Antibacterial Activity of Crude Extracts from Medicinal Plants *Carissa spinarum* Linn and *Carica papaya* Linn. *European Journal of Medicinal Plants*, 4, 1513-1523.

Sahaya SS, Janakiraman N and Johnson M (2012): Phytochemical Analysis of *Vitex altissima* L. using UV-VIS, FT-IR and GC-MS. *International Journal of Pharmaceutical Sciences and Drug Research*, 4, 56-62.

Sainkhediya J and Ray S, (2012): Preliminary Study of Flowering Plant Diversity of Nimar Region. *Bioscience Discovery*, 3, 70-72.

Saxena M and Saxena J (2012): Evaluation of Phytoconstituents of *Acorus calamus* by FT-IR and UV-VIS Spectroscopic Analysis. *International Journal of Biological and Pharmaceutical Research*, 3, 498-501.

Schultes RE (1978): *The Kingdom of Plants*. In W.A.R. Thomson (ed), McGrow-Hill Book Co., New York, p. 208.

Sen A, Dhavan P, Shukla KK, Singh S and Tejovathi G (2012): Analysis of IR, NMR and Antimicrobial Activity of β-Sitosterol isolated from *Momordica charantia*. *Science Secure Journal of Biotechnology*, 1, 9-13.

Senthilkumar PK and Reetha D (2011): Isolation and Identification of Antibacterial Compound from the Leaves of *Cassia auriculata*. *European Review for Medical and Pharmacological Sciences*, 15, 1034-1038.

Sharma V and Kaur RK (2014): Identification and Characterization of Medicinally Important Plants of Kanger Valley with Synergistic Effects of Traditional Antibiotics against Microbial Infections. *The Journal of Phytopharmacology*, 3, 102-112.

Sharma V and Paliwal R (2013): Isolation and Characterization of Saponins from *moringa oleifera* (moringaeceae) Pods. *International Journal of Pharmacy and Pharmaceutical Sciences*, 5, 179-183.

Shihabudeen HMS, Priscilla DH and Thirumurugan K (2010): Antimicrobial and Phytochemical Analysis of Selected Indian Folk Medicinal Plants. *International Journal of Pharma Science and Research*, 1, 430-434.

Silva O, Duarte A, Cabrita J, Pimentel M, Diniz V and Gomes E (1996): Antimicrobial Activity of Guinea-Bissau Traditional Remedies. *Journal of Ethnopharmacology*, 50, 55-59.

Sirkar NN (1989): *Pharmacological basis of Ayurvedic Therapeutics. In: Cultivation and Utilization of Medicinal Plants*. Atal CK and Kapoor BM, Published by CSIR.

Stefanovic O and Comic L (2012): Synergistic Antibacterial Interaction between *Melissa officinalis* Extracts and Antibiotics. *Journal of Applied Pharmaceutical Science*, 2, 1-5.

Sukanya SL, Sudisha J, Prakash HS and Fathima SK (2011): Isolation and Characterization of Antimicrobial Compound from *Chromolaena odorata*. *Journal of Phytology*, 3, 26-32.

Sumathi BM and Uthayakumari F (2014): GC-MS Analysis of Leaves of *Jatropha* Maheswarii. *Science Research Reporter*, 4, 24-30.

Syed HA, Khalid A, Sikander KS and Shahana UK (2015): Synergy between Antibiotics and Natural Agents Results in Increased Antimicrobial Activity against *Staphylococcus epidermidis*. *The Journal of Infection in Developing Countries*, 9, 925-929.

Teow SY and Ali SA (2015): Synergistic Antibacterial Activity of Curcumin with Antibiotics against *Staphylococcus aureus*. *Pakistan Journal of Pharmaceutical Science*, 28, 2109-2114.

Williamson EM (2001): Synergy and other Interactions in Phytomedicines. *Phytomedicine*, 8, 401-409.

Wong RW, Hägg U, Samaranayake L, Yuen MK, Seneviratne CJ and Kao R (2010): Antimicrobial Activity of Chinese Medicine Herbs against Common Bacteria in Oral Biofilm. A Pilot Study. *International Journal of Oral Surgery*, 39, 599-605.

World Health Organization (2000): Drug Information. *Herbal Medicine*, 14, 237-243.

World Health Organization (2001): *Essential Drugs and Medicines Policy*, WHO Geneva.

Yadav S, Patgiri BJ and Prajapati PK (2015): Review of Bio-active Principle of *Butea monosperma* (Lam.) Kuntze. *Indian Journal of Ethnophytopharmaceuticals*, 1, 45-51.

Index

A

Algal foods, 16
Allahabad Safeda guava, 94
Alloxan diabetic rats, 136
Aloe vera gel, 95
Amino acid, 55
Anthraquinones, 104
Antibiotics, 146
Antimicrobial compounds, 146
Antimicrobial therapy for combating multi-drug resistance, 145-160
    advances in antimicrobial therapy, 147-152
    introduction, 146-147
    structural elucidation of plant bioactive molecules, 152-156
Anti-oxidant ability of guava, 94
Antioxidants, 18
Apple of tropics, 82-96
    enzymatic browning, 85
    guava, 83
    introduction, 83
    nature and its duration for storage, 83-84
    papayas and litchis, 84
    review on current research, 86-95
    storage atmosphere and its metabolites, 84
    storage atmosphere, 84
Appollonius of Memphis, 113
Aravinth, V., 54
Aretaeus of Cappadocia, 113
Ascorbic acid, 84
Aspergillus fumigatus, 107
Athrospira, 9
Ayurveda, 135
Azad, Tariq Parvez, 99, 112

B

Beeswax, 94
Bhat, Showkat Ahmad, 99, 112
Bifidobacterium, 36
    bifidum, 44
Blue-green algae, 3

C

Candida albicans, 106
Cheddar cheese, 45
Chemical carcinogens, 40
Chinese Rhubarb, 101
Chromophore phycocyanobilin (PCB), 16
Cultured dairy foods, 40

D

Dey, Shipa Rani, 23, 82
Diabetes and medicinal plants, 112-144
    Abelmoschus moschatus, 122
    Acacia Arabica, 122
    Achyranthes aspera, 122
    Achyrocline satureioides, 123
    Acosmium panamense, 123
    Acute Presentation, 116
    Aegle mar, 123
    Agrimony eupatoria, 123
    Ajuga iva, 123
    Allium cepa, 124

Allium sativum, 124
Aloe barbadensis, 124
Aloe vera, 124
Andrographis paniculat, 124
Annona squamosa, 125
Artemisia dracunculus, 125
Artemisia herba-alba, 125
Astragalus membranaceus, 125
Averrhoa bilimbi, 125
Azadirachta-indica, 126
Bauhinia candicans, 126
Bauhinia forficate, 126
Bidens pilosa, 126
Biophytum sensitivum, 127
Bixa orellana, 127
Brassica nigra, 127
Bryonia alba, 127
Bumelia sartorum, 127
Caesalpinia bonducella, 128
Cajanus cajan, 128
Carum carvi, 128
Casearia esculent, 128
Cassia auriculata, 128
Catharanthus roseus, 129
Causes of Diabetic Complications, 120
Chamaemelum nobile, 129
Cichorium intybus, 129
Clausena anisata, 129
Clinical Presentation of Diabetes, 116
Coccinia indica, 129
Complications as the presenting feature, 116
Complications of Diabetes, 117
Coriandrum sativum, 129
Cuminum cyminum, 130
Cuminum nigrum, 130
Cyamopsis tetragonolob, 130*a*
diabetes and macrovascular complications, 119
diabetes medicinal plants, 121
diabetic nephropathy, 118-119
diabetic neuropathy, 119
diabetic retinopathy, 118
Dioscorea dumetorum, 130
Eclipta alba, 130
Emblica officinal, 130
Enicostema littorale blume, 130
Ficus bengalensis, 130
Fraxinus excelsior, 130
Garcinia kola, 130
Gongronema latifolium, 130
Helicteres isora, 131
history, 113
hypertension, 120
Hypoxis hemerocallidea conn, 131
insulin secretion, 117
introduction, 113
Inula racemosa, 131
Lagerstroemia speciosa, 131
Lepidium sativum, 131
lipid abnormalities, 121
Low Density Lipoprotein, 121
Macrovascular complications, 119
Major Risk Factors, 120
Mangifera indica, 131
Momordica charantia, 131
Morinda lucida, 132
Myrcia uniflora, 132
Nigella sativa, 132
Ocimum sanctum, 132
Origanum vulgare, 134
Otholobium pubescens, 134
Paeonia lactiflora, 134
Panax ginseng, 134
Pathophysiology and Major Risk Factors, 116
Phyllanthus amarus, 134
Psidium guajava, 134

Pterocarpus marsupium, 135
Retama raetam, 135
Salacia reticulate, 135
Smoking, 121
Spergularia purpurea, 135
Suaeda fruticosa, 135
Subacute Presentation, 116
synthetic drugs and herbal medicine, 136
Syzigium cumini, 136
Tamarindus indica, 136
Telfaria occidentalis, 136
Tinospora cordifolia, 136
Trigonella foenum, 136
Types of Diabetes, 114
Diabetes mellitus (DM), 112-144

E

Edible coating of fruits and vegetables, 85
Encapsulated probiotics, 49
Ethanol 147
Exo-polysaccharides, 49
Extrusion and emulsion techniques, 50

F

Fermented probiotic products, 44
Fermented products, 41
Foliar nutrition in green gram, 51-81
after care, 62
available nitrogen, 64
phosphorus, 64
potassium, 64
biometric observations, m62
crop and variety, 58
management, 61
dry matter production, 63, 66
economics, 58, 64
effect of foliar nutrition on
growth, 56-57
yield parameter and yield, 57-58
electrical conductivity, 64
experimental design, 58
fertilizer application, 61
foliar application, 55
nutrients, 62
foliar nutrition, 55
gap filling, 62
growth components of green gram, 63, 65, 72, 74
harvesting, 62
introduction, 54
leaf area index, 65
location of the experiment farm, 58
mechanical analysis, 64
number of
pods per plant, 63
seeds per pod, 63
organic carbon, 64
plant height, 65
pod length, 67
seeds and sowing, 62
soil analysis, 64
soil characteristics, 58
treatment details, 61
water management, 62
yield components, 67, 73, 74
of green gram, 63
yield, 63

G

Garlic cloves coated with acetic acid, 93
Gastrointestinal infections, 36
Gastrointestinal tract, 45, 48
Geriatric patients, 18
Green gram, 54-81
Green Gram: Growth of, 56
Guava, 83
Gupta, A.K., 145

H

Hassan, Tehseen, 99, 112

I

Immune system, 41
Impaired insulin action, 116
Indo-Gangetic plains, 83
Infectious diseases, 147
integration of traditional and modern medicine, 146

K

Kumar, Prasann, 23, 82

L

Lactic acid bacteria (LAB), 35
Lactobacillus, 36, 37
  acidophilus, 39
  johnsonii, 41
Lactose, 41

M

Madhumeha, 113
Majid, Sabhiya, 99, 112
Manimala, M.R.A. 3, 33
Medicinal plant(s), 99-111, 112-144, 146, 156
Metformin, 137
Methanol 148
mildly diabetic (MD), 128

N

Nano chitosan based coating on apple, 95
Napthoquinones, 101
Neuroblastoma cells, 18
Nutrient Deficiency in Plants, 23-32
  deficiency symptoms
    B, 31
    Ca, 28
    Cu, 29
    Fe, 30
    K, 27
    Mg, 28
    Mn, 30
    N, 27
    P, 27
    S, 29
    Zn, 30
  highly susceptible to deficiencies, 31
  introduction, 23
  macronutrient deficiencies & soils, 26
  nutrient deficiencies, 25
Nutritious fruit, 83
Nutritive value and importance of probiotics, 33-53
  anticarcinogenic activity, 40
  application of probiotics in food industry, 41
  fermented milk products, 44
  introduction, 33
  maintenance of normal micro flora, 36
  methods for improving probiotic viability, 49
  nondairy products, 45
  prebiotics, 46
  probiotic challenges, 47
  probiotic dairy products, 43
  probiotics, 34-38
    concept of, 35
    dietary supplements, 44-49
    health benefits, 36
    ice-cream, 45
    hypothesis, 38
    therapeutic or prophylactic properties of probiotic, 37
  protection against
    allergies/eczema, 41
    ulcers, 41
  reduction of
    lactose intolerance, 39
    serum cholesterol levels, 40
  therapeutic applications, 39, 42

O

Oral administration of aqueous extract of root, 128
Oral hypoglycemic drugs, 136

P

Pandey, Dhananjay, 145
Phycocyanorubin, 16
Plant molecular medicine, 145-160
Polysaccharides, 17
Preventive healthcare, 19
Probiotic consumption on heart disease, 40
Probiotic cultures, 48
Pulse crop, 54

R

Revand-chini, 100
Rheum emodi as valuable medicinal plant, 99-111
- anticancer activity, 106
- antidiabetic effect, 106
- antidyslipidemic activity, 106
- antifungal activity, 106
- anti-inflammatory activity, 107
- antimicrobial activity, 107
- antiplatelet and anticoagulant activities, 107
- antiulcer activity, 108
- contraindications, 108
- hepatoprotective activity, 108
- historic overview, 102
- immune-enhancing activity, 108
- names in different languages, 102
- nephroprotective effect, 108
- occurrence and distribution, 103
- pharmacological actions and traditional uses, 103
- physicochemical study, 104
- phytoconstituents, 104
- plant description, 102
- uses of rhubarb, 105

S

Singh, Gurjinder, 99, 112
Spirulina, 3-22
- agitation, 12
- beneficial uses and nutritional value of *spirulina*, 17
- biochemical composition of *spirulina platensis, 4*
- carbon source, 10
- composition of spirulina, 4
- contamination, 12
- cyanobacteria, 13
- essential
  - amino acids, 13
  - fatty acids, 4, 5
- health benefits of spirulina, 6
- historical background, 7
  - aztec messenger, 7
  - historical use, 7
  - kanembu population, 7
  - rediscovery of spirulina, 8
  - spanish invaders, 7
- inoculum size, 12
- introduction, 3-4
- mass cultivation, 13
- mechanism of action, 6
- minerals, 5
- morphology and taxanomic status, 8
- natural sources, 4
- nutrient
  - medium, 10
  - profile, 5-7
  - value, 4
- other growth factors, 12
- pH, 11
- photosynthetic pigments, 5
- phytopigments, 5
- *Spirulina* species, 3
  - *gigantean*, 9
  - *platensis*, 9, 11, 13, 14
- temperature, 10
- therapeutic uses of *spirulina*, 15-18
  - anti-cancer effects, 18

anti-inflammatory effects, 16
anti-viral activity, 15-16
cures eye disease, 16
effects against nephrotoxicity, 16
protein source for malnutrition, 15
role of spirulina in immunity, 17
spirulina as antioxidant, 18
in anaemia, 17
substitute for animal meat, 16
vitamins, 5
water quality, 11
Sulfolipids, 17
Sulfonylureas, 137
Synthetic antibiotics, 146

T

Thiazolidinediones, 137
Trichophyton mentagrophytes, 106

U

Use of organic solvents, 50

V

Vigna radiate, 54-81

W

Water loss, 94

Y

Yield potential of green gram, 55
Yoghurt, 36, 39,

❑ ❑ ❑ ❑ ❑ ❑